JOURNAL FOR THE STUDY OF THE OLD TESTAMENT
SUPPLEMENT SERIES

107

JSOT Press
Sheffield

THE ALIEN IN ISRAELITE LAW

Christiana van Houten

Journal for the Study of the Old Testament
Supplement Series 107

Published by JSOT Press
JSOT Press is an imprint of
Sheffield Academic Press Ltd
The University of Sheffield
343 Fulwood Road
Sheffield S10 3BP
England

Typeset by Sheffield Academic Press
and
Printed on acid-free paper in Great Britain
by Billing & Sons Ltd
Worcester

British Library Cataloguing in Publication Data

Van Houten, Christiana
The Alien in Israelite law.—(JSOT supplement
series. ISSN 0309-0787; 107)
I. Title II. Series
933.02

ISBN 1-85075-317-2

PREFACE

This book is based on a thesis entitled *The Legal Status of the Alien: A Study of the Pentateuchal Laws Pertaining to the Alien* which was submitted to the University of Notre Dame for the degree of PhD in November, 1989. The greater part of the work remains unchanged except for the chapter dealing with the Priestly laws. The recent book by Daniel Smith, *The Religion of the Landless* (Bloomington: Meyer Stone Books, 1989) convinced me that I had to rethink the dating of the laws calling for equality between the alien and the native. These laws, I concluded, did not fit in with the social dynamics of the community in exile, but rather with the conflicts that group experienced upon returning to their homeland.

I have followed the translation of the New Revised Standard Version which happily now translates *ger* as 'alien', rather than as 'stranger' or 'sojourner' as it did previously. When the translation was not precise enough for our purposes, I have noted that in a footnote.

I wish to thank especially my advisor, Dr Joseph Blenkinsopp, for his encouragement and support for what turned out to be a long haul. My readers, Dr John Collins, Dr Eugene Ulrich and Dr John H. Yoder, made many helpful suggestions which have made this a stronger, more clearly argued presentation. I also wish to acknowledge the assistance of Dr Norbert Lohfink, who very kindly gave me a copy of his speech, 'The Option for the Poor: Views of an Old Testament Scholar', which he delivered at the Annual Meeting of the Catholic Biblical Association in August 1990. His enthusiasm that we had embarked on similar projects and had come to similar conclusions was very encouraging to me. Calvin College has also supported me in this endeavor by granting me a reduced teaching load so that I could revise this manuscript. I am grateful for their commitment to promoting excellence in scholarship. Finally, special thanks are due to the editors of the *Journal for the Study of the Old*

Testament for their insightful comments and for their graciousness in including this work in their Supplement Series.

Christiana de Groot van Houten
February 1991

ABBREVIATIONS

AnBib	Analecta biblica
ANET	J.B. Pritchard (ed.), *Ancient Near Eastern Texts*
ATR	*Anglican Theological Review*
BA	*Biblical Archaeologist*
CBQ	*Catholic Biblical Quarterly*
HSM	Harvard Semitic Monographs
HTR	*Harvard Theological Review*
ICC	International Critical Commentary
IDB	G.A. Buttrick (ed.), *Interpreter's Dictionary of the Bible*
IDBSup	*IDB*, Supplementary Volume
Int	*Interpretation*
JAOSSup	*Journal of the American Oriental Society Supplement*
JBL	*Journal of Biblical Literature*
JNES	*Journal of Near Eastern Studies*
JSOT	*Journal for the Study of the Old Testament*
JSOTSup	Journal for the Study of the Old Testament Supplement Series
JSS	*Journal of Semitic Studies*
NCB	New Century Bible
NICOT	New International Commentary on the Old Testament
OTL	Old Testament Library
OTS	*Oudtestamentische Studiën*
RB	*Revue biblique*
SBLDS	SBL Dissertation Series
SBT	Studies in Biblical Theology
SJT	*Scottish Journal of Theology*
SOTSMS	Society for Old Testament Study Monograph Series
TynBul	*Tyndale Bulletin*
VT	*Vetus Testamentum*
VTSup	Vetus Testamentum, Supplements
ZAW	*Zeitschrift für die alttestamentliche Wissenschaft*

Chapter 1

THE ALIEN IN BIBLICAL RESEARCH

1. *Introduction*

The study of Old Testament law today stands in the tradition of de Wette and Wellhausen.[1] Their method and assessment of the biblical legal tradition is continued in the work of A. Alt[2] and M. Noth,[3] among others.[4] These scholars did much of the historical-critical groundwork which is still the starting point for discussions on the law today. Unfortunately, they have also bequeathed to us a tradition which denigrates a law-centered religion. Wellhausen, for example, who dated the formation of most of the legal tradition to the post-exilic period, understood it to be a sign of the spiritual demise of Israel. The centrality of the law in Judaism indicated to him that the creativity and spontaneity of the Israelite religion had ceased. In his own words,

> The Creator of heaven and earth becomes the manager of a petty scheme of salvation; the living God descends from his throne to make way for the law. The law thrusts itself in everywhere; it regulates and sets limits to the understanding of the divine working on earth. As far as it can, it takes the soul out of religion and spoils morality. It demands a service of God, which though revealed, may yet with truth be called a self chosen and

1. J. Wellhausen, *Prolegomena to the History of Israel* (trans. J.S. Black and A. Menzies; Gloucester, MA: Peter Smith, 1983 [repr. Meridian Edition, 1957]).

2. A. Alt, 'The Origins of Israelite Law', in *Essays on Old Testament History and Religion* (trans. R.A. Wilson; Oxford: Basil Blackwell, 1966), pp. 79-132.

3. M. Noth, 'The Laws in the Pentateuch', in *The Laws in the Pentateuch and Other Studies* (trans. D.R. Ap-Thomas; Philadelphia: Fortress Press, 1967), pp. 1-107.

4. For a presentation of the history of scholarship on the laws in the Pentateuch see R.J. Thompson, *Moses and the Law in a Century of Criticism since Graf* (VTSup, 19; Leiden: Brill, 1970).

> unnatural one, the sense and use of which are apparent neither to the understanding nor the heart. The labor is done for the sake of the exercise; it does no one any good, and rejoices neither God nor man.[1]

This estimation of law was carried over into works on biblical theology. Contemporary theologies of the Old Testament trace the development of law from its beginning in a covenant context, in which law has a place within the total relationship of the people to God, to its end in the post-exilic period when it became divorced from its moorings and became an end in itself.[2] At that point, it is said, the living fellowship between God and Israel was replaced by mere outward obedience to the laws.[3] However, in the recent past monographs have been published which testify to a new appreciation for law. Works by anthropologist M. Douglas have brought insights from the study of taboos to bear on the laws regulating clean and unclean.[4] M. Fishbane has made a major contribution by focusing on the development of laws within

1. Wellhausen, *Prolegomena to the History of Israel*, p. 509.

2. See, for example, G. von Rad, *Old Testament Theology*, I (trans. D.M.G. Stalker; Edinburgh: Oliver and Boyd, 1962), pp. 200-203; W. Eichrodt, *The Theology of the Old Testament*, I (trans. J.A. Baker; OTL; London: SCM Press, 1961), p. 168. J. Blenkinsopp, in 'Tanakh and the New Testament: A Christian Perspective', in *Biblical Studies: Meeting Ground of Jews and Christians* (ed. L. Boadt, H. Croner and L. Klenicki; New York: Paulist Press, 1980), pp. 100-11, discusses the devaluation of the second temple period in biblical theologies of the nineteenth and twentieth centuries.

3. J.D. Levenson, in 'The Theologies of Commandment in Biblical Israel', *HTR* 73 (1980), pp. 17-21, describes the assessment of law by nineteenth- and twentieth-century scholars such as Wellhausen, Eichrodt, von Rad, Mendenhall and G.E. Wright. He notes how covenant was seized upon by these theologians as a way of redeeming law by placing it in a covenant context. However, when describing the post-exilic period in which the idea of covenant is not central, these same theologians return to Wellhausen's assessment that at this point in its history Israel lost sight of its spiritual tradition and fell into the wasteland of law.

4. Her book *Purity and Danger* (London: Pelican, 1970) has been the basis for the exposition in G.J. Wenham's recent commentary, *The Book of Leviticus* (NICOT; Grand Rapids: Eerdmans, 1979), and represents a great advance on the conclusion reached by M. Noth in his commentary, *Leviticus* (trans. J.E. Anderson; OTL; Philadelphia: Westminster Press, 1965), p. 92. Noth concluded that the distinctions found in the text were simple and superficial and that the real reason for the laws had been forgotten. According to Noth, the real reason was that these animals were considered sacred in a foreign religion and therefore were considered abhorrent to the Israelite tradition.

the Old Testament, drawing attention to the fact that the legal tradition is a living tradition.[1] The laws have also come to be studied as vehicles of theology by J.G. McConville[2] and E. Feldman.[3] All of this scholarly activity is slowly laying to rest the long held notion that a law-centered religion is necessarily legalistic, lacking in genuine piety, social concern and historical awareness.

I hope that this study of the laws pertaining to the alien (Hebrew גר) in the Pentateuch will contribute to the recent blossoming of inquiry. In particular, I intend to enhance the appreciation of the distinctive theologies found in the various legal collections in the Old Testament. Although it is true that within each of the law collections (the Covenant Code, the Decalogue, the Deuteronomic laws, and the Priestly laws) development has occurred, it is still possible to speak of the distinctive nuances of the individual collections.

In addition, I hope to contribute to our understanding of the development of Old Testament law. We have already seen how Wellhausen has characterized that development, and I expect that on the basis of this study I can demonstrate that his assessment is inadequate.[4]

Because the laws pertaining to the alien are found in sufficient number in all the bodies of law in the Pentateuch, a study of them would contribute both to an appreciation of the theologies of the legal collections and to an assessment of their development. The Book of the Covenant contains three references, the Decalogue one, Deuteronomy eighteen, and the Priestly laws thirty.[5]

1. M. Fishbane, *Biblical Interpretation in Ancient Israel* (Oxford: Clarendon Press, 1985).

2. J.G. McConville, *Law and Theology in Deuteronomy* (JSOTSup, 33; Sheffield: JSOT Press, 1984).

3. E. Feldman, *Biblical and Post-Biblical Defilement and Mourning: Law as Theology* (New York: Ktav, 1977).

4. J. Blenkinsopp, *Prophecy and Canon* (Notre Dame, IN: University of Notre Dame Press, 1977), pp. 7, 19-22, attributes Wellhausen's depiction of the development of Israelite religion to his Hegelianism and Romanticism, as well as to his anti-Semitic cultural background.

5. The Book of the Covenant refers to the alien in Exod. 22.20 (ET: 21); 23.9, 12; the Decalogue in Exod. 20.10; Deuteronomy in 1.16; 5.14; 10.18, 19; 14.21, 29; 16.11, 14; 23.7; 24.14, 17, 19, 20, 21; 26.11, 12, 13; 27.19; and the Priestly laws in Exod. 12.19, 48, 49; Lev. 16.29; 17.8, 10, 12, 13, 15; 18.26; 19.10, 33, 34; 20.2; 22.18; 23.22; 24.16, 22; 25.23, 35, 47; Num. 9.14; 15.14, 15, 16, 26, 29, 30; 19.10; 35.15.

Furthermore, a study of the laws pertaining to the alien would help us reconstruct the history of this class. There are others who have examined the identity of the alien, and who have used the references in the Pentateuchal laws in order to do this. However, these studies are few, generally do not deal at length with the material, and seem content to repeat uncritically previous scholarship.[1] The reason that a major study has not been produced is not due to insufficient evidence. There is sufficient data available to make a significant contribution. In addition to the references to the alien in the legal material, there are many other references in the Old Testament. As well as fleshing out the historical picture, these provide a measure of control in our reconstruction of the development of the legal status of this class.

2. *Survey of Past Research*

My survey of scholarship on this topic begins in this century with M. Weber's work on Judaism (1921). Although I am critical of the way in which he used his sources, and of his resulting historical reconstruction, he made a lasting contribution by drawing attention to the way the definition of the alien changed as the definition of the people of Israel changed. He noted that as Israel developed from a tribal society to a monarchical state to a confessional community, the identity of the alien also developed.[2] Furthermore, his sociological analysis, for example, of the dualism of in-group and out-group morality, helps illuminate the social dynamics reflected in the laws, and enhances our understanding of that society. However, his work needs to be refined and extended. His conclusions cannot simply be

1. For example, M. Weber's description of the alien as a metic in *Ancient Judaism* (trans. and ed. H.H. Gerth and D. Martindale; Glencoe: Free Press, 1952), pp. 32-36, is repeated, without reference to him, or to the possible limits of the analogy, by many ensuing scholars. See, for example, D. Kellerman, 'גור', in *Theological Dictionary of the Old Testament*, II (ed. G.J. Botterweck and H. Ringgren; trans. J.T. Willis; Grand Rapids: Eerdmans, 1975), p. 443; and K.G. Kuhn, 'προσήλυτος', in *Theological Dictionary of the New Testament*, VI (ed. G. Friedrich; trans. G.W. Bromiley; Grand Rapids: Eerdmans, 1968), p. 728. Because the metics were not allowed to own land, it is assumed by these scholars that the alien was also not allowed to buy land. This is not demonstrated by them on the basis of biblical texts, nor, as I shall show later, was it satisfactorily demonstrated by M. Weber.

2. M. Weber, *Ancient Judaism*, pp. 28-32.

repeated. Criticisms of his work need to be taken into account.[1]

M. Sulzberger published a monograph in 1923 on the status of labor in ancient Israel,[2] and did much with the person of the alien. However, his uncritical use of sources and now questionable historical reconstruction have made his work outdated. Similarly, J. Pedersen's anthropological study of Israel in 1927 devoted a section to the alien,[3] but because he used the legal material uncritically, his conclusions need to be revised. He is the first, I believe, who suggested that aliens were the defeated Canaanites, and this is another questionable hypothesis which has been repeated ever since.[4]

G.F. Moore included a brief description of the alien in the course of his presentation of Jewish proselytism.[5] However, his main interest was in describing those aspects of Judaism, such as its monotheism, which predisposed it to an acceptance of converts.

T.J. Meek's article in 1930 on the translation of גר and its bearing on the documentary hypothesis is a major step forward.[6] He traces the meaning of the term through the documents of the Hexateuch, distinguishing between its occurrence in JE, the Covenant Code, the Holiness Code and the Priestly Writings. He concludes that in JE, גר denotes a Hebrew living in a foreign land and is best translated as 'immigrant'. In Deuteronomy, the Covenant Code and a few passages in the Priestly source, it refers to the indigenous population of Israel

1. See D.L. Petersen's 'Max Weber and the Sociological Study of Ancient Israel', in *Religious Change and Continuity* (ed. H.M. Johnson; San Francisco: Jossey–Bass, 1979), pp. 117-50, for a presentation of the major theses of Weber's work as it relates to the history of Israel and its impact on subsequent biblical scholarship. A more critical appraisal is given by S. Talmon in 'The Emergence of Jewish Sectarianism in the Early Second Temple Period', in *King, Cult and Calendar in Ancient Israel* (Jerusalem: Magnes Press, 1986), pp. 165-201.

2. M. Sulzberger, *The Status of Labor in Ancient Israel* (Philadelphia: Dropsie College, 1923).

3. J. Pedersen, *Israel: Its Life and Culture*, I (London: Oxford University Press, 1973 [1927]), pp. 39-46.

4. See, for example, T.M. Mauch's description of the alien as the indigenous population of Canaan in his article 'Sojourner', in *IDB*, IV, p. 398. I will discuss the inadequacies of this identification in Chapter 2.

5. G.F. Moore, *Judaism in the First Centuries of the Christian Era*, I (Cambridge, MA: Harvard University Press, 1966), pp. 323-39.

6. T.J. Meek, 'The translation of *Ger* in the Hexateuch and its Bearing on the Documentary Hypothesis', *JBL* 49 (1930), pp. 172-80.

who have been conquered and are now in a subordinate position to the Israelites. This is best translated as 'resident alien'. Finally, in some passages in the Holiness Code and Priestly source, the status of the alien has become equal with that of the native-born. Here the LXX generally translated גר as προσήλυτος, and Meek agrees that in these passages it means convert.[1] In time, he argues, the conquered Canaanites moved up socially and cultically to be on the same level as the native-born Israelite.

Meek's conclusions need to be tested. His treatment of the references to the alien in the Pentateuchal legislation has not considered their form, nor the genre of legal collections. His dating of the various documents, as well as his delineation of documents has been much revised in scholarship since 1930. In addition, his organization of the references to the alien does not persuasively demonstrate the conclusions he reaches. In his first category he includes only references attributed to JE, and in his final category only references from H and P. However, his middle category includes references from the Covenant Code, Deuteronomy, the Holiness Code and the Priestly source. The criteria by which they have been grouped together has to do only with content. In all these occurrences the alien is subordinate to the Israelite. To posit any progression from resident alien to proselyte on this basis is not very convincing. Much more needs to be done in terms of the editorial activity within each of the documents before the historical development that Meek proposes can be substantiated.

Other articles concerning the alien have not contributed much to our understanding of the legal status of the alien. Those articles by T.M. Horner,[2] L.M. Muntingh[3] and N.L. Levison[4] use the material in order to present theological themes and give only passing attention to historical or form-critical issues. Both B.J. Bamberger[5] and

1. See W.C. Allen, 'On the Meaning of προσήλυτος in the Septuagint', in *The Expositor* IV/10 (1894), pp. 264-75, for a discussion of the LXX's tendency to translate גר with προσήλυτος.

2. T.M. Horner, 'Changing Concepts of the "Stranger" in the Old Testament', *ATR* 42 (1960), pp. 49-53.

3. L.M. Muntingh, 'Die Begrip "Ger" in die Ou Testament', in *Nederduits Gereformeerde Teologiese Tydskrif* 3 (1962), pp. 534-58.

4. N.L. Levison, 'The Proselyte in Biblical and Early Post-Biblical Times', *SJT* 10 (1957), pp. 45-56.

5. B.J. Bamberger, *Proselytism in the Talmudic Period* (New York: Ktav, 1939), pp. 13-16.

M.M. Rothschild[1] use the material briefly in the same way, in order to discuss the background to the phenomenon of Jewish proselytism. W.J. Braude's book on Jewish proselytizing is helpful in depicting how the alien was treated in the rabbinic literature, but does not deal with the biblical material in any systematic way.[2]

The article in the *Interpreter's Dictionary of the Bible* by T.M. Mauch[3] does not contribute new information to the study of the alien. However, he does draw attention to the motivation clauses which attach to some of the laws pertaining to the alien. He notes especially the motivation given in Deuteronomy, and this is not surprising in light of Deuteronomy's parenetic style. However, the motivation clauses found in the Covenant Code and the Priestly writings also merit attention. In addition, more study is needed on what motivating clauses reveal about the genre of the law, the self-identity of the Israelites, and how their communal history functioned *vis-à-vis* their legal and ethical tradition.[4] B. Gemser and R. Sonsino have addressed this issue in part, and I shall be building on their contributions.[5]

The article on προσήλυτος in the *Theological Dictionary of the*

1. M.M. Rothschild, 'Aliens and Israelites—Pt. 1, 2, 3', in *Dor le Dor*, 9, 10, 11 (1981, 1981–82, 1982), pp. 196-202, 118-21, 35-39.

2. W.G. Braude, *Jewish Proselytizing in the First Five Centuries of the Common Era* (Providence: Brown University, 1940).

3. T.M. Mauch, 'Sojourner', pp. 397-99.

4. The relationship of narrative to community to ethics has been addressed by S. Hauerwas, 'The Moral Authority of Scripture: the Politics and Ethics of Remembering', in *A Community of Character* (Notre Dame, IN: University of Notre Dame Press, 1981), pp. 53-72. I hope to build on his notion that the kind of narrative a community reflects on determines its life, and that narratives can and must be reinterpreted as the community undergoes change.

5. B. Gemser, 'The Importance of the Motive Clause in Old Testament Law', *VTSup*, I (1953), pp. 50-66, makes a comparative study on the frequency and content of the motivation clauses in the various legal collections in the Pentateuch, and briefly addresses the relationship of Old Testament law to ancient Near Eastern law in this regard. He concludes that biblical law is unique in attaching motive clauses to laws. R. Sonsino's study *Motive Clauses in Hebrew Law: Biblical Forms and Near Eastern Parallels* (Dissertation Series, 45; Chico, CA: Scholars Press, 1980) focuses on the relationship of biblical law to ancient Near Eastern law and comes to different conclusions. He claims that although there are many more motivations clauses in the Pentateuchal law, and although their content is different, they are not unique to biblical law (pp. 172-74).

New Testament [1] uses the sources in a disciplined way, but of necessity is only sketchy. D. Kellerman's article on the root גור in the *Theological Dictionary of the Old Testament* [2] provides a good survey of the extra-biblical occurrences of the root גור.[3] However, his major section entitled 'The Legal Position of the גר' is not clear. He begins with an overview of the causes for becoming an alien, then follows with a survey of the individuals in the Old Testament who were designated as aliens and then discusses the alien in the monarchical period, the alien in Deuteronomy, and in P. The rationale for this organization is not obvious, and his use of sources is not disciplined. In discussing the monarchical period he draws on narrative material from Samuel, Kings and Chronicles as well as Genesis, without considering the historical-critical issues associated with these texts or evaluating them as witnesses to the monarchical period. He also discusses the patriarchs as aliens, the laws of the Book of the Covenant, and the laws of assembly in Deuteronomy 23, all without indicating why this is pertinent in a presentation on the alien in the monarchical period. In the course of the article he repeats the consensus that the alien could not own land, and that the aliens were the defeated Canaanites. Apart from its discussion of extra-biblical references, this article does not represent an advance on the state of the question.

An excellent article on the Israelites as גרים was published by F.A. Spina in 1983.[4] In it he discusses the authenticity of the tradition that the Israelites were aliens before their settlement in the land. He notes the references to the patriarchs as aliens in Gen. 23.4; Exod. 6.4; Ps. 39.13; 105.12; 1 Chron. 29.15, and to the Israelites as aliens in Egypt in Gen. 15.13; Exod. 22.20; 23.9; Lev. 19.33-34; Deut. 10.19; 16.11, 12; 23.8; 24.17, 18, 19-22. He concludes that Israel as a unified people did not exist before their settlement, and that therefore any statements

1. K.G. Kuhn, 'προσήλυτος', pp. 727-44.

2. D. Kellerman, 'גור', pp. 439-50.

3. D. Kellerman ('גור', pp. 440, 442) notes that the Akkadian *geru*, meaning 'to be hostile', and occurring most often as a participle meaning 'enemy, opponent', can be regarded as the etymon of the Hebrew root גור. The Arabic substantive *gar* frequently means 'neighbor', but can also denote 'protector, patron, protective companion'.

4. F.A. Spina, 'Israelites as *gerim*: Sojourners in Social and Historical Context', in *The Word of the Lord Shall Go Forth: Essays in Honor of David Noel Freedman in Celebration of his Sixtieth Birthday* (ed. C.L. Meyers and M. O'Connor; Winona Lake, IN: Eisenbrauns, 1983), pp. 321-35.

about the identity of the Israelites before then are suspect. However, if we read this statement as meaning that there were various groups which later became Israel, then Spina is proposing that the tradition that some of the proto-Israelites were aliens is reliable. Although this tradition has been artificially applied to all Israel, it is still a bona fide recollection of the past.[1] He argues against the notion that this tradition is a creation of the exilic period by noting that the Israelites in Babylon are never referred to as aliens. Only in Ezra 1.4 is the verbal form *gar* used to describe their stay in Babylon.[2]

Spina notes that the semantic range of גור in the Old Testament includes: (1) to sojourn; (2) to stir up strife, create confusion, quarrel; (3) to dread, be afraid.[3] He suggests, noting that this cannot be proven, that the roots are related and that the connotation of social conflict and unrest underlies all three meanings.[4] On this basis he proposes that the word 'immigrant' is the best English translation of the word גר since it captures the connotations of social and political upheaval which are part of the origins of the גר, and clearly distinguishes him from the pastoralist who moves from place to place as part of his occupation.[5] I would suggest that the translation 'alien' also accomplishes this, as well as leaving open whether or not the person has settled down. An immigrant is someone who comes from elsewhere and is now settled, whereas an alien may be settled or may still be on the move.

Spina does not go on to discuss the different meanings that came to be associated with the term, although in the footnotes he demonstrates that he is aware that in the Priestly legislation it sometimes means 'proselyte'. The reason for this lacuna would seem to be that he is mostly interested in the term as it depicts Israel in its pre-settlement period. For that time, and for most of the references in the Old Testament his definition of the alien fits very well:

> ... *ger* in the Hebrew Bible refers to people who are no longer directly related to their original social setting and who have therefore entered into dependent relationships with various groups or officials in a new social

1. Spina, 'Israelites as *gerim*', p. 322.
2. Spina, 'Israelites as *gerim*', p. 329.
3. F. Brown, S.R. Driver, C.A. Briggs, *A Hebrew and English Lexicon of the Old Testament* (Oxford: Clarendon Press, 1975), pp. 157-58.
4. Spina, 'Israelites as *gerim*', p. 325.
5. Spina, 'Israelites as *gerim*', pp. 323-24.

> setting. The *ger* was of another tribe, city, district or country who was without customary social protection or privilege and of necessity had to place himself under the jurisdiction of someone else.

This definition is helpful in that it notes the ways in which one's group may be defined, and the resulting different ways in which an alien may be defined. One may belong to a tribe or city or district or country, and through Israel's history the primary group to which an Israelite belonged changed. Concomitantly, the גר in the period of the Judges was anyone from another tribe or village, while the גר in the monarchical period was a citizen from a foreign country.

The alien has also been discussed by scholars in the course of presentations on Israel's history and theology. These contributions do not aim at a comprehensive description of the status of aliens, but they do provide valuable contributions on certain aspects of their identity and development. In particular, M. Smith,[1] H. Cazelles[2] and P. Grelot[3] have enhanced our understanding of the historical development of the status of the alien, and J. Blenkinsopp[4] has enriched our appreciation of how the development of the status of the alien goes hand in hand with the development of theological themes, such as universalism, in the Old Testament.

3. *Proposal and Method*

This survey indicates that there is a need for a study which will use the biblical evidence in the context of ancient Near Eastern culture and literature, paying attention to dating, genre, and to the society presupposed by the literature, as well as to its theological agenda, and on this basis attempt to reconstruct the legal status of the alien, its rationale, and how both developed through Israel's history.

I intend to focus attention on the laws in the Pentateuch, but I also propose to use the references to the alien found in the rest of the Old Testament when they are illuminating. In fact, they are very impor-

1. M. Smith, *Palestinian Parties and Politics that Shaped the Old Testament* (New York: Columbia University Press, 1971), pp. 178-83.

2. H. Cazelles, 'La mission d'Esdras', *VT* 4 (1954), pp. 113-40.

3. P. Grelot, 'La dérnière étape de la rédaction sacerdotale', *VT* 6 (1956), pp. 174-89.

4. J. Blenkinsopp, 'Yahweh and other Deities: Conflict and Accommodation in the Religion of Israel', *Interpretation* 40 (1986), pp. 362-66

tant to my task since they help fill out the historical and social context of the laws.

I will proceed by studying each legal collection on its own, since each has had its own literary history and reflects a particular view of God, Israel and the alien. Of course, these documents are not monolithic entities, and developments not only between legal collections but also within a particular collection will sometimes be traced.

Because the current discussion on the composition of the Pentateuch is in such a state of flux, one can assume neither the Documentary Hypothesis, nor any other hypothesis concerning the dating and delineation of sources in the Pentateuch.[1] This means that we cannot merely refer to a consensus when working with the legal collections, but must argue for their date, provenance and authorship. It should also be noted that even were the Documentary Hypothesis intact, it would not contribute much to historical-critical questions surrounding the law collections. These collections have generally been dated on the basis of their narrative context; however, they did not originate in the narrative context in which they are now located.[2] For these reasons, I propose to argue for the date and provenance of the various layers of

1. See, for example, the statement by R. Rendtorff, 'The "Yahwist" as Theologian? The Dilemma of Pentateuchal Criticism', *JSOT* 3 (1977), pp. 2-9, and the responses to it by R.N. Whybray, J. Van Seters, N.E. Wagner, G.W. Coats and H.H. Schmid in *JSOT* 3 (1977), pp. 2-45. More recently, R.N. Whybray's *The Making of the Pentateuch* (JSOTSup, 53; Sheffield: JSOT Press, 1987) discusses the pitfalls of both the Documentary Hypothesis and the reconstruction of the Pentateuch based on form criticism.

2. According to the Documentary Hypothesis, both J and E contain decalogues as part of their narrative. J's decalogue is found in Exod. 34.14-26 and E's in Exod. 20. For the rest, the legal material in the Pentateuch was not originally part of any of the narrative strands. Phrasing typical of J, E and P which has been traced through the narrative of the Pentateuch is not discernible within the legal collections. The Book of the Covenant, the Deuteronomic laws and the Holiness Code are each said to have had their own prehistory. Their present positions are due to the work of redactors. See presentations on the documentary hypothesis and the legal collections in the Pentateuch in O. Eissfeldt, *The Old Testament: An Introduction* (trans. P.R. Ackroyd; New York: Harper & Row, 1965), pp. 158-81, 212-38; and G. Fohrer, *Introduction to the Old Testament* (trans. D.E. Green; Nashville: Abingdon Press, 1968), pp. 103-85. Whybray (*The Making of the Pentateuch*, pp. 127-28) draws attention to the fact that the documents of the Documentary Hypothesis are seen to be narratives, and that there has been little discussion on the relationship between the narrative material and the legal material.

the legal collections on the basis of internal evidence.

I shall first study the phenomenon of legal collections and aliens in the ancient Near East, and then the references to the alien in the legal collections in the Pentateuch, beginning with the Book of the Covenant and Decalogue, proceeding to the laws in Deuteronomy, and ending with the Priestly laws. In the concluding chapter, I suggest what sort of development has occurred in the status of the alien, and indicate what this tells us of the development and character of the legal traditions in the Pentateuch.

Chapter 2

The Ancient Context

In order to evaluate the historical and theological significance of the laws pertaining to the alien in the Old Testament, we need to put them in the context of ancient Near Eastern legal texts. These texts can provide a framework within which we can appreciate the distinct nuances of the Old Testament laws, as well as the traditions which they have in common with their neighbors. There are two aspects of Near Eastern culture which are of importance to a study of the legal status of the alien: (1) the nature of ancient legal collections: their purpose, intended audience, literary and subsequent historical value; and (2) the social and legal status of aliens in these cultures. Strangers are a phenomenon that all societies, both ancient and modern, must deal with. We can expect that some societies will include their treatment in legal precepts, and in other societies, social mores regarding strangers will not become inscribed in law. We will study, when data permits, how other ancient Mediterranean societies dealt with aliens.

1. *Ancient Near Eastern Legal Collections*

A. *Historical Connections*

The rationale for studying Old Testament laws in the context of ancient oriental law presupposes that the laws in the Old Testament are in some way related to other legal collections in the ancient Near East, and that there are historical connections between the people of Israel and other peoples of the Fertile Crescent. It is indeed the case that there was much contact between the peoples of the Fertile Crescent, that there was a common culture in ancient Mesopotamia, and that this is reflected in a common customary law.[1] This 'cultural

1. G.R. Driver and J.C. Miles, *The Babylonian Laws* (Oxford: Clarendon Press,

continuum', as R. Sonsino describes it,[1] is due to the history and geography of the region, and is evidenced in the material remains as well as in the written traditions. Palestine, as the bridge between the great civilizations of Egypt and Mesopotamia, was in contact with both cultures.

However, Old Testament law does not seem to have been influenced by Egyptian legal practice.[2] Egypt has left behind no body of law which is analogous to the law collections of Mesopotamia or those in the Old Testament. There are no textual references to laws, nor accounts of law-giving by the king or an official until the tradition of King Bocchoris, c. 700 BC.[3] Since the pharaoh was believed to be divine, law proceeded from his mouth. The codification of law was neither necessary nor proper. Since each new pharaoh was a new god, it would not be fitting for him to be heir to a standing tradition outside of himself.[4]

Similarly, the laws of the Hittites do not seem to have had much influence on Old Testament laws.[5] The content of the Hittite laws is quite distinct from Old Testament laws and reflects a different traditional culture.[6]

1952), p. 9. Also, E.A. Speiser ('Cuneiform Law and the History of Civilization', in *Proceedings of the American Philosophical Society* 107 [1963], pp. 538-39), argues that the strength of Mesopotamian law is indicated by its use in Assyria at a time when Assyria was an enemy of Babylon, and by its existence in Ugarit. More recently, R. Westbrook, in *Studies in Biblical and Cuneiform Law* (Cahiers de la Revue Biblique, 26; Paris: Gabalda, 1988), has demonstrated that the laws of ancient Israel were an integral part of the legal tradition of the Fertile Crescent.

1. Sonsino, *Motive Clauses in Hebrew Law*, p. 1.
2. H.J. Boecker, *Law and the Administration of Justice in the Old Testament and Ancient East* (trans. J. Moiser; Minneapolis: Augsburg, 1980), p. 17. Westbrook, in *Studies in Biblical and Cuneiform Law*, p. 1 n. 1, also concludes that Egyptian law is not part of the Mesopotamian legal tradition.
3. J.A. Wilson, 'Authority and Law in Ancient Egypt', *JAOSSup* 17 (1954), p. 5.
4. Wilson, 'Authority and Law in Ancient Egypt', p. 7.
5. E. Neufeld, *The Hittite Laws* (London: Luzac and Co., 1951), p. 95.
6. According to T.J. Meek ('The Origin of Hebrew Law', in *Hebrew Origins* [New York: Harper & Row, 1936], p. 62), there is one Hittite law which is close to an Old Testament law, i.e. Deut. 22.23-27. Both laws deal with the rape of a woman, and make a distinction between a woman raped in the city and a woman raped in the country, and declare her innocent if raped outside of the city. See also

Nor did Syria-Palestine have a separate legal tradition which exerted much influence on Old Testament law.[1] This conclusion is based partly on arguments from silence since no codes of law have been recovered in Syria, and because there is evidence that Syrian-Palestinian law was itself influenced by the Babylonian legal tradition. Indeed, there appears to have been much contact with and influence from Mesopotamia. At the scribal schools in Hazor and Megiddo, in levels which pre-date the Israelite occupation, legal documents were found. These were not written in the local language, but in Akkadian. Akkadian, it seems, functioned as the language of law, even though Canaan was at that time under Egyptian sway.[2]

The many similarities between Mesopotamian law and Old Testament law are to be explained by a common legal tradition which was an integral part of a similar underlying culture.[3] The judicial principles, such as equal retribution, which underlie the laws, produced a similar customary law.[4]

H.G. Guterbock, 'Authority and Law in the Hittite Kingdom', *JAOSSup* 17 (1954), pp. 16-24, for a description of the legal functions within the state.

1. I. Mendelsohn ('Authority and Law in Canaan-Israel', *JAOSSup* 17 [1954], pp. 25-30) suggests that the social organization of the territory into small city-states, with the king functioning as a local chieftain, contributed to the weakness of an independent legal tradition. He attributes the lack of a powerful centralized government in Canaan to its being a rain-culture, as opposed to the irrigation cultures of Egypt and Babylon.

2. Westbrook, *Studies in Biblical and Cuneiform Law*, p. 3; Meek, 'The Origin of Hebrew Law', p. 69; E.A. Speiser, 'Authority and Law in Mesopotamia', *JAOSSup* 17 (1954), p. 15.

3. R. de Vaux, *Ancient Israel: Its Life and Institutions* (trans. J. McHugh; London: Darton, Longman and Todd, 1961), p. 146.

4. See the discussion of the principle of equal retribution in Near Eastern law and Old Testament law by T. Frymer-Kensky, 'Tit for Tat: The Principle of Equal Retribution in Near Eastern and Biblical Law', *BA* 43 (1980), pp. 230-34. This is in disagreement with B.S. Jackson, 'Reflections on Biblical Criminal Law', in *Essays in Jewish and Comparative Legal History* (Leiden: Brill, 1975), pp. 30-31, who understands that the endeavor to find underlying principles in ancient law codes is premature. However, although the principles are not explicitly stated, and there is no argument within the legal collections which derives laws from over-arching principles, Frymer-Kensky demonstrates that there are principles of justice operative in these texts.

B. *The Literary Genre of Ancient Near Eastern Law*

Having made the case that our understanding of Old Testament law will be enriched and refined by examining other law collections from the Fertile Crescent, I now need to investigate what the nature of those law codes was. The law codes to which I am comparing the Old Testament laws are:

Laws of Eshnunna, dated to c. 1930 BC[1]
Lipit-Ishtar Law Code, dated to c. 1868–1857 BC[2]
Code of Hammurabi, dated to c. 1728–1686 BC[3]
Middle Assyrian Laws, dated to c. 1112–1074 BC[4]

If we define a law code as a body of law which seeks to be comprehensive and to which judges are bound when deciding cases, then none of the law collections qualify as a law code. Firstly, it is clear that they are not intended to be exhaustive. For example, the Laws of Hammurabi contain no laws pertaining to murder or the giving of loans, yet evidence from contract tablets of the time indicate that these were dealt with according to a known legal procedure.[5]

The function of Mesopotamian legal collections is difficult to ascertain. They are never cited as an authority in judgments, nor do any

1. The original texts are located in the Iraq Museum (texts 51059 and 52614). They were excavated at Tell Abu Harmel by the Iraq Directorate of Antiquities, in the pre-Hammurabi layers. One was discovered in 1945, the other in 1947. I shall be using the translation of A. Goetz, *ANET*, pp. 161-63.

2. The code is inscribed on tablets, six of which were excavated at Nippur and are now located in the University Museum in Philadelphia. They were discovered by F.R. Steele in 1947. Prior to this only brief fragments of Sumerian laws were known. One tablet of unknown provenance is in the Louvre. All seven are from the pre-Hammurabi period. I shall be using the translation of S.N. Kramer, *ANET*, pp. 159-61.

3. The code was inscribed on a diorite stela which was excavated in Susa by a French expedition in 1901–2 and is now located in the Louvre. The stela was not original to Susa, but had been brought there by the Elamites as a trophy of war. Some of the laws were chiseled off by them, but these have been preserved in other copies. I shall be using the translation of T.J. Meek, *ANET*, pp. 163-80.

4. The laws were inscribed on tablets and were excavated by a German team in 1903–14 at Qal'at Shergat (ancient Ashur), and dated to the reign of Tiglath Pileser I. Some of the tablets were missing and some were fragmentary, and these lacunae have not been filled in. I shall be using the translation of T.J. Meek, *ANET*, pp. 180-88.

5. Meek, 'The Origin of Hebrew Law', p. 54.

collections state that judges must refer to these laws when deciding cases.[1] In the epilogue to the Laws of Hammurabi we find the only statement within the law codes about the intended human audience:

> Let any oppressed man who has a cause
> come into the presence of the statue of me, the king of justice,
> and then read carefully my inscribed stele,
> and give heed to my precious words,
> and may my stela make the case clear to him;
> may he understand his cause;
> may he set his mind at ease! [2]

However, it is doubtful that the laity was helped by the laws inscribed on this stele. It has been pointed out that most members of society would have been illiterate, and would not have been allowed into the temple precinct where the stele was displayed.[3] And even if a literate oppressed person had managed to read the stele, they would have discovered that there are no laws which protect the oppressed inscribed on it.[4]

On the basis of the prologue and epilogue sections it has been suggested that these documents are a royal *apologia*. Prologue and epilogue are extant for the Laws of Hammurabi and in part for the Lipit-Ishtar collection, and it has been argued that all the Mesopotamian law collections evinced this three-part structure.[5] They indicate that the legal collections have been promulgated soon after a change in government.[6] The main purpose of publication would be to give legal credence to the new state.[7] The law codes would serve to justify the king's position as the head of state.[8] They emphasize that he has

1. R. Westbrook, 'Biblical and Cuneiform Law Codes', *RB* 92 (1985), p. 249.

2. *ANET*, p. 178.

3. S.M. Paul, *Studies in the Book of the Covenant in the Light of Cuneiform and Biblical Law* (Leiden: Brill, 1970), p. 22.

4. This was emphasized by Norbert Lohfink in his address, 'The Option for the Poor: Views of an Old Testament Scholar', delivered at the Catholic Biblical Association Annual Meeting, 1990.

5. Paul, *Studies in the Book of the Covenant*, p. 11.

6. D.J. Wiseman, 'The Laws of Hammurabi Again', *JSS* 7 (1962), p. 163.

7. G.E. Mendenhall, 'Ancient Oriental and Biblical Law', *BA* 17 (1954), pp. 32-34.

8. K.W. Whitelam, *The Just King: Monarchical Judicial Authority in Ancient Israel* (JSOTSup, 12; Sheffield: JSOT Press, 1979), p. 22.

fulfilled his divine mandate as the faithful shepherd and judge of his people.

The relief at the top of the stele containing the Laws of Hammurabi contributes to its function as a royal apology. It depicts the king being offered a rod and a ring from the god Shamash. Although the relief has been interpreted to mean that Shamash is giving the law to Hammurabi, S.M. Paul argues that this is not the case. Instead, he claims that the ring and rod are symbols of sovereignty, justice and authority. It is these which are being given to the king. In addition, the relief at the top of the stele served to place the image of Hammurabi permanently in the presence of the god Shamash.[1] Hence, the publication of the law code assured the citizens that the king was chosen of the gods, that he was being faithful to his mandate, and that therefore there would be justice and prosperity in the land.

Consistent with its being an apology for the king, the Code of Hammurabi, as an imperial code, strove to unify the empire by means of a single legal tradition.[2] Publication of a unified law code is part of his task as overseer of justice in the land. This purpose is articulated in the prologue:

> When Marduk commissioned me to guide the people aright, to direct the land,
> I established law and justice in the language of the land,
> thereby promoting the welfare of the people.[3]

This leads to the conclusion that Hammurabi brought together various laws of his empire, put them into a common language, and made them a more or less consistent whole.[4] This law code therefore contains traditional material as well as laws which have been modified or added.

There are some major difficulties, however, in explaining all ancient Near Eastern legal collections as royal *apologia*. Because in the later texts the prologue and epilogue are missing, and because it is here that the royal apology was present, this description of the literary

1. Whitelam, *The Just King*, p. 23.
2. Boecker, *The Administration of Justice*, p. 77; Meek, 'The Origin of Hebrew Law', p. 55.
3. *ANET*, p. 165.
4. Meek, 'The Origin of Hebrew Law', p. 55.

genre cannot account for all collections of Mesopotamian law.[1] In fact, Westbrook argues that the very different style of the prologue and epilogue from the bodies of law indicates that the law collections existed separately and were only sometimes inserted into a framework.[2] He continues his discussion on the genre of the law collections by arguing that law collections and omen collections in Mesopotamia are similar in that both are compilations of precedents which are referred to by practitioners.[3] As evidence of the law collections being referred to in adjudicating legal disputes, he points to the finding of Assyrian laws in a Gate House—the normal location of the court in Mesopotamia. Furthermore, the process of recopying laws over a series of centuries revealed both that archaic language was retained, and that substantive changes in laws were made.[4] Westbrook argues that this process indicates that the laws were being used and hence needed to be revised in order to remain current. Here, then, is evidence of the laws being collections of legal precedents which were used in the adjudication of legal disputes at the gate.

The fact that the Code of Hammurabi was recopied for more than a millennium with no significant changes indicates to him that at some point it had changed its genre. It had become canonical literature and was recopied in scribal schools for its own sake.[5] In conclusion, Westbrook claims that when the legal texts are copied without changes being made, then they are no longer functioning as references for judges, but that when legal collections are being revised, this indicates that they are being applied in the courts.[6]

We may conclude that the legal collections so far unearthed in Mesopotamia fall into three distinct literary genres. When the laws are sandwiched between a prologue and epilogue which proclaims the deeds and divine mandate of the king, then the law collection is part of a royal *apologia*. When the laws are preserved without the prologue

1. Westbrook, 'Biblical and Cuneiform Law Codes', pp. 249-50.

2. Westbrook, 'Biblical and Cuneiform Law Codes', p. 251. In the case of biblical law, they are inserted into a narrative framework.

3. Westbrook, 'Biblical and Cuneiform Law Codes', pp. 251-56.

4. Westbrook, 'Biblical and Cuneiform Law Codes', p. 256. My selection of laws dealing with the family abandoned by the patriarch is an example of laws being reworked over time. See section 2A, below.

5. Westbrook, 'Biblical and Cuneiform Law Codes', p. 236.

6. Westbrook, 'Biblical and Cuneiform Law Codes', p. 256.

and epilogue, when there is evidence that they are being recopied with changes and additions being made, and when they are uncovered in a location at which legal disputes are settled, then the laws are functioning as a set of precedents which are referred to in the process of adjudication. Finally, when the laws are uncovered in scribal schools, and show no signs of revision, then the laws have become canonical, or classical literature—part of the venerated tradition which is passed on unchanged.

C. *Comparison of Mesopotamian and Biblical Law*

What comparisons can be drawn between ancient Mesopotamian legal collections and biblical law? Studies in the past have sometimes stressed the similarities, and at other times the differences between the traditions.[1] A discussion of the individual points of comparison is not pertinent. However, it is important for this study of the legal status of the alien to keep in mind the nature, purpose and scope of these ancient Mesopotamian law codes. In these matters, the Old Testament laws seem to be very similar. As the Laws of Hammurabi were not referred to in legal practice, so also the biblical laws are not referred to by the judges, or any other practitioners of the law in the biblical text. For example, when Boaz seeks to carry out a legal transaction at the city gate (Ruth 4), no law collection is cited or referred to, yet it seems that all parties understood and agreed to the legal procedure and the consequences. There was clearly an authoritative legal tradition operating, and yet the text gives us no indication whether it was written or oral or both. If we compare the account in Ruth 4 to laws regulating the levirate and goel institutions in the Pentateuch, there are a great number of discrepancies.[2] Yet because the authors of the

1. The Book of the Covenant and the Laws of Hammurabi have been the focus of the discussion, since the greatest resemblances exist between the laws of these two codes. Mendenhall ('Ancient Oriental and Biblical Law', p. 37) points out that the Laws of Hammurabi reflect a class society which values human life on the basis of class, whereas the Covenant Code, with one exception, advocates impartial justice. Eichrodt (*Theology of the Old Testament*, I, pp. 77-78) describes the Covenant Code as more humane because it does not legislate bodily mutilation except in the case of the *lex talionis*, and because it values human life more highly than property.

2. See D.A. Leggett's dissertation, *The Levirate and Goel Institutions in the Old Testament* (Cherry Hill, NJ: Mack, 1974) for a discussion of the differences between the narrative accounts of these institutions and biblical laws which regulate them.

biblical text did not deem it important to set out clearly the judicial procedures that they followed, we do not have the information needed to draw any firm conclusion from these discrepancies. The texts are silent on this issue, and hence we do not know precisely what relationship existed between written laws and legal practice.[1]

Also, like other ancient oriental law codes, the Old Testament laws are not comprehensive in scope. For example, marriage laws are absent, yet there were clearly social conventions to be followed. The account of the choice of a marriage partner for Isaac (Gen. 24) presumes a host of customs—the arranging of the marriage by the parents, the criteria for an acceptable bride, the woman's right of refusal—and yet none of these are part of Israel's legal tradition.

Furthermore, biblical laws like Mesopotamian laws are not arranged in an easily observable order. In the three legal collections in the Pentateuch, the order of the laws has been the subject of debate, but has yet to be satisfactorily resolved.

The connection of Old Testament law codes with the establishment of a new government, and with the king as the law giver, is not so easily demonstrated. Whitelam's study concludes that the king in Israel had legislative powers, but that the ascription of laws to Yahweh through the mediation of Moses did not allow this to be stated in the text.[2] He further concludes that there is no evidence for a 'law book' being promulgated by a king, in similar manner to Hammurabi publishing the laws in order to establish his rule.[3]

The process of revising the laws, which was the basis of Westbrook's argument that some of the law collections did have practical import, is apparent in the biblical legal material. This will be demonstrated below with regard to the legal status of the alien. That evidence will lead to the conclusion that the biblical legal collections did function in the courts.

I would also like to consider whether biblical and Mesopotamian law collections can be characterized as reform documents. In some sense, all revisions are reforms, but the relationship of the law to

1. Jackson, 'Reflections on Biblical Criminal Law', p. 29.

2. See Whitelam's discussion of the pertinent texts in the Old Testament which point to the legislative legacy of the king, in *The Just King*, pp. 207-18.

3. Whitelam, *The Just King*, p. 212.

accepted practice is what is at issue here. Do the laws at times attempt to change customary practice, or do they only respond to new situations as they occur? Westbrook documents the changes that occurred through time to a law dealing with a bride's dowry, and concludes that the original law in the Code of Hammurabi was an innovation which was not taken up in practice.[1] Biblical law, we will notice, also evinces both types of revisions—both those which are in response to a new situation (1 Sam. 30.25) and those which attempt to reform existing institutions and would most likely not have become accepted practice (Deut. 17.18-20).

Finally, we need to consider whether motivating clauses are part of the ancient Mesopotamian legal tradition to which Israelite law was heir. Sonsino's study of this feature found that motivation clauses do occur in oriental collections, although not as frequently. For example, six per cent of the laws in the Code of Hammurabi contain motivation clauses as compared to sixteen per cent of the laws in the Book of the Covenant. Furthermore, the contents of the motivation clauses differ. In cuneiform law they serve to reinforce the main point of the law. For example, in the law of Hammurabi, which I shall discuss below, the husband is not allowed to reclaim his wife if he has voluntarily left the city, 'Because he rejected his city and fled'.[2] The motive clause emphasizes the main point at issue here. There are no cuneiform laws which are motivated by reference to an event, promise of well-being, or by being tied to the divine will.[3] Hence, although Israelite law was not unique in attaching motivating clauses to the laws, it was different in terms of the content of many of the motivation clauses, and the frequency with which they occurred.

In conclusion: the comparison between the genre of Mesopotamian law and biblical law indicates that both had some relation to existing legal practice, that neither are exhaustive compendiums of law but are lists of precedents of difficult cases. There are connections to the king, but it is not clear whether law collections are in all cases royal inscriptions or royal apologies. The differences noted above concerning the number of motivation clauses attached to biblical law may indicate that they came to function in other settings than the court. I

1. Westbrook, 'Biblical and Cuneiform Law Codes', p. 257.
2. *ANET*, p. 171.
3. Sonsino, *Motive Clauses in Hebrew Law*, pp. 153-54, 173-74.

will consider this in more detail when I deal with the individual collections in the Pentateuch.

D. *Comparisons between Treaties and Biblical Law*

Comparisons have also been made between biblical law and laws which functioned as stipulations of international treaties in the ancient Near East. Much has been made of the covenant form as a context to laws in the Old Testament.[1] Most of the legal collections in the Old Testament are placed in a context which contains elements of the treaty form.[2] They often begin with a historical introduction, conclude with blessings and curses, contain a document clause, call on witnesses, and list stipulations which regulate the relations between the two parties to the treaty. However, the stipulations of the Hittite international treaties are limited to regulating the dealings between the two states.[3] For example, they require the mutual renunciation of aggression, and provide for a defensive alliance. Hence, the content of the stipulations argues against seeing international treaties as a major influence on the biblical laws.

However, the discovery of the Hittite treaties has laid to rest the hypothesis of A. Alt that the apodictic form was unique to the Old Testament.[4] These treaties contain imperatives formulated using the direct form of address and which do not stipulate a punishment for the crime. They differ from biblical apodictic law in that they do not occur in lists which deal with a wide range of topics, as, for example, the Decalogue.[5] Hence, on the basis of content, the stipulations of international treaties do not seem to have influenced biblical law,

1. See, for example, Eichrodt's *Theology of the Old Testament*, I, pp. 70-97, in which the theology of the laws is discussed under the heading 'The Covenant Statutes'.

2. See D.J. McCarthy's *Treaty and Covenant* (AnBib, 21; Rome: Pontifical Biblical Institute, 1963), pp. 1-106, for a full discussion of the treaty form in the ancient Near East.

3. The Hittite treaties are found in *ANET*, trans. A. Goetz, pp. 201-206.

4. Alt, 'The Origins of Israelite Law', p. 103. His thesis that the casuistic law in the Old Testament was influenced by Mesopotamian law, while apodeictic law was original to the Israelites, was widely accepted. It constituted a central point of comparison between biblical law and laws of the ancient Near East. See, for example, Eichrodt's *Theology of the Old Testament*, I, p. 71.

5. McCarthy, *Treaty and Covenant*, pp. 159-60.

although the apodictic form of law and treaty form itself was very significant in shaping the context in which biblical laws came to be framed.

2. *The Alien in the Ancient Mediterranean*

It would be illuminating to this study of how the Pentateuchal laws deal with the alien if we could compare them with the way in which other ancient legal collections treated them. In looking for comparative material, I am presuming that the existence of aliens was not confined to the people of Israel, nor to the land of Canaan. The causes of leaving one's homeland which are described in the Old Testament, i.e. famine, war, family conflict and blood guilt, are common to all peoples.

A. *The Alien in Mesopotamian Law*

My search for laws which would regulate how the citizens of the land are to treat an outsider who needs to stay among them for some time yielded nothing in the Mesopotamian legal collections. Instead, the Laws of Eshnunna, the Code of Hammurabi and the Middle Assyrian laws each contained only one law pertaining to the alien, and in each case it dealt with the phenomenon of the alien only from the vantage point of the family left behind. The Laws of Eshnunna legislate:

> If a man hates his town and his lord and becomes a fugitive, (and if) another man takes his wife—when he returns, he shall have no right to claim his wife.[1]

The Code of Hammurabi states:

> If, when a seignior deserted his city and then ran away, his wife has entered the house of another after his (departure), if that seignior has returned and wishes to take back his wife, the wife of the fugitive shall not return to her husband because he scorned his city and ran away.[2]

The Middle Assyrian Laws stipulate, in a more detailed way than the Laws of Eshnunna, the legal status of the wife left behind.[3] There are then, no laws dealing with the legal status of the alien.

1. *ANET*, p. 162.
2. *ANET*, p. 171.
3. *ANET*, p. 183.

In the biblical laws, the treatment of aliens is sometimes included in laws which protect the widow, orphan and poor. The concern shown for the widow, the orphan and the poor is not unique to the Old Testament. To demonstrate this, F.C. Fensham investigated the legal and wisdom literature of the ancient Near East, and found numerous texts which stated the king's intent to protect the weak.[1] For example, in the stele of Hammurabi we read in the prologue that

> at that time Anum and Enlil named me to promote the welfare of the people,
> me, Hammurabi, the devout, god-fearing prince,
> to cause justice to prevail in the land,
> to destroy the wicked and the evil,
> that the strong might not oppress the weak[2]

and in the epilogue that

> I always governed them in peace;
> I sheltered them in my wisdom.
> In order that the strong might not oppress the weak,
> that justice might be dealt the orphan (and) the widow.[3]

However, it is significant that all these references are found in the prologue and epilogue to the laws. The protection of the widow, orphan and poor is not regulated by the case laws, but is part of the statement made by the king in order to demonstrate that he has carried out his mandate of establishing justice.

The laws in the Pentateuch which protect the dependent members of society differ, therefore, in two important respects. First, their protection is formulated as a law. It is a law addressed to the head of the household, as are all the laws. It is significant that the protection of the needy is not seen as an in-house area completely under the jurisdiction of the *paterfamilias*, as was, for example, the arranging of marriages. Second, the alien is not specifically mentioned along with the widow, orphan and poor in the Mesopotamian law collections. Members of their own community who are in need are singled out as worthy of

1. See his references to the law collections of Mesopotamia in 'Widow, Orphan and the Poor in Ancient Near Eastern Legal and Wisdom Literature', *JNES* 21 (1962), pp. 130-33.
2. *ANET*, p. 164.
3. *ANET*, p. 178.

protection by the king, but an outsider entering their community in need of protection is not mentioned.

The fact that the alien is mentioned in all the law collections in the Pentateuch, and not at all in the Mesopotamian codes, does not necessarily mean that the Babylonians and Assyrians were unsympathetic to the plight of the alien. Hospitality to the stranger may have been one of the accepted mores of the culture and yet may not have been included in the legal tradition. The omission can be explained by noting that these law codes are addressed to the citizens of a land in order to establish justice among them. The aliens as non-citizens are not part of the intended audience, although they may in fact be members of the society.

The place to look for an explanation of this difference is perhaps in the particular history of the Israelite people. The patriarchs are portrayed as aliens, both in Canaan and Egypt.[1] The Israelites were aliens in the land of Egypt. These traditions play an important role in the legal collections in the Old Testament. Their sojourn in Egypt is often referred to in order to motivate the Israelites to be kind to those less fortunate than themselves (Exod. 22.21; 23.9). It may also have led to the formation of laws which protected not only the widow, orphan and poor, but also the alien.

B. *The Alien in Bedouin Society*

Scholars have drawn analogies between the alien referred to in the Old Testament and other fringe peoples. Since there are no helpful comparisons to be drawn from the legal material, they have turned to other material and other societies when making analogies. R. de Vaux, for example, when discussing the practice of hospitality in the Old Testament, shown, for example, by Abraham's receiving of guests at Mambre (Gen. 18.1-8) and Laban welcoming Abraham's servant (Gen. 24.28-32), refers to the customs of nomads. The law of asylum which he sees operative in modern Bedouin societies is reflected, he claims, in the Old Testament institution of protecting the alien.[2] Similarly, V.H. Kooy describes the duty of hospitality to a stranger in

1. Spina ('Israelites as *gerim*', p. 322) has investigated the historicity of this tradition, and concluded that it represents an authentic history of some proto-Israelites.

2. De Vaux, *Ancient Israel*, p. 10.

terms of present-day Bedouin customs.[1]

Both of these scholars have made assumptions which are questionable. First, they have assumed that the desert has somehow preserved for four thousand years the sort of life lived by the patriarchs.[2] Second, they have identified the patriarchs as Bedouins, nomads or semi-nomads. This description has come under attack. Rogerson concludes that we know too little about mobility and livestock breeding and their relationship to be able to describe ancient people as nomadic or semi-nomadic, and that the meaning of 'Bedouin' is also so vague as not to be helpful.[3]

C. *The Alien in Ancient Greece*

De Vaux also compares the status of the alien in the Old Testament with that of the *perioikoi* of Sparta.[4] He is not suggesting any historical connection, as with the comparison with Arabic nomadic society, but points out that there are similarities in the way these two societies dealt with non-residents who were free. When comparing the alien to the *perioikoi*, he is working only with those references to a group of aliens, i.e. the references which describe the Israelites as aliens in Egypt (Exod. 22.20). According to de Vaux, the *perioikoi* were the original inhabitants of the Peloponnesus, who retained their freedom and could own property, but had no political rights. This, he suggests, is analogous to the status of the conquered Canaanites, although the Canaanites were less fortunate in that all landed property was in Israelite hands. The Canaanites, i.e. the aliens, had to work for pay and as a rule were poor.[5]

It is not de Vaux's purpose in this survey to be exhaustive, or to

1. V.H. Kooy, 'Hospitality', in *IDB*, II (Nashville: Abingdon Press, 1976), p. 654.

2. See J.W. Rogerson, *Anthropology and the Old Testament* (Oxford: Basil Blackwell, 1978), pp. 1-4, 37, for a description of the history of the anthropological study of the Old Testament, and the need to rethink many assumptions.

3. Rogerson, *Anthropology and the Old Testament*, pp. 42-45. He applauds the work of de Geus and Mendenhall because they have taken into account the work of recent anthropology and reject the classification of the Hebrews as a semi-nomadic people when they entered the land.

4. De Vaux, *Ancient Israel*, pp. 74-75.

5. It should be noted that this comparison is based upon the conquest theory of the settlement of Israel in Canaan.

defend every aspect of the comparison. Thus, it would not be fair to disagree with him because he has not mentioned certain features of the status of the *perioikoi* or the alien. Since my intent is to study the status of the alien more thoroughly than de Vaux's survey is able to do, it may be helpful to understand the status of the *perioikoi* in more detail so that any subsequent discussion can be seen against the backdrop of how another ancient society dealt with residents who were neither slaves nor full citizens.

Sparta in the classical period was an *ethnos* as opposed to a *polis*. An *ethnos* was a state without a city center, whereas a *polis*, such as Athens, had an urban center. The *ethnos* type of state was less developed than the *polis*, and preceded it chronologically.[1] Within Sparta there were three classes of people: the *homoioi* (the citizens with full rights); the *perioikoi* (communities of free people who were subject to Sparta); and the Helots (the native people who became dependent due to conquest but were not slaves). About the *perioikoi* there is not much information. They formed small communities which were somewhat independent in internal matters, but were completely dependent on Sparta in war and foreign relations. They were in some way part of the state, although as second-class citizens. The communities of *perioikoi* were homogeneous and owned their own land and engaged in all manner of economic activities, agriculture and manufacturing.[2] This description, as de Vaux has noted, may shed light on the relations which Israel had with some of the tribes in Canaan. The Gibeonites especially might function within the Israelite state in a way analogous to that in which the *perioikoi* functioned within Sparta. I will defer further investigation of this possibility until I turn to a study of the pertinent texts.

In his study of ancient Judaism, Max Weber draws many analogies between the pre-exilic alien and the metic (*metoikos*) of the Athenian *polis*. He does this not to draw any historical connections, but because he sees similarities between the way in which the Athenian state dealt with the variety of people living within Attica, and how the Israelites

1. M.M. Austin and P. Vidal-Naquet, *Economic and Social History of Ancient Greece: An Introduction* (trans. and rev. M.M. Austin; Berkeley: University of California Press, 1977), pp. 78-79.

2. Austin and Vidal-Naquet, *Economic and Social History of Ancient Greece*, pp. 84-85.

treated the variety of people living in Palestine.[1]

In Athens there were also three classes of people: the citizen, the metic and the slave, and the distinction between them was legally quite precise. There is abundant material, both in the literary and legal texts, which make it clear what the requirements and privileges of each class were. There is also enough material to indicate that changes occurred in these requirements. For example, until the law of Pericles, it was sufficient that a father was a citizen for his children to be considered citizens. However, the law of Pericles, formulated in 451–450 BC, required that both parents be citizens in order for their children to be considered citizens.[2] One of the privileges of citizenship was owning land. As non-citizens, agriculture was closed to the metics and they became involved largely in trades and commerce.[3] The metics were free, ethnically Greek and non-Greek, and lived in Athens or Attica more or less permanently. The evidence for their legal status dates from the fourth century BC, and it is not certain whether the same rules applied before then. These rules specify that when foreigners entered Athens, they had to register as metics within a certain time (Austin suggests a month), otherwise they could be sold as slaves. Metics had to pay a tax on their person (*metoikion*) and if remiss could be sold into slavery. They also had to pay for the right to trade in the *agora*, in addition to the war taxes and liturgy taxes which were levied on citizens as well. Metics could be granted equality of taxation with a citizen, but that still did not make them full citizens, it merely excused them from paying the *metoikion* and certain other taxes. Metics also had to find a patron (*prostates*), whose function seemed to be to represent the metic in court. Failure to do so would again result in being sold into slavery. In law, they were treated as second-class citizens. They had to register as resident in a *deme*, but had no political rights. They served in the army in separate contingents, and also in the navy, as rowers. Austin concludes that the metics were, in fact, indispensable to the economic life of the city.[4]

1. Weber, *Ancient Judaism*, pp. 32-36.

2. Austin and Vidal-Naquet, *Economic and Social History of Ancient Greece*, p. 95. At approximately the same time, in the province of Judah, Ezra was attempting to enforce laws which prohibited Jews from marrying foreigners.

3. Austin and Vidal-Naquet, *Economic and Social History of Ancient Greece*, p. 97.

4. Austin and Vidal-Naquet, *Economic and Social History of Ancient Greece*,

Weber's description of the pre-exilic alien sounds very much like the description of the metic. On the basis of Lev. 25.35 he concludes that landlessness is the criterion of the גר. This is more basic than his being a non-Israelite, since Israelites out of their tribal territory are also considered aliens. Aliens are under the private protection of an individual, and their rights are protected by the political organization in the village. The phrase 'the alien who is in your gate' is understood to denote the legal status of an alien. That is, like metics, they were under the jurisdiction of the city and were also protected by it. It is unclear whether or not they were required to have a legal patron, but since the law requires that they not be oppressed, Weber assumes that aliens can appear in court.[1]

In addition, Weber claims that aliens were often tradespeople, musicians and artisans. The description of aliens as tradespeople is based on an analogy with the social organization of the Bedouins which did not grant full citizenship to artisans and merchants, as well as concluding that the artisans described as descendants of Cain (Gen. 4.17, 21, 22) were a guest people.[2]

There are many points on which I would differ with M. Weber, such as the dating of the texts he uses, as well as the social inferences that he draws from them. It seems that the analogy with the metics has been forced onto the material, and this is indeed the danger of any analogy. His conclusion that the aliens are landless on the basis of Lev. 25.35 is a clear example of this. The law requires that:

> If one of your countrymen becomes poor and is unable to support himself among you, help him as you would an alien or temporary resident, so he can continue to live among you.

From this Weber concludes that 'impoverished' Israelites are aliens, and that impoverished means landless, and that the defining characteristic of an alien is landlessness.[3]

These connections cannot be sustained on the basis of the text. For example, the wording of the law, 'Help him as you would as alien or temporary resident', indicates that the Israelite does not become an

pp. 99-101, contains a description of the status of the metic, and a discussion of the sources from which this reconstruction is drawn on pp. 263-88.

1. Weber, *Ancient Judaism*, p. 33.
2. Weber, *Ancient Judaism*, p. 28.
3. Weber, *Ancient Judaism*, p. 33.

alien but should only be treated like an alien. In addition, Lev. 25.47 presumes that aliens can become wealthy, hence the connection between aliens and poverty is not definitive. Neither is there evidence to suggest that aliens are always landless. Although poverty and landlessness often go together in the traditional agricultural society presumed by Leviticus 25, that is not necessarily the case. In fact, on the basis that Leviticus 25 does presume an agricultural society, we could argue that the wealthy alien of Lev. 25.47 would own land. Elsewhere we read that Abraham, though an alien, could buy land (Gen. 23.4), and in the visions of Ezekiel, aliens are allocated land (Ezek. 47.23). Although there may be connections between how *perioikoi* and metics were treated in Greek society, and how aliens were treated in Israelite society, they are not strong enough to warrant our reading into biblical laws the particular features of these two groups.

D. *The Alien and the Habiru*

Finally, we need to ask if there is any connection to be made between the Israelites as Hebrews and Israelites as aliens. The discussion on the identity of the *habiru/apiru* and their connection with the Hebrews and the Israelites has been long-standing and is not easily resolved. It is significant to note that the presence of the *apiru* is no longer attested after 1500–1200 BC. No group of people, however defined, were called that throughout Israelite's history, whereas גר continued to be used to describe certain individuals and tribes.[1] The reason for this is perhaps because the terms *apiru/habiru* were not epithets by which these people referred to themselves. Spina argues that they had a pejorative connotation and were usually applied by the insiders to the outsiders. In the Old Testament, the term Hebrew is most often used by non-Hebrews, except when the word refers to their ethnic identity or when talking to foreigners.[2]

Spina has made some interesting observations on the possible relationship between aliens and Hebrews. He argues that these words refer to the same social type. That is, both refer to individuals or groups who are alienated from their original social context. Further, as the tradition referring to proto-Israelites as aliens is reliable, so also is the

1. See M.C. Astour, 'Habiru', in *IDBSup* (Nashville: Abingdon Press, 1976), pp. 382-85, for an overview on the scholarship and data.

2. Spina, 'Israelites as *gerim*', p. 331.

tradition referring to proto-Israelites as Hebrews.[1]

For the moment, I want to conclude this brief survey on the analogies which have been made between the aliens we meet in Pentateuchal law and other fringe groups by noting only that Israel was not unique in having within its borders a variety of people whose presence there was due to a variety of reasons. Because of the movements of people, and the existence of powerful states, ancient societies had to deal with a plurality of peoples. In addition, conditions of famine, family upheaval and war also meant that individuals or families apart from their tribal group would occasionally enter a village and require assistance. Different societies reacted differently to the challenge of incorporating newcomers. Various factors can be discovered which will be helpful in illuminating one society's response over against another. The contrasting status of the *perioikoi* and the metics was understandable on the basis of geographical, historical, social, religious, economic, political and ethnic factors. I hope that my study of the changing status of the alien in Israel will also be able to uncover the various factors which were at work.

1. Spina, 'Israelites as *gerim*', pp. 330-31.

Chapter 3

THE PRE-DEUTERONOMIC LAWS

My study of the legal status of the alien begins quite modestly with an examination of the three references to the alien (גר) in the Book of the Covenant (Exod. 20.22–23.33).[1] In the second section of this chapter I shall consider the single reference to the alien that occurs in the Sabbath command of the Decalogue in Exodus 20.

1. *The Book of the Covenant*

The three references to the alien in the Book of the Covenant occur in Exod. 22.20 (ET 21); 23.9, 12. Interestingly, the first two are quite similar, and instruct the Israelite not to mistreat the alien, while the last is the Sabbath command amplified to include the animals, slaves and the alien. Before I analyse these particular texts, it is necessary to examine the sources, form and possible dating of the pertinent sections of the Book of the Covenant.

A. *Introductory Matters*

The Book of the Covenant is part of the Sinai narrative, but it is clear that it has been inserted here. The narrative breaks off at Exod. 20.21 and resumes in Exod. 24.1.[2] The law collection which is set within

1. I am using the traditional name of this collection deriving from Exod. 34.7.

2. See Eissfeldt, *The Old Testament: An Introduction*, p. 213; Fohrer, *Introduction to the Old Testament*, p. 133; and B.S. Childs, *The Book of Exodus: A Critical, Theological Commentary* (OTL; Philadelphia: Westminster Press, 1962), pp. 453-54, for a presentation of how the Book of the Covenant was incorporated into its present context. They argue that the original narrative sequence was Exod. 20.18-21; 20.1-17; 24.3. The references in Exod. 24.3 to the 'words and laws' are attributed to the redactor. Furthermore, it is argued that the phrase 'all the words' referred only to the Decalogue, which formed the basis for the following covenant renewal ceremony.

this framework seems to have existed independently in some form prior to its being incorporated into the narrative.[1] Because it is not one with its context, I will not use the narrative framework in my discussion of the dating, purpose and audience of the Book of the Covenant in its independent form.

Furthermore, the Book of the Covenant as it now stands does not seem to have originally been a single work. Because it contains both casuistic and apodictic laws, and because these different forms occur in clusters which are formulated consistently within themselves, as in Exod. 21.2–22.17; 22.18-22; 23.1-3, I conclude that smaller collections have been combined. There have been several attempts to outline the process of growth which resulted in the law collection we now have.[2] I do not need to involve myself in that discussion, but it is important to be aware of the genre and intent of the final form of the law collection, since that is the immediate context of the laws concerning the alien. We will also need to be aware of the form-critical issues connected with apodictic law, since the pertinent laws are all cast in the apodictic form.

Although the genre of the Book of the Covenant may seem obvious, i.e. it is a legal collection, that simple designation is not sufficient. The Code of Hammurabi is also a legal collection, and yet it is very different from the Book of the Covenant. The Code of Hammurabi has a threefold structure; the laws are sandwiched between a prologue and epilogue. The laws are consistently casuistic in form, and deal only with civil affairs. The Book of the Covenant does not have these features.[3] Rather than being framed by a poetic prologue and epilogue,

1. See D. Patrick, *Old Testament Law* (Atlanta: John Knox, 1985), pp. 63-65; J. Blenkinsopp, *Wisdom and Law in the Old Testament* (Oxford: Oxford University Press, 1983), p. 82; M. Noth, *Exodus: A Commentary* (trans. J.S. Bowden; OTL; Philadelphia: Westminster Press, 1962), p. 169; Boecker, *Law and the Administration of Justice*, p. 136.

2. See, e.g., P.D. Hanson, 'The Theological Significance of Contradiction within the Book of the Covenant', in *Canon and Authority: Essays in Old Testament Religion and Theology* (ed. G.W. Coats and B.O. Long; Philadelphia: Fortress Press, 1977), pp. 113-15; and Patrick, *Old Testament Law*, pp. 65-66.

3. Paul, *Studies in the Book of the Covenant*, pp. 29-35, argues that the Book of the Covenant as well as Deuteronomy and the Holiness Code evince signs of the same structure as the Laws of Hammurabi. He claims that Exod. 19.3-6 is parallel to the Mesopotamian Prologue, and Exod. 23.20-33 is parallel to the Epilogue. Hence the law is in a framework of redemptive history. However, showing that the present

the Book of the Covenant is framed by cultic laws (Exod. 20.22; 23.14-19). It includes not only casuistic laws dealing with civil cases, but also personally addressed laws dealing with cultic matters, and ethical obligations. These differences indicate that the purpose and social location of the intended audiences of the two legal collections are quite different.

The framing of the Book of the Covenant with cultic laws is important for understanding its intent. These laws provide a civic code with a religious framework.[1] Boecker claims that this structure makes a theological statement. It places the laws which regulate how the Israelites are to relate to one another in the context of laws which regulate how they are to be related to God.[2] Because the opening law of the altar is polemical in tone, part of the purpose of the law code is to oppose foreign cults.[3]

N. Lohfink has noticed that the laws dealing with the alien are significant for the structuring of the Covenant Code. He suggests that the doubling of the law prohibiting the oppression of the alien (Exod. 22.20; 23.9) creates a frame which begins and ends a series dealing with *personae miserae*. In addition, the law in Exod. 22.20 differs from those preceding it in the text in its strongly parenetic character. He concludes that by means of their placement, their repetition and their form, the laws dealing with the alien are emphasized.[4]

context of the Book of the Covenant includes a prologue and an epilogue does not indicate a relationship to the form of Mesopotamian law collections. The purpose and form of the Prologue and Epilogue of the cuneiform legal collections is quite different from the purpose and form of the context of the Book of the Covenant, as described by S.M. Paul himself. Rather than finding a point of similarity with the Mesopotamian collections, it seems more correct to draw a contrast. The Book of the Covenant, unlike Mesopotamian laws, now stands in a narrative context.

1. Blenkinsopp, *Wisdom and Law in the Old Testament*, p. 82.
2. Boecker, *Law and the Administration of Justice*, pp. 138, 144, 145.
3. Childs, *Exodus*, p. 459.
4. He argues that the Code's final form shows a hebdomadarian structure:

1.	A	20.22-26	Cult: idols and altar
2.	B	21.1-11	6 + 1: liberation of slaves
3.	C	21.12–22.19	Civil law collection
4.	C′	22.20–23.9	Collection 'ger'
5.	B′	23.10-12	6 + 1: fallow year and sabbath
6.	A′	23.13-19	Cult: feasts and sacrifices
7.		23.20-33	Epilogue.

In addition, Childs has characterized the Covenant Code as a national law because it distinguishes between the stranger and the native. I would wish to qualify this since the distinction between the native and the stranger (גר) is not necessarily between the Israelite and non-Israelite. The stranger may be a member of another Israelite tribe.[1] Since it is by no means certain that the Covenant Code is dated to the monarchic period, it is premature to call it a national law.[2] However, since it is true that the law is addressed to the people of Israel, it could be classed as an ethnic law.

In contrast with cuneiform laws which are not personally addressed and which do not bear signs of being widely published, the laws of the Book of the Covenant seem to have been delivered orally. S.M. Paul argues that because the personal form of address predominates, and because the laws have a didactic purpose as demonstrated in the motive clauses, we can conclude that they were delivered orally.[3] D. Patrick further substantiates this thesis by demonstrating that the personal sections of the code overshadow the impersonal. He claims that the impersonal judgments are the imports into the personal sections, and that the resulting combination bears the marks of being an address.[4] Childs and Hanson also argue that the judgments (משפטים) have been incorporated into an existing body of apodictic law. As evidence they cite its consistent and uniform casuistic style, as well as the fact that it has its own introduction in Exod. 21.1.[5]

The discussion of the genre of the whole law book now proceeds to a discussion of the separate genre of the apodictic sections. It is now appropriate to enter into the discussion on the formal characteristics

Lohfink's table is from a hand-out which was distributed at the occasion of his address on 'The Option for the Poor', to the Catholic Biblical Association 1990 Annual Meeting.

1. See, for example, Judg. 17, where the Levite is described as 'sojourning'.

2. I will discuss the dating of the Covenant Code later in this section.

3. Paul, *Studies in the Book of the Covenant*, p. 39.

4. D. Patrick, 'I and Thou in the Covenant Code', in *Society of Biblical Literature Seminar Papers 1978* (Missoula, MT: Scholars Press, 1978), pp. 72-77.

5. Hanson, 'The Theological Significance of Contradiction', pp. 124-25, and Childs, *Exodus*, pp. 456-57. Childs dates these casuistic laws early on the basis of the parallels to ancient Near Eastern legal collections, and because the society depicted by them points to the period immediately after the occupation.

of apodictic law, and the *Sitz im Leben* of this form. I am primarily concerned with the apodictic laws since it is in this section, and not in the judgments section, that the laws referring to the alien occur.

There has been an extensive discussion on the form of apodictic law. The classic description of the form occurs in Alt's study,[1] and the most thorough overview of the scholarship is found in S.M. Paul's monograph.[2] Apodictic laws can be characterized as personally addressed, brief prohibitions. The grammatical construction often involves a verb preceded by the particle לא: a very forceful negative. In addition, apodictic laws often occur in a series.[3]

In the Book of the Covenant we find the apodictic commands bunched together in three relatively homogeneous sections: the law of the altar (Exod. 20.23-26); moral commands and duties (Exod. 22.21–23.9); and Sabbatical times and cultic calendar (Exod. 23.10-19).[4] The fact that they often occur in series, which are rhythmical, lends support to the claim that they were recited.[5] Alt proposed that it was the annual covenant renewal ceremony at which these laws were recited. This *Sitz im Leben* rests on the hypothesis that Israel was organized as an amphictyony in the pre-monarchic period. This thesis has come under attack and can no longer be assumed.[6] However, the supposition that these laws were proclaimed publicly at a cultic ceremony does not necessarily require the existence of an amphictyony.[7] In addition, the

1. Alt, 'The Origins of Israelite Law', pp. 79-132.

2. Paul, *Studies in the Book of the Covenant*, pp. 118-23. See also W. Malcolm Clark, 'Law', in *Old Testament Form Criticism* (ed. John H. Hayes; San Antonio: Trinity University Press, 1974), pp. 99-140, for a survey of scholarship on the form of biblical law.

3. This is the definition given by K. Koch, *The Growth of the Biblical Tradition: The Form-Critical Method* (trans. from the 2nd German edn by S.M. Cupitt; New York: Scribner's, 1969), pp. 9-10.

4. I am using the headings and divisions suggested by Patrick, *Old Testament Law*, pp. 65-67.

5. Alt, 'The Origins of Israelite Law', pp. 111-12, 129.

6. See A.D.H. Mayes, *Israel in the Period of of the Judges* (SBT [2] 29; Naperville, IL: SCM Press, 1974), pp. 7-83 for a presentation of the amphictyony theory and its refutation.

7. Hanson, 'The Theological Significance of Contradiction', p. 119, and Patrick, *Old Testament Law*, p. 66, for example, argue that the laws are addressed to all Israel, and that they show signs of oral proclamation, without claiming that Israel was organized around a central shrine.

apodictic form requires that a person speaks for God. This is further evidence that the cultic setting is the most likely *Sitz im Leben*, and it has been suggested that a priest would be the most likely mouthpiece for God.[1] The existence of motive clauses attached to the laws again points to their didactic function. Although they are not so common in the Book of the Covenant as in the laws in Deuteronomy,[2] it should be noted that all the motive clauses in the Book of the Covenant are attached to the apodictic laws.

Although all scholars agree that the characteristics of apodictic law already mentioned indicate that they were used in oral setting, they are not agreed on the original *Sitz im Leben*. Alt's contention that apodictic law is unique to Israel[3] has long been disputed. Mendenhall pointed to the similarities between the laws of the Decalogue and Covenant Code and the Hittite treaties[4] and argued on that basis that Old Testament apodictic laws should be considered as stipulations of a covenant between Yahweh and his people, Israel. Koch follows Mendenhall in concluding that although the form is not identical, it was inspired by the Hittite treaties. What is unique to Israel, he concludes, is the tendency to form apodictic laws into a series.[5]

The other major thesis regarding the origin of apodictic laws is Gerstenberger's. He theorizes that these laws are parallel to wisdom maxims, both in their form and content.[6] It is only in the wisdom

1. Alt, 'The Origins of Israelite Law', pp. 125-29; Hanson, 'The Theological Significance of Contradiction', p. 119.

2. According to Gemser ('The Importance of the Motive Clause in Old Testament Law', p. 51) nine out of fifty-nine laws in the Book of the Covenant contain motive clauses, as opposed to sixty-one out of ninety-nine in Deuteronomy.

3. Alt, 'The Origins of Israelite Law', p. 103. R.A.F. MacKenzie ('The Formal Aspect of Ancient Near Eastern Law', in *The Seed of Wisdom* [ed. W.S. McCullough; Toronto: University of Toronto Press, 1964], pp. 40-44) claims that the apodictic form occurs in Egyptian royal edicts and in the Code of Hammurabi. Although the form is similar, the content of Egyptian and Babylonian apodictic laws is very different from Old Testament apodictic law. MacKenzie does not discuss the possible *Sitz im Leben* of the apodictic laws in the Old Testament, but assumes that they were heard by individual Israelites who were then held responsible for their own conduct.

4. Mendenhall, 'Ancient Oriental and Biblical Law', p. 30.

5. Koch, *The Growth of the Biblical Tradition*, p. 21.

6. E. Gerstenberger ('Covenant and Commandment', *JBL* 84 [1965], pp. 50-51) cites the example of the negative prohibition found, for example, in Prov. 3.27-30. The form is not strictly parallel, since the prohibition in Proverbs does not use the particle לא, but אל.

literature, he argues, that we find instruction on ethical matters. Clan instruction, he suggests, rather than covenant stipulation, is the *Sitz im Leben* in which apodictic law originated.

The discussion is difficult to resolve, because the analogies all fall short of being strictly parallel. There is no extra-biblical form analogous to the apodictic law in the same way that cuneiform law is analogous to the casuistic law of the Covenant Code. As Blenkinsopp has noted, the hypothesis that the laws arose out of clan instruction can account for the wide-ranging content of apodictic law. Although the grammatical form of wisdom maxims is different from apodictic laws, this can be accounted for by the use of the 'laws' in a different context.[1] However, Gerstenberger's further thesis that proverbial sayings originate in clan instruction is not widely accepted. Many see the instruction of an elite class in the royal court as the original context. Although we may agree that the laws embody tribal wisdom, that is a step removed from arguing for clan instruction as the original setting.

Similarly, although Mendenhall claims that treaty stipulations cover the wide range of topics found in the Book of the Covenant,[2] he has been criticized on this point.[3] Treaty stipulations deal with the relationship between a vassal and sovereign, and do not deal with the cultic and moral issues that are addressed in the Book of the Covenant.

The evidence on both sides is suggestive but not conclusive. Aspects of apodictic law are analogous to laws found in extra-biblical literature, however the particular combination of features found in this collection has not, to date, been found elsewhere. We have not discovered apodictically formulated laws which regulate cultic, moral and civil affairs, and which tend to occur in series in any other ancient Mesopotamian text. It does seem very likely that these laws were used in a cultic setting in which the people of Israel were addressed by a

1. Blenkinsopp, *Wisdom and Law*, p. 81. He points to the admonitions in Prov. 3.29-31 as examples of proverbial sayings which seem closely related to apodictic laws.

2. Mendenhall ('Ancient Oriental and Biblical Law', p. 39) argues that the covenant was made with each individual. Hence the laws regulating relations between Israelites are analogous to the stipulations in Hittite treaties which regulate relations between vassals.

3. Gerstenberger ('Covenant and Commandment', p. 47) rightly claims that the covenant partner of Yahweh is always the people of Israel, not individual Israelites.

speaker representing Yahweh. It is also apparent that these laws were not only to be known and followed, but also to some extent understood and internalized. The motivation clauses, which do not specify punishment, indicate that the law should be obeyed as a result of choosing the right. These aspects also set apart this oldest Israelite legal collection from other ancient Near Eastern collections.

Although I have indicated that the law is addressed to all Israel,[1] some individuals are more responsible under the law than others. These laws are primarily addressed to the patriarch and instruct him in his various capacities as a participant in the cult, a judge in the court, and a man of substance in the economy.[2] It is not necessary to conclude that different people were holding these different offices. In pre-monarchic Israel, society was fairly undifferentiated, and the patriarch could be involved in settling legal disputes at the gate (Exod. 23.1-9); could participate in the cult (Exod. 23.10-19); and be required to be charitable (Exod. 22.22-27). Hence, the social location of the addressee is that of an Israelite male who is a powerful member of the society.

In the preceding discussion I have already alluded to, but not demonstrated that the final form of Book of the Covenant is prior to Deuteronomy. This is not a conclusion that all scholars agree with.[3] The laws dealing with the alien, widow and orphan have been described as belonging to a later stage in the development of the Covenant Code, and showing signs of deuteronomistic redaction. However, although the widow, orphan and alien are mentioned in the Covenant Code, they are mentioned in separate laws. Exodus 22.20 legislates for the alien; Exod. 22.21 for the widow and orphan. The widow and orphan are mentioned again in Exod. 23.11, the law regulating the fallow year, and this is followed in Exod. 23.12 by the Sabbath law which includes the alien. The fixed formula, 'the alien, widow and orphan' which is so prevalent in and typical of Deuteronomy does not occur here. For this reason, Lohfink argues that the laws pertaining to the poor in the Covenant Code are prior to

1. See the discussion by Patrick, 'I and Thou', p. 74, where he demonstrates that the 'thou' is Israel.

2. Patrick, 'I and Thou', pp. 75-76.

3. Lohfink briefly reviewed the recent scholarship on the issue in his address, 'The Option for the Poor', pp. 7-9.

the laws in Deuteronomy.[1] A thorough discussion of the evidence is presented in S.R. Driver's introduction to Deuteronomy. He clearly sets out the many instances in which Deuteronomic laws are dependent on those in the Book of the Covenant.[2]

Furthermore, on the basis of the society depicted by these laws, both in the apodictic and casuistic sections, we can date them to the period of the Judges.[3] In that time as in the Book of the Covenant, the patriarch is the locus of authority, and the extended family (בית־אב) is the basic social unit. Laws punishing offenses are addressed to the injured party or the next of kin, rather than judges and courts. The laws presuppose an agrarian, non-urban society which would have existed before and following the occupation of the land.[4] In addition, there are several arguments from silence which support this dating. There are no laws dealing with the monarchy, no laws dealing with an established priesthood, and no laws concerning commercial dealings.[5]

Finally, before I turn to the pertinent texts, it is necessary to address the issue of the historical value of these laws. In what way may they be used to illuminate the actual legal and social status of the alien in the community? The genre of the law code is the most significant factor in deciding what relationship these laws have to historical reality. Because we have placed apodictic law in the context of

1. Lohfink, 'Option for the Poor', pp. 7-9.

2. S.R. Driver, *Deuteronomy* (ICC; Edinburgh: T.&T. Clark, 3rd edn, 1902), pp. iv-ix.

3. This is earlier than the traditional dating based on the Documentary Hypothesis. Both Fohrer (*Introduction to the Old Testament*, pp. 136-37) and Eissfeldt (*The Old Testament: An Introduction*, p. 219) argue for a date in the early monarchy, partly on the basis of its incorporation into E. Furthermore, they connect the polemical law of the altar (Exod. 20.24-26) with the reforms of Jehu or Elijah.

4. See Mayes, *Judges*, pp. 72-73, for a presentation of tribal society at this time as analogous to the segmentary society found in African tribal societies, and his conclusion that the Book of the Covenant would be an appropriate legal code for such a society.

5. Paul, *Studies in the Book of the Covenant*, pp. 44-45. I. Lewy's discussion of the dating of Exod. 22.21-28 and Exod. 22.31–23.9, in 'Dating of the Covenant Code Sections on Humaneness and Righteousness', *VT* 7 (1957), pp. 322-26, is not convincing. He hypothesizes that these sections are presupposed by the literary prophets, and hence must be dated between Samuel and the division of the kingdom. The nature of the evidence is sufficiently imprecise for us to be unable to say that the prophets knew these particular laws rather than that the prophets stood in a tradition of moral exhortation.

the cult, it follows that it does not function in society as a modern law code functions. We cannot assume that when the law prohibits the Israelite from oppressing the alien, that Israelites disobeying this law would be punished. Instead, these laws present the Israelites with normative conduct. They attempt to persuade them to behave in this gracious and charitable way by their own choice. From this genre of preached morality we can conclude that there were strangers who had been oppressed, and that the Israelites had been the oppressors. Because these laws had to be intelligible to both their author(s) and listeners/readers, we can argue that although it may not be an accurate reflection of what was actually practiced, it presents behavior which was within the realm of possibility.

B. *Laws Pertaining to the Alien*

> a. You shall not wrong or oppress a resident alien, for you were aliens in the land of Egypt (Exod. 22.20).[1]

Exod. 22.20 (ET 21) is cast in the apodictic form; employing the particle לא followed by the hiphil imperfect of ינה.[2] The meaning of ינה is 'to oppress' or 'be violent'. It is often used in the context of the rich and powerful ill-treating the poor and weak. It describes the oppression of the weak Israelite by the powerful Israelite.[3] Only in Isa. 49.26 is the oppressor a foreigner. This law is thus prohibiting not neglect, but active abuse of the alien.

The second injunction in the same command is also cast in the apodictic form; employing the particle לא followed by the qal imperfect of לחץ.[4] The verb can mean 'press' in a physical sense, or 'oppress'. It is consistently used to refer to foreigners oppressing Israel.[5] Its use here to refer to an Israelite oppressing an alien is an exception. Because of its connotation with foreign oppressors, this law might be paraphrased, 'Do not be oppressors to them as the Egyptians,

1. All translations are taken from the NRSV unless otherwise noted.

2. Some ancient translations, the LXX, the Syriac and the Targums, have the second person plural form of the verb.

3. See Lev. 19.33; 25.14, 17; Deut. 23.17; Jer. 22.3; Ezek. 18.7, 12, 16; 22.7, 29; and 45.8.

4. In addition, some ancient translations, the LXX, the Syriac and the Targums, give the second person plural form with no object.

5. See Exod. 3.9; Judg. 2.18; 4.3; 6.9; 10.12; 1 Sam. 10.18; Amos 6.14; 2 Kgs 13.4, 22; Jer. 30.20; Ps. 106.42.

Philistines, etc., have been oppressors to you'. Because the alien was probably a foreigner, i.e. someone outside one's clan, tribe or village, it is appropriate to use a term which refers to the oppression of one people by another people.

The two verbs thus connote oppression between two differently related groups of people. The first refers to the oppression, within a society, of the weak by the powerful. The second refers to the oppression of one people by another. The alien as a vulnerable foreigner needs to be protected from both types of oppression.

This law also includes a motivation clause, i.e. 'for you were aliens in Egypt'. Childs states, but does not demonstrate, that this is one of several Deuteronomic glosses found in the Book of the Covenant. Others he cites are Exod. 22.24; 23.9b.[1] The latter is the motivational clause which is attached to another law prohibiting the oppression of an alien. In both the Israelites are reminded of their past as aliens in Egypt.

The argument favoring these motivation clauses as glosses could be based on considerations of genre. If apodictic law is described as a brief imperative, found in a series, which exhibits a regular rhythm, then these and all motivation clauses are secondary. However, the Book of the Covenant has nine motivation clauses, many of which Childs does not seem to consider glosses. This law in particular does not seem to be in a series of similarly formulated laws. Hence, on the basis of genre, it need not be seen as a secondary addition.

Childs does not argue the point, but I would surmise that his attribution of these glosses to the Deuteronomist is based on content. As we shall see, in the book of Deuteronomy, the Exodus experience is determinative for creating and defining the people of God, and was often appealed to in order to motivate obedience. However, in the book of Deuteronomy, the reference to Israel's time in Egypt is most often phrased as, 'remember that you were *slaves* in Egypt' (Deut. 5.15; 16.12; 24.18, 22). Only twice does it refer to the Israelites as aliens in Egypt (Deut. 10.19; 23.7). Furthermore, the Exodus is mentioned in the Book of the Covenant in connection with the Feast of Unleavened Bread (Exod. 23.15). Childs does not classify this latter reference as a secondary addition, and indeed, it is not a parallel usage of the Exodus event. In Exod. 23.15 it is referred to in order to

1. Childs, *Exodus*, p. 454.

provide the rationale behind holding the Feast of Unleavened Bread in the month of Abib. Therefore, because the release from slavery is mentioned elsewhere in the Book of the Covenant, and because these motivation clauses do not obviously interrupt a series of apodictic laws, and because Deuteronomy prefers to describe the Israelites as slaves in Egypt, I will conclude that they are not secondary glosses added by the Deuteronomist.

I now need to analyse the significance of tying the status and treatment of the alien to the Israelites' memory of their ancestors' time as slaves in Egypt.[1] Depicting the alien as a person who now occupies the position that their forebears had occupied serves to close the gap between the alien and the Israelite. It does not allow the Israelites to hold the alien at arm's length, but causes them to be sympathetic to and identify with the alien. The memory of their stay in Egypt mitigates the apparently universal exclusivism common to all social, political and religious communities.[2] Using their history in order to motivate obedience contributed to an openness to outsiders which would have far-reaching results. This is an example of a community shaping its ethic on the basis of remembering and retelling their narrative. The motivation clause argues that certain actions are appropriate because of what has happened to them in the past.

It is instructive to note that this prohibition is followed by a similar law protecting the widow and the fatherless. These laws are grouped together because of a common subject. Together they protect the weaker members of society. All three groups mentioned are socially and economically dependent. Because they have lost or have been separated from their *paterfamilias* they are particularly vulnerable to abuse. The law prohibits this abuse. Because it is stated negatively, it does not tell us much of how an Israelite is to treat them. The alien, widow and fatherless are clearly dependent on charity, but the law does not go so far as to require charity.

> b. You shall not oppress a resident alien; you know the heart of an alien, for you were aliens in the land of Egypt (Exod. 23.9).

The second command concerning the alien is a doubling of the first.

1. See Spina, 'Israelites as *gerim*', p. 322, for a discussion of the authenticity of the tradition. He concludes that various groups of proto-Israelites were aliens in Egypt, and that this memory has been applied to Israel as a whole at a later time.
2. Blenkinsopp, 'Yahweh and other Deities', p. 366.

As Lohfink had indicated, this is striking and functions as a framing device. That it is the laws dealing with the alien that is used this way emphasizes the importance of these laws within the Covenant Code.[1]

This law occurs at the beginning of a series which pertains mostly to the legal system (Exod. 23.1-9). These apodictic laws, minus their motivation clauses include:

1. Do not spread false reports (Exod. 23.1);
2. Do not follow the crowd in doing wrong (Exod. 23.2);
3. Do not show favoritism to the poor (Exod. 23.3);
4. Do not deny justice to your poor people in their lawsuits (Exod. 23.6);
5. Do not accept a bribe (Exod. 23.8); and
6. Do not oppress an alien (Exod. 23.9).

All these apodictic laws employ the form לא plus the imperfect. The law concerning the alien (Exod. 23.9) again uses the verb לחץ, and again the ancient translations differ on the number of the verb.[2]

On the basis of the context of this law, it is likely that the oppression referred to is oppression in the courts. Stated positively, it is claiming that the alien has legal rights and must be accorded a fair hearing. This law also will have far-reaching implications. It provides for the alien being reckoned as an equal in some respects with an Israelite. We will see that the laws in Deuteronomy and the Priestly Code begin to work out in what sense aliens must be treated in the same way as Israelites, and in what situations they are to be treated differently.

It is appropriate to pause here to consider what the legal system might look like at this period in Israel's history in order to understand what 'oppression' this law is referring to. R.R. Wilson has studied the mechanisms of judicial authority and concludes that they are strongly linked to the society's social structure.[3] The judicial procedures of the

1. Lohfink, 'The Option for the Poor', pp. 7-9.

2. The LXX, the Syriac and the Targums have the second person plural form of the verb.

3. For example, R.R. Wilson, in 'Enforcing the Covenant: The Mechanisms of Judicial Authority in Early Israel', in *The Quest for the Kingdom of God: Essays in Honor of George E. Mendenhall* (ed. H.B. Huffmon; Winona Lake, IN: Eisenbrauns, 1983), pp. 60-61, describes society during the time of the monarchy as hierarchically ordered, with the king at the top of the pyramid. Judicial authority in such

pre-monarchic period are difficult to reconstruct. There are few biblical sources, and there are differences among scholars regarding the structure of the social system. Wilson bases his description of the legal system on the premise that the basic social unit at this time was the extended family (בית־אב). At this level, judicial authority resided with the patriarch, who had virtually absolute control (see the accounts of Genesis 31 and 38).[1] In the case of disputes between extended families, proceedings took place at the level of the clan (משפחה). These proceedings occurred at the village gate, where the elders gathered to hear the case.[2] Presumably, this is the level at which the laws of the Book of the Covenant would function, and it would be at this court that the rights of the alien to a fair hearing were to be upheld. Wilson concludes, on the basis of lack of evidence, that there were no proceedings at the tribal level, and that no case can be made for a central office of judge. According to him, the Samuel narratives envision a court at the level of the clan, and not at the national level.[3]

> c. Six days you shall do your work, but on the seventh day you shall rest, so that your ox and your donkey may have relief, and your homeborn slave, and the resident alien, may be refreshed (Exod. 23.12).

The final law concerning the alien in the Book of the Covenant occurs in the series of laws regulating the cultic life of the Israelite (Exod. 23.10-19). The law of the Sabbath is formulated as a positive law here; 'Six days you shall do your work, but on the seventh day you shall rest' (Exod. 23.12a). The reference to the alien occurs in the following dependent clause which gives the rationale, 'so that your ox and your donkey may have relief and your homeborn slave, and the resident alien, may be refreshed' (Exod. 23.12b). The rationale here is not tied to the creation order as in Exod. 20.8-11, or to the deliverance from Egypt as in Deut. 5.15. The concern shown in the motivating clause seems to be purely humanitarian.[4] It ensures that the ox, donkey, slave and alien (in that order) may rest. The verb used here, as well as in the decalogue of Deuteronomy (Deut. 5.14) is the qal

a society was centralized in the king and delegated to his representatives. The king established and maintained the legal system and enforced judicial decisions.

1. Wilson, 'Enforcing the Covenant', p. 64.
2. *Ibid.*
3. Wilson, 'Enforcing the Covenant', pp. 64-65.
4. Childs, *Exodus*, p. 482.

as well as in the decalogue of Deuteronomy (Deut. 5.14) is the qal imperfect of נוח. This verb is also used in the Sabbath command of the Decalogue in Exodus (Exod. 20.11), but there the subject is God rather than people or animals.

The mention of the animals, slave and alien could be a secondary addition. In part, the argument depends on whether one is convinced that the original form of any apodictic law lacked motivation clauses.[1] Phillips and Nielsen have suggested that the addition of the animals and slave and alien to the Sabbath law is due to the change of Israelite culture from a Bedouin culture to a sedentary culture. They set the original Sabbath law in the wilderness period, and assume that animal husbandry is possible only in a sedentary culture.[2] However, I have already indicated that it is doubtful that the Israelites ever were Bedouin, and that it is incorrect to posit that semi-nomadism and agricultural activity are mutually exclusive.[3]

Although I do not agree with the historical reconstruction which is used to explain the additions to the Sabbath command, it does seem correct to conclude that the observance of a day of rest is an ancient custom. The origin of this custom has been the subject of much study. It has been connected with the taboo of the Kenites against lighting fires on certain days; with the custom of ceasing most labor on market day, as one of a series of feast days in a calendar which is based on the number seven, and on analogy to Babylonian *sabattu* (evil days), on which the king and his courtiers were not allowed to function officially.[4] N.E. Andreasen's tradition-history study of the institution of the Sabbath concludes that the most fundamental part of the Sabbath legislation is the formula which requires that work be done on six

1. A.C.J. Phillips, *Ancient Israel's Criminal Law* (Oxford: Blackwell, 1970), p. 64, for example, argues that the original command had no motivation clause.

2. Phillips, *Ancient Israel's Criminal Law*, p. 68; E. Nielsen, *The Ten Commandments in New Perspective: A Traditio-Historical Approach* (ABT 2/7; Naperville: Alec R. Allenson, 1968), p. 122.

3. See Mayes, *Judges*, pp. 53-55 for a discussion of the nature of tribal Israel as a pastoral society. He demonstrates that the hypothesis that Israel was nomadic or semi-nomadic until the settlement in the land cannot be substantiated. He concludes that semi-nomadism belongs with agriculture in this non-urban mode of society.

4. See J. Morgenstern, 'Sabbath', in *IDB*, IV (Nashville: Abingdon Press, 1962), pp. 135-37; and N.A. Andreasen, *The Old Testament Sabbath: A Traditio-Historical Investigation* (SBLDS, 7; Missoula, MT: Scholars Press, 1972), pp. 123-24.

days and abstained from on the seventh. He suggests that Exod. 23.12 and 34.21 are the oldest formulations of this command.[1] The motivating clauses, he suggests, do not explain the origin of the custom, but were added over time to a tradition which was ancient.[2] The strength of this tradition is indicated in Exod. 23.12. The law requires that the animals, slave and alien rest on the Sabbath, while nothing is said of their participation in the other festivals (Exod. 23.14-17). We will see that the cultic inclusion of the alien was dealt with differently by the different law collections. Here I will note only that the strength of the Sabbath as a day for ceasing from work necessitated that the alien be included in the rest, and that this was the beginning of what was to become his complete cultic integration into the people of Israel.

The concern shown here, not only for the patriarch or his immediate family, but for animals and dependent members of the household is very significant. It is the first positive statement of how the aliens are to be treated. Their social position is also made clear. They are members of the household, in a dependent position. Although they are distinguished from the slave, they rely on the charity of the patriarch, who, it seems, decides when they can rest and when they must work.

In all the laws pertaining to aliens in the Book of the Covenant, they have been treated as socially and economically less fortunate members of the society. The concern of the laws is that they not be abused, but treated with the kindness that is appropriate to dependants. There is no concern here to regulate their responsibilities *vis-à-vis* the cult, or to legislate whether they may own land or slaves. If we understand that the alien is dependent on the patriarch, then this silence is understandable. The alien, under the protocol of hospitality, would be under the authority of the patriarch. For a similar reason the laws in the Book of the Covenant are silent regarding marriage laws. Because a daughter and son come under the authority of their father, these decisions rest with him. The laws regulate only the public communal life of the Israelites, or, to put it differently, the relations between extended families, not within the family.[3]

C. *The Social Location of the Alien*

On the basis of these texts, I will try to create a picture of the identity

1. Andreasen, *The Old Testament Sabbath*, p. 168.
2. Andreasen, *The Old Testament Sabbath*, p. 135-36.
3. Boecker, *Law and the Administration of Justice*, p. 139.

of aliens, and how they fit into Israelite society in the pre-monarchic period. First, we can conclude that the laws pertaining to the alien are not regulating how the Israelites are to deal with large numbers of homeless people. All the references to the alien are in the singular, and would seem to refer to individuals. Furthermore, because the Sabbath law envisions taking the alien into one's household, I would suggest that the laws are legislating against taking advantage of the occasional stranger or family from afar. The moral imperative here concerns hospitality, rather than resettling masses of refugees.

If this is correct, we will need to reconsider the prevailing historical reconstructions regarding the identity of the alien referred to in the Covenant Code. From Pedersen's work in 1927,[1] to the survey article in the *Interpreter's Dictionary of the Bible*,[2] the alien has been identified with the indigenous population of Palestine which had been conquered by the Israelites.[3] The description given by Pedersen of the alien, thus identified, is the description of a class of people, i.e. those between free Israelite citizens and slaves. He draws an analogy between this group and the *perioikoi* of Sparta, and concludes that they are poor because they are not land-holders.[4]

The laws referring to the alien in the Book of the Covenant do not substantiate this thesis. Rather, the narrative material in Judges 17, 19 provides a description of the sojourner which accords with the legislation concerning him in the Covenant Code. Aliens are more or less permanently part of the Israelite tribal community, and need to be taken in if they are to survive.

It should be noted that the above identification of the alien with the Canaanites is based on a conquest or infiltration model for the occupation of Israel.[5] What becomes of the alien within the hypothesis of Mendenhall or Gottwald? J. Milgrom discusses the status of the alien as presented by revolt hypothesis, and claims that because the alien maintains a distinct identity over against the Israelite, the revolt hypothesis fails. Furthermore, he maintains that the revolt model pre-

1. Pedersen, *Israel: Its Life and Culture*, I, p. 41.
2. Mauch, 'Sojourner', pp. 397-99.
3. Cf. de Vaux, *Ancient Israel*, p. 74; Kellerman, 'גור', p. 445.
4. Pedersen, *Israel: Its Life and Culture*, I, p. 41.
5. See the discussion of the different settlement models in N.K. Gottwald's *The Tribes of Yahweh: The Sociology of the Religion of Liberated Israel 1250–1050* BCE (Maryknoll, NY: Orbis Books, 1979), pp. 191-228.

supposes the phenomenon of religious conversion. Yet Milgrom claims that religious conversion is neither attested nor possible in ancient Israel in the time before the Second Temple period.[1] The only way an outsider could become an Israelite in pre-exilic times was through intermarriage.[2]

Milgrom's critique misses the mark because he is speaking only of the conversion of individuals, while the revolt model presupposes the conversion of large groups. Gottwald's hypothesis envisions entire tribes or villages joining the Israelites.[3] Biblical evidence for or against this thesis would rest in part on whether tribes or villages ever joined Israel. This is quite a different phenomenon from the conversion of an individual to another religion.

In his description of the social make-up of the tribe, de Vaux discusses how tribes join Israel, and how some tribes effectively disappear as identifiable entities.[4] He traces how the tribe of Caleb, originally not part of the confederation, becomes incorporated. This sort of movement allows for the phenomenon of conversion which Gottwald's model presupposes. However, his reconstruction does not result in the creation of a group of second-class citizens. Hence, the revolt model does not substantiate the thesis of Pedersen that the aliens were a class between the free Israelite and the slave.

Evidence for the existence of second-class citizens is found in the relationship between the Israelites and the Gibeonites and Shechemites, both of whom were ethnically dissimilar to the Israelites, being of Hurrian descent.[5] Blenkinsopp discusses the account of the Gibeonite treaty (Josh. 9.3-27) and the evidence of a treaty with the people of

1. J. Milgrom, 'Religious Conversion: the Revolt Model for the Formation of Israel', *JBL* 101 (1982), pp. 169-76. He notes the fact that non-Israelites seem to be worshipers of God in the pre-monarchic and monarchic period. He cites Doeg the Edomite (1 Sam. 21.8), Uriah the Hittite (2 Sam. 11.11) and Ittai the Gittite (2 Sam. 15.21), but does not use this as evidence for or against the possibility of individual conversion. He claims that the legal material should be the basis of the discussion. Why he limits himself to this material when addressing a historical problem is not clear.

2. Milgrom, 'Religious Conversion', p. 175.

3. Gottwald, *The Tribes of Yahweh*, pp. 555-84.

4. De Vaux, *Ancient Israel*, p. 6.

5. See J. Blenkinsopp's discussion of the ethnic identity of the Gibeonites in *Gibeon and Israel* (SOTSMS, 2; Cambridge: Cambridge University Press, 1972), pp. 14-27.

Shechem (Gen. 34), and suggests that these people were incorporated into the tribal structure by means of a disparity treaty. They were not to be citizens of equal status with the Israelites, but were 'hewers of wood and drawers of water' (Josh. 9.23, 26).[1] He argues that although the text as it now stands reflects the polemic against foreign people and gods that is typical of the Deuteronomist, there is yet sufficient evidence to posit that a disparity treaty was made with the Gibeonites.[2] Here, then, is evidence for the creation of a group of second-class citizens along the lines suggested by Pedersen.

However, it is another step to argue that the alien mentioned in the Book of the Covenant is to be identified with these people. Again, I would suggest that the evidence does not favor this identification. The Gibeonites, although in a servant class, were not aliens in the land; they were not without family; and they were not dependent on charity. In addition, they are a group of people, distinguished by their race and culture, rather than individuals. Regulating how a society is to deal with an ethnically identifiable group of people is quite different from regulating how the *paterfamilias* is to treat an individual (and perhaps his family) who comes from afar and is in need of hospitality. The two may be related, but I will not be examining how Israel dealt with conquered peoples, such as the Gibeonites, since this is not the concern of the laws pertaining to the alien.

Milgrom's second hypothesis, that at this time it is only through intermarriage that an individual foreigner becomes assimilated into the Israelite community, does seem to be correct. R.R. Wilson's description of Israelite society in the period of the Judges as a lineage system concurs with this.[3] Lineage systems grow by means of birth and marriage. The latter is an especially significant mechanism for incorporating outsiders into the lineage.[4] He also claims that

1. J. Blenkinsopp, 'Are There Traces of the Gibeonite Covenant in Deuteronomy?', *CBQ* 28 (1966), pp. 207-209, 213-19.

2. Blenkinsopp, 'Are There Traces', pp. 207-19; also his *Gibeon and Israel*, pp. 28-40.

3. R.R. Wilson, *Sociological Approaches to the Old Testament* (Philadelphia: Fortress Press, 1984), pp. 37-47. The analysis of the social organization of Israel during the period of the judges is a blossoming field. The latest review of scholarship, and discussion of the social structure of Israel is found in N.P. Lemche, *Early Israel: Anthropological and Historical Studies on the Israelite Society before the Monarchy* (VTSup, 37; Leiden: Brill, 1985).

4. Wilson, *Sociological Approaches to the Old Testament*, p. 45.

foreigners may be incorporated by other means, but unfortunately does not elaborate on what these might be.[1]

We may conclude that on the basis of the pertinent texts in the Book of the Covenant, and on the basis of the lineage structure of Israelite society in the pre-monarchic period, that aliens are not to be identified with the conquered Canaanites. They are not indigenous inhabitants, recently defeated, but outsiders, who are vulnerable in a new place. They must rely on the protection of a powerful member of the Israelite society, and fall under the jurisdiction of the patriarch of the family in most things.

2. *The Decalogue*

> Remember the sabbath day, and keep it holy. Six days you shall labor, and do all your work; but the seventh day is a sabbath to the LORD your God; you shall not do any work—you, your son or your daughter, your male or female slave, or your livestock, or the alien who is within your towns. For in six days the LORD made heaven and earth, the sea and all that is in them, but rested the seventh day; therefore the LORD blessed the sabbath day and consecrated it (Exod. 20.8-11).

The alien is referred to once in the fourth command of the Decalogue in Exodus 20. He is mentioned at the end of a list which enumerates all who are required to cease work on the Sabbath (Exod. 20.10). The list includes the patriarch (and his wife?), the sons and daughters, the male and female slaves, the livestock as well as 'your alien within your towns' (וגרך אשר בשעריך). The NRSV is translating 'within your towns' with what is in Hebrew literally, 'within your gates.' This translation makes clear what seems to be the case. The 'gates' in other references are clearly the gates of the town. It is just within the gates that the alien would wait for someone to take him in. That is where Lot meets the two angels who come to Sodom (Gen. 19.1-2) and where the Levite and his concubine wait in Gibeah (Judg. 19.15-21). Once the aliens are taken in, they become dependent members of the patriarch's household, and hence must observe the Sabbath with the rest of the household.

The stipulation is part of the series of apodictic commands comprising the Decalogue, and hence we must consider what can be learned about the Sabbath command from this context. It is beyond the scope

1. Wilson, *Sociological Approaches to the Old Testament*, p. 45.

of this thesis to review the state of the question on the date and authorship of the Decalogue. It has been the focus of much attention, and I would refer the reader to the work of J.J. Stamm and M.E. Andrew for a presentation of scholarship on the issue up to 1967.[1] I will be relying heavily on the work of E. Nielsen in my discussion of the date, form and tradition history of the Sabbath command.[2]

Several attempts to reconstruct the original Decalogue are analysed by Nielsen before offering his own rendition.[3] For my purpose it is sufficient to note that the phrase concerning the alien is clearly not part of the original Decalogue. In its present form it disrupts the regularity of the series. The basic prohibition here concerns the cessation of work on the seventh day. This injunction is found in Exod. 35.3 in a shortened negative form, and leads Nielsen to conclude that the original command was, 'Thou shall not do any work on the sabbath day'.[4]

My task has thus been narrowed to dating not the entire fourth command (Exod. 20.8-11), but only the expansion. Traditionally, the reasons given for the Sabbath rest in Exod. 20.11 are seen to be connected to the Priestly account of creation in Gen. 1.1–2.4a. For this reason, it is dated later than the Deuteronomic version of the Sabbath command.[5] However, this has been disputed. Even Stamm, who accepts that the expansion attests to the work of the Priestly author, notices that the last words of Exod. 20.11 do not correspond exactly with Gen. 2.3.[6] Nielsen argues for a pre-Deuteronomic date for the expansion by demonstrating that the Deuteronomic version of the Decalogue depends on the Exodus version, and that the expansion in Exodus shows no literary dependence on the creation account found in Gen. 1.1–2.4a.[7] It is necessary to examine this argument in detail, since upon it hangs the dating of the reference to the alien.

When the divergences between the Exodus Decalogue and the Deuteronomic Decalogue are compared, the evidence suggests that the

1. J.J. Stamm and M.E. Andrew, *The Ten Commandments in Recent Research* (SBT 2/2, II; Naperville: Alec R. Allenson, 1967).
2. Nielsen, *The Ten Commandments in New Perspective*.
3. Nielsen, *The Ten Commandments in New Perspective*, pp. 78-86.
4. Nielsen, *The Ten Commandments in New Perspective*, pp. 84, 88.
5. Stamm and Andrew, *The Ten Commandments in Recent Research*, p. 15.
6. *Ibid.*
7. Nielsen, *The Ten Commandments in New Perspective*, pp. 39-41.

Deuteronomic Decalogue is later. The Deuteronomic version is more precise (compare the listing of ox, donkey or animals in Deuteronomy with 'your animals' in Exodus); it upgrades the status of women (compare the placing of the wife first in the list in Deuteronomy, and second in Exodus in the tenth command); and it is more repetitious (introducing the phrase 'the Lord your God' many times where it does not occur in Exodus). All of these changes are consistent with the expansionist style of the Deuteronomist.[1] They are understandable if the Deuteronomist had the Exodus text before him, but not vice versa.

The two versions of the Sabbath command also point to the Exodus command as the basis of Deuteronomy's expansion and refinement. First, Deuteronomy adds the phrase, 'as the Lord your God commanded you' (Deut. 5.12b). The same expansion occurs in Deut. 5.16. Deuteronomy and Exodus differ in the verb used in the Sabbath command. Exodus uses 'recall' or 'remember', and Deuteronomy 'observe'. Nielsen argues on this basis that the Exodus version would be earlier since it is easier to understand the Deuteronomist changing 'remember' to 'observe' than vice versa. In the Deuteronomic work, the word 'observe' (שמור) is the preferred word for obeying the law.[2] In the list of those included in this command, Deuteronomy and Exodus follow the same order: you, your son, your daughter, your male or female slave, animals and alien (Exod. 20.10; Deut. 5.14). However, Deuteronomy again expands the list by inserting 'ox and donkey and any livestock' (Deut. 5.14).

The greatest difference between the two commands occurs in the motivation clauses attached to the commands. The Sabbath law in Deuteronomy is reinforced by referring back to Israel's deliverance from Egypt. The transition to the motivating clause is clumsy.[3] The repetition of male and female slave serves as a link tying the preceding list to the remembrance that the Israelites were slaves in Egypt. The male and female slave stand as representatives for all the others previously mentioned. The subsequent reference to salvation history contains two elements. First, they are to remember their own past as slaves—a typical motivating theme of the Deuteronomist. Second, they are to remember that the Lord delivered them from their oppression.

1. Nielsen, *The Ten Commandments in New Perspective*, pp. 35-44, for a fuller comparison.

2. Nielsen, *The Ten Commandments in New Perspective*, p. 38.

3. Nielsen, *The Ten Commandments in New Perspective*, p. 39.

Making a connection between God's acting and their behavior happens more often in Deuteronomy. It occurs in a fuller form in Deut. 15.12-15. There it is clear that God's deliverance of them entitles him to make claims on them, and also that they are to model themselves on God's gracious behavior towards them.[1] Although the reason given in Deuteronomy is not as clearly stated as that in Exodus, it does not indicate which version was the original. However, the other points of difference do indicate that the Exodus version of the Sabbath command was earlier.

The Sabbath law in Exodus 20 is motivated by harking back to creation. In order to date this clause, it is necessary to examine the connection between the creation account in Gen. 1.1–2.4a, and especially Gen. 2.2, 3, and the reason given for sabbath rest in Exodus 20. This was the second point in the traditional argument which attributed the expansion of the Sabbath command to the Priestly writer. Nielsen points out several differences between the two. First, he notes that whereas Gen. 1.1ff. consistently uses ברא for 'create', Exod. 20.11 employs עשׂה.[2] However, this is not entirely the case. God 'made' the sun, moon and stars (Gen. 1.16), the wild animals (Gen. 1.25), and people (Gen. 1.26). A more significant difference is that in Exod. 20.11 the text states that the Lord made the heavens, the earth and the sea and all that is in them, while in the introductory and closing lines of the creation account, God made only the heavens and the earth (Gen. 1.1; 2.1). The sea, according to Genesis 1, was there before creation, and had to be put in its rightful place.[3] Nielsen's conclusion that there is no literary dependence of Exod. 20.11 on the Genesis creation account attributed to the Priestly writer seems justified.

I have arrived, therefore at a date for this expansion sometime before the Deuteronomic Decalogue. A more precise dating of this command and the entire Decalogue is not possible. Because the Decalogue contains no references to a specific historical period or to a particular institution, it is very difficult to connect it with any particu-

1. Nielsen, *The Ten Commandments in New Perspective*, p. 40, goes on to hypothesize that the change in the Sabbath command came about in response to the poverty experienced in Judea when it was under the control of Babylon. The reference to salvation history is to remind them that God has delivered them in the past, and to instill the hope that he will deliver them again if they are obedient.

2. Nielsen, *The Ten Commandments in New Perspective*, p. 41.

3. Nielsen, *The Ten Commandments in New Perspective*, p. 41.

lar time.[1] In addition, because it is generally agreed that the Decalogue has been inserted into its present context, it cannot be dated with regard to its narrative framework.[2]

The significance and possible *Sitz im Leben* of apodictic law has already been discussed in connection with the laws in the Book of the Covenant and need not be repeated. The specific genre of the Ten Commandments, as opposed to the cultic decalogue of Exodus 34; or the curse ritual of Deuteronomy 27, the list in Lev. 18.6-18 and Lev. 20.2-16 has been discussed at length, but no one *Sitz im Leben* can account for these lists of ten prohibitions or curses.[3] The tendency to create series of ten is most likely accounted for as a mnemonic device, and suggests only that these were meant to be recited.

There is not much information to be learned from this one reference to the alien that we have not already learned from the Sabbath command in the Book of the Covenant. The fact that the Sabbath command is part of the Decalogue testifies to the strength and antiquity of the tradition of resting one day out of seven. The inclusion of aliens at the end of the list, again after the animals, while the servants are mentioned before the animals, testifies to their low social position. The second person singular suffix attached to the word alien also indicates that they are in a dependent position. In some sense the alien belongs to the patriarch. This indicates that the alien referred to here is not a self-sufficient individual who participates independently in society. This alien is not a second-class citizen living alongside Israelites; but is a member of a large household under the authority of the patriarch.

3. *Conclusion*

The four references to the alien which I have examined in the pre-Deuteronomic laws have dealt with aliens in three different ways.

1. In reaching this conclusion, I am in the good company of Childs, *Exodus*, pp. 396-97, who after surveying the various attempts to date the Decalogue concludes that the evidence is not specific enough to establish any thesis.

2. See W. Harrelson, *The Ten Commandments and Human Rights* (Overtures to Biblical Theology, 8; Philadelphia: Fortress Press, 1980), pp. 44-45; Childs, *Exodus*, p. 392; Nielsen, *The Ten Commandments in New Perspective*, p. 55.

3. See Harrelson, *The Ten Commandments and Human Rights*, pp. 28-40, for a survey of the literature and discussion of the distinguishing features of the four series of ten.

They have been protected from general abuse; they have been protected from unfair treatment in the courts, and they have been included in the Sabbath rest. It is possible to categorize the laws as requirements dealing with charity, equity and cultic activity. We will see that these three areas of concern will be expanded on and developed in the subsequent legal collections.

It is also significant that the identity of the alien in all references was that of an individual, or perhaps a family. The alien was someone who was taken into a household, and hence could not be identified with the defeated Canaanites or any other large group of people. Instead, the aliens, and possibly their families,[1] are strangers who are vulnerable and need protection and charity because they are out of their familial context.

This legal and social status of the alien was understandable in the sociopolitical context of pre-monarchic Israel. The laws do not evince a national consciousness, but only a clan consciousness. The alien thus is someone from another tribe, whether Israelite or non-Israelite.

Although the laws are to be understood in this context, we cannot describe the context as determinative of the legal status accorded the alien. Law, if it is understood as the outcome of a struggle between competing interest groups, cannot explain the phenomenon of these laws which protect those vulnerable people who are not part of one's extended family or community. It is in fact surprising that outsiders who have no social clout are given the fair treatment which the Decalogue and Book of the Covenant accord them. It seems likely that behind this legislation stands the custom of hospitality to the stranger. Perhaps the surprising thing, the new thing, is that this custom has been formulated as a law. This is a significant step however. It gives what was perhaps a generally accepted moral norm the new status of being part of the written legal tradition. It is this written tradition that we can trace to some extent. In the subsequent legal tradition we will see these laws change and develop because they had to be rethought and reapplied as the people of Israel changed and developed through time. These laws thus stand at the beginning of a process which eventually would allow the inclusion of outsiders as equal members of the Israelite community.

1. For example, the family of Elimelech went to Moab, to sojourn (לגור), because there was a famine in Bethlehem (Ruth 1.1, 2).

Chapter 4

THE DEUTERONOMIC LAWS

Because there are more references to the alien in the book of Deuteronomy than in the Book of the Covenant[1] and because the laws in Deuteronomy are more comprehensive than those in the Book of the Covenant, we can look forward to getting a more complete picture of how the author(s) understood the people of Israel and how they were to be related to the resident aliens in their midst.

Before I can begin my examination of the references to the aliens, it is necessary to gain an understanding of the literary work in which they occur. The historical-critical work on the book of Deuteronomy has been extensive.[2] Unfortunately, this has not resulted in a consensus concerning authorship, date(s) of composition, or *Sitz im Leben*. Even de Wette's thesis that the law book discovered by Josiah was some form of Deuteronomy is now challenged by many.[3] The wide variety of opinion testifies to some extent to the ambiguity of the evidence. My presentation will not aspire to resolve all the problems, but to indicate my point of departure on issues pertinent to this study of the alien.

1. The eighteen references to the alien occur in Deut. 1.16; 5.14; 10.18, 19; 14.21, 29; 16.11, 14; 24.14, 17, 19, 20, 21; 26.11, 12, 13; 27.19; 29.11; 31.12.

2. For an overview of the criticism of the work of the Deuteronomist, from Deuteronomy to 2 Kings, see A.D.H. Mayes, *The Story of Israel between Settlement and Exile* (London: SCM Press, 1983), pp. 1-21. For a summary of the critical work on Deuteronomy alone see the introductory section in Mayes' commentary, *Deuteronomy* (The New Century Bible Commentary; Grand Rapids: Eerdmans, 1979), pp. 25-108.

3. See Mayes, *Deuteronomy*, pp. 98-102, for a discussion, using form-critical arguments, demonstrating that the finding of the law book is not part of the basic account of Josiah's reform.

1. *Introductory Matters*

A. *Unity and Form*

Von Rad opened a new chapter in the form-critical research on Deuteronomy by noting that Deuteronomy has a fourfold structure: (a) a historical introduction in chs. 1–11; (b) the reading of the law in chs. 12.1–26.15; (c) the sealing of the covenant in ch. 26.16-19; and (d) the blessings and curses in chs. 27–28.[1] This structure is analogous to ancient Near Eastern treaty documents, and it seems clear that Deuteronomy as well as other literature in the Old Testament has been influenced by this treaty tradition.[2] The similarities between Deuteronomy and the Hittite and Assyrian texts have given rise to two theories concerning the genre and unity of Deuteronomy. On the one hand, Weinfeld argues that Deuteronomy is formally an oration based on the treaty form represented by the Esarhaddon treaty (dated 672 BC), and on this basis argues for the unity of Deuteronomy.[3] On the other hand, Mayes argues that, although the treaties between a sovereign and a vassal have influenced the form, language and theology of Deuteronomy, it is not closely related to one treaty in particular, and it cannot be argued that Deuteronomy is the work of one author on that basis.[4] The latter theory does more justice to the text of Deuteronomy as it now stands. The last three chapters of the book, which include the Song of Moses, the Blessings of Moses and the account of his death, find no analogy in a treaty form. Neither do the laws conform to the stipulations of a covenant. Covenant stipulations deal with matters which define and control the relationship between the two parties involved in the treaty. The laws of Deuteronomy are much more extensive in that they seek to govern the whole communal life of a people.

The form in which the individual laws are cast distinguishes Deuteronomic law from other Pentateuchal law. In the Priestly collection and the Book of the Covenant, the laws are styled as the words of God to Moses and Aaron, whereas in Deuteronomy the laws are given

1. G. von Rad, 'The Form-Critical Problem of the Hexateuch', in *The Problem of the Hexateuch and Other Essays* (trans. E.W. Trueman Dicken; Edinburgh: Oliver and Boyd, 1966), pp. 26-33.

2. See the study by McCarthy, *Treaty and Covenant.*

3. M. Weinfeld, *Deuteronomy and the Deuteronomic School* (Oxford: Oxford University Press, 1972), pp. 59-157.

4. Mayes, *Deuteronomy*, pp. 32-34.

as words of Moses. They are clearly invested with God's authority, and yet Moses is the intermediary through whom the Israelites come to know God's law.

They also differ from other law collections in that they can be characterized as 'preached law'.[1] They are almost always formulated using the personal form of address. There are very few laws formulated in the impersonal casuistic style. In addition, the laws are usually accompanied by motivation clauses. These encourage obedience by explaining the rationale behind the law, by reminding the Israelites of their history, inculcating virtue, or stating the blessings and curses that will follow on disobedience or obedience.

The content of the laws also points to their character as 'preached law'. Laws such as those requiring generosity to the poor (Deut. 15.7-11) are clearly unenforceable by the courts. In other instances the laws are utopian. The regulations for the offices of judge, priest, king and prophet (Deut. 16.18–18.22) read like the constitution for an ideal society. The transmitters of these laws were not the judges or elders who adjudicated cases at the city gate, and their goal is not so much to regulate daily life as to present the way daily life ought to be lived.

The content as well as the parenetic style point to their originating in a public setting. Von Rad suggests that the preaching style indicates a cultic setting.[2] Whether or not we can also agree that the covenant form of the whole book, as well as the parenetic style of the individual laws, points to the festival of covenant renewal at Shechem as its original *Sitz im Leben* is another matter.[3] Suffice it to say that although Moses in Deuteronomy gives instructions for a covenant making ceremony at Shechem, this does not necessarily mean that there was a yearly covenant renewal festival or that Shechem was the place where these laws originated.[4]

1. G. von Rad, *Studies in Deuteronomy* (trans. D. Stalker; SBT, 9; London: SCM Press, 1953), p. 16, described them in this way, and it is still an apt description.

2. Von Rad, *Studies in Deuteronomy*, p. 14. See also Nicholson's arguments that the parenetic style of Deuteronomy points to its origin in the cultus (E.W. Nicholson, *Deuteronomy and Tradition* [Philadelphia: Fortress Press, 1967], pp. 46-47).

3. See Nicholson, *Deuteronomy and Tradition*, pp. 37-57 for a discussion of the scholarship on Deuteronomy's relationship to the covenant renewal ceremony.

4. G.J. Wenham's discussion of the theme of centralization in Deuteronomy is helpful in illuminating the role that Shechem plays in Israelite history. See his

I conclude then, first, that the overall structure of Deuteronomy is related to the structure of the international treaties of the Hittite and later Assyrian empires. Second, upon examining the form and content of the individual laws, I conclude that in scope they resemble the laws of a law code rather than a treaty document. Hence it is likely that the legal collection has been inserted into this covenant framework and is not original to it.

In style, the laws are unusual in that they almost always employ the personal form of address and abound in motivational clauses. This peculiar character points to an original *Sitz im Leben* of public preaching. This preaching would most certainly be done by someone with authority, because these laws, though spoken by Moses, are portrayed as deriving from God himself.[1] Passages in Deuteronomy (for example, Deuteronomy 27) suggest a cultic setting for this proclamation—specifically a covenant renewal ceremony.

I have already indicated that although there is an overall structure and fairly consistent style and theology, I do not conclude that it is the work of one author. One argument against unity which I have already discussed is the discrepancy between the content of the laws and the treaty form in which they are now found. I conclude from this that some form of the law book once existed independently of the treaty

'Deuteronomy and the Central Sanctuary', *TynBul* 22 (1971), pp. 103-18. He notes that Shechem was never the central sanctuary, but rather that it was the place where traditions of inheriting the land were localized. He cites as evidence the promise to Abraham (Gen. 12.6, 7), God's appearance to Jacob after his return to Canaan (Gen. 35.1-4), and Jacob's purchase of a plot of ground (Gen. 33.19)—all of which are located at Shechem. Joshua's renewal of the covenant (Josh. 8.30; 24) also occurs at Shechem, as does Rehoboam's coronation as king (1 Kgs 12.1-17). Especially the crowning of Rehoboam as king at a time when Jerusalem had been established as a sanctuary containing the ark leads him to conclude that Shechem was the site appropriate for covenant renewals which had to do with the gaining of the land. On this basis he also concludes that there is no contradiction between the call for a central sanctuary and the naming of Shechem as the place for a covenant renewal ceremony.

1. B. Lindars' study of the use of the word תורה in Deuteronomy illuminates the author's concept of this law code. He notes that Deuteronomy for the first time uses the word in the singular to denote the entire law code. It is used to convey their notion that the law is a complete expression of the will of God. The use of תורה to express this notion, rather than חק or משפט, is indicative of the didactic character of the laws. The laws are to be understood and learned by the people. See his 'Torah in Deuteronomy', in *Words and Meaning* (ed. P.R. Ackroyd and B. Lindars; Cambridge: Cambridge University Press, 1968), pp. 117-37.

context. The interchange of second person singular and plural forms of address also points to the disunity of particular passages.[1]

B. *Date of Composition of the Law Book*

Because the law book seems to have existed apart from its present context, I will not concern myself with the composition history of the whole book of Deuteronomy.[2] However, it is important to consider the composition history of the law book (Deuteronomy 12–26). It is clear from the laws on the sanctuary that a process of editing has occurred within the law book.[3] In my presentation I will assume that the law book has been redacted, but I will not now attempt to isolate the levels of redaction. Rather, I intend later to see what evidence emerges from the examination of the laws concerning the alien, and whether it can contribute to the discussion .

In this introductory section, I wish to consider the date of composition of the law book as a whole. There are two aspects to this dis-

1. This vacillation by itself is not enough to prove disunity. Mayes, for example, in his article, 'Deuteronomy 4 and the Literary Criticism of Deuteronomy', *JBL* 100 (1981), pp. 23-51, argues that ch. 4 is a unity, and that the interchange between the second singular and plural forms of address can be explained on stylistic grounds. However, in other places Mayes uses the interchange of second singular and second plural as important evidence on which to base his theories on the literary development of Deuteronomy. He argues that the original introduction to the laws of chs. 12–26 is now found in chs. 5–11, and consists of those passages which use the second person singular form of address. The author who incorporated this law code into the larger deuteronomic work by giving it a historical prologue in chs. 1–3 and continuing the narrative at the end of the laws consistently used the second person plural form. See his *Deuteronomy*, pp. 35-37.

2. See a full discussion of this topic in Nicholson, *Deuteronomy and Tradition*, and more recently, in the introduction to Mayes' commentary, *Deuteronomy*, pp. 29-57.

3. For example, the duplication of the laws on slaughtering and centralization in Deut. 12 have led Mayes, *Deuteronomy*, p. 43, to attribute Deut. 12.8-12, 16 to the deuteronomistic editor. Not much has been done on the history of redaction within the law book. Von Rad, in his *Studies in Deuteronomy*, p. 43, is an exception to this. He theorized that the demand for centralization in Deuteronomy is a comparatively late addition to the legal material, and is easily removed. This view has not gained many adherents. Instead, the call for centralization and concomitant interest in the role and support of the Levites are seen to be major themes, and integral to the law book. See the arguments of Mayes, *Deuteronomy*, pp. 52-53; and Nicholson, *Deuteronomy and Tradition*, p. 55.

cussion: first, what date is suggested solely on the basis of the type of society presupposed by the legal material in Deuteronomy; second, what date is suggested when we connect this evidence with the particular events in Israel's history. In the latter case, it will be necessary to examine the relationship that exists between these laws and the law book discovered during the reign of Josiah, and between these laws and the reforms of Jeroboam.

The society presupposed by the laws of Deuteronomy 12–26 is an urban society.[1] I mean by this that although the economic base of the society was predominantly agricultural, there were now fortified cities upon which the rural population depended for safety, for a market and for administrative matters. In the time of the monarchy, there was an interdependence of city, village and field. The urban community, rather than the tribe, had become the basic political unit.[2]

Urbanization in Israel was accompanied by a weakening of the tribal structures of society.[3] This resulted in a limiting of the patriarch's authority, as is indicated by the regulations concerning the rights of the first-born (Deut. 21.15-17), and by the legislation which requires that parents bring a rebellious son to the gate of the town when they have a serious complaint against him (Deut. 21.18-21). The authority to enact the death penalty now lies with the elders of the town and not with the *paterfamilias*, as in the case of Judah and Tamar (Gen. 38).[4] The weakening cohesion of the family in an urban society is indicated by the law releasing the family members from being liable for each other's crimes (Deut. 24.16).[5] In place of the family, the city is now the responsible body under the law. In Deut. 21.1-9 it is the

1. For a presentation on the occurrences of the word 'city' in Deuteronomy, see D.C. Benjamin, *Deuteronomy and City Life* (New York: University Press of America, 1983).

2. See F.S. Frick, *The City in Ancient Israel* (SBLDS, 36; Missoula, MT: Scholars Press, 1977), pp. 77-114, for a discussion of the physical, social, economic and political aspects of the city in the time of the monarchy.

3. This disintegration was not caused by the process of urbanization, according to Frick (*The City in Ancient Israel*, p. 110), but was a consequence of the heavy economic burden of the monarchy.

4. See Whitelam, *The Just King*, p. 40, for a discussion of this account as an example of the judicial authority of the head of the family to impose the death penalty on members of his extended family.

5. See Weber's further discussion of the economy and society presupposed by Deuteronomy in *Ancient Judaism*, pp. 66-67.

city closest to the murder victim which must carry out the ritual of atonement.[1]

The level of organization presumed here is more sophisticated than that presupposed in the Book of the Covenant. For example, there is now a court instituted for those cases too difficult for the local judiciary to handle (Deut. 17.8-13). The community addressed is now organized into a state with a king at its head (Deut. 17.14-20). Although this legislation has been described as utopian, it still presupposes and provides for the existence of the king. On this basis, the legal material is dated in the period of the monarchy at the earliest.

The internal evidence which has been used to pinpoint its date more precisely is the law book's demand for centralization. Deuteronomy 12 opens the law book by instructing the Israelites several times that they are to seek the Lord 'only in *the* place where he will put his name' (Deut. 12.5, 11, 14, 18, 26).[2] These laws are clearly teaching something new. They necessitate the reform of the old laws of slaughter which presupposed that every city had a sanctuary. They are instituting a new procedure when, for example, they instruct the Israelites to slaughter their domestic animals as they were used to slaughtering their wild animals (Deut. 12.15, 16).

The laws concerning the Levites can also be understood as instituting a new status and a new means of support which is necessitated by calling for the eradication of the local sanctuaries. Their status is precisely delineated in the laws. Levites are cultic personnel with a right to tithes (Deut. 14.27-29), to participate in the festivals (Deut. 16.11, 14) and to a share of the sacrifices (Deut. 18.1-8). The status of the Levites is one of the arguments for the pre-exilic dating of much of the legal material. The Levites in Deuteronomy are not a lower level of clergy as they are in the exilic and post-exilic literature.[3]

1. For this reason, Frick, *The City in Ancient Israel*, p. 125, claims that the laws in Deuteronomy may properly be called municipal laws.

2. The exact meaning of this phrase has been disputed. On the basis of grammar and syntax alone, Nicholson, in *Deuteronomy and Tradition*, p. 8, demonstrates that it is possible to translate Deut. 12.14 as, 'in every place which Yahweh shall choose in any of your tribes'. This is achieved by giving the definite article in במקום a distributive interpretation, and the indefinite article in באחד a general meaning. However, he goes on to say that this meaning is not possible because of the context in which the law is found.

3. See the articles on the role of the Levites/priests in Deuteronomy by G.E. Wright, 'The Levites in Deuteronomy', *VT* 4 (1954), pp. 325-30; and J.A. Emerton,

Because of the reforms advocated in the laws, many scholars identify the Deuteronomic law book with the 'Book of the Law' found in the temple in Jerusalem in the eighteenth year of Josiah's reign (2 Kgs 22.8-23).[1] This historical connection has come under attack on several fronts,[2] and yet is defensible. For example, Nicholson's presentation draws attention to the discrepancies between the account in 2 Kings 22–23.25 and 2 Chronicles 34–35.19.[3] In Chronicles the sequence of events is somewhat different than in Kings. Josiah first begins to seek the Lord and purge the land of foreign gods and goddesses, and then discovers the law book. Nicholson's reconstruction of the events draws from both accounts, as well as the history of the Assyrian empire at that time. He theorizes that Josiah's reform had two phases. The first was basically an independence movement. Due to weakening Assyrian control, Josiah began to rid the land of Assyrian cult emblems and practices, since these were a sign of their sovereignty. The second stage of the reformation, the purifying of the cult of Yahweh, came in response to finding the law book. This law book is characterized in 2 Chronicles as the Book of the Law of the Lord that has been given through Moses (2 Chron. 34.14). Here the author clearly makes the identification with the laws of Deuteronomy. Although the two accounts differ, and although it is clearly the intent of both authors that we make the identification, Nicholson yet con-

'Priests and Levites in Deuteronomy', *VT* 12 (1962), pp. 129-38. Wright first argues for a distinction between priests in the central sanctuary and client Levites in the countryside. Emerton, in response, argues that the priests in the central sanctuary are a fluctuating minority of the tribe of Levi, and that Deut. 18.1-8 legislates that all Levites have the right to serve in the sanctuary. Hence, although in practice there may be a difference between rural Levites and levitical priests in the sanctuary, this was not a difference based on Deuteronomy's laws. In particular, the law makes no distinction based on heredity within the tribe of Levi.

1. See, for example, Patrick's conclusion in his *Old Testament Law*, p. 99.

2. Mayes, for example, in *Deuteronomy*, pp. 88-103, argues against this identification. On form-critical grounds he divides the account in 1 Kgs 22 into a pre-deuteronomic basis, the deuteronomistic redaction and a post-deuteronomistic redaction. He concludes that only the oracle of Huldah, now in an edited version in 2 Kgs 22.12-20, is pre-deuteronomistic and based on historical tradition. Rather than dating the law book to the reign of Josiah, he dates it to the late monarchic period in Judah. He does this on the basis of its language, which has affinities with later parts of Jeremiah, and its theological ideas. Although he concedes that isolated sections may have had a long prehistory, the law book is dated to the seventh century BC.

3. Nicholson, *Deuteronomy and Tradition*, p. 8.

cludes that there is a historical connection between the laws of Deuteronomy and the law book found by Josiah.

The call for centralization, which is an important theme in the legal material, has also been used to determine the date(s) of the laws. However, there is a great deal of evidence that the call for centralization of worship in response to apostasy had occurred at several junctures in Israel's history as a state. According to the Deuteronomist, the establishing of the altars at Dan and Bethel marked the beginning of the end for the northern kingdom. Evidence from 2 Chron. 11.14 (cf. 1 Kgs 12.31; 13.33) suggests that this negative judgment on Jeroboam because of his building of new sanctuaries is not merely based on hindsight. The call for centralization of worship in Jerusalem, which then required new positions for the deposed Levites, may well have begun in response to Jeroboam's disregard of traditional cultic sites, rituals and personnel.[1] In addition, the reforms of Hezekiah involved removing the high places, the sacred stones and Asherah poles, and requiring that worship be conducted in Jerusalem (2 Kgs 18.4, 22). There were in fact, religious reforms in Judah from the time of Asa, and in connection with these reforms we read of covenants being made.[2] Josiah's reform is best seen as one in a series of reforms which differs in that it involved the discovery of a law book. The deuteronomic law, although it cannot be connected with any one of these reforms with certainty, is most likely to be connected with this pre-exilic nationalistic and cultic reform movement in Judah.

If there is any consensus on the historical-critical questions related to Deuteronomy, it involves the provenance of the legal material. The book contains both northern and southern traditions, and any theory about its provenance must be able to account for both. The northern origin of the book is demonstrated by its designation of Shechem as a site for covenant renewal; the affinities between Deuteronomy and Hosea on cultic matters, and the connections between its laws and the laws of the Book of the Covenant.[3] It also includes southern traditions, the most significant being the call for centralization of worship in what must be Jerusalem.[4] If the account of a law book being found in

1. Blenkinsopp, *Prophecy and Canon*, p. 34.

2. Blenkinsopp, *Prophecy and Canon*, pp. 28-29.

3. See Nicholson, *Deuteronomy and Tradition*, pp. 67-73, for a full discussion of the northern traditions present in the law.

4. Nicholson, *Deuteronomy and Tradition*, p. 80.

Jerusalem during Josiah's reign is granted any historical credence, this also indicates that at some point its authors came to be involved with Judah and the sanctuary in Jerusalem, and to work toward its renewal and reform.

The migration south of many Levites during the reign of Jeroboam (1 Kgs 12.31; 2 Chron. 11.13, 14), and their new location in and allegiance to Judah would explain the existence of both northern and southern traditions in the book. Nicholson argues for another historical occasion for the movement from north to south, namely, the fall of the northern kingdom. The date of composition of the bulk of the law book is then put in the reign of Manasseh.[1] This is also possible. The evidence is ambiguous enough that it cannot be precisely dated. However, it is possible to locate the law book as part of a reform movement which included both northern and southern traditions, and came to play a strategic role in the reign of Josiah.

2. *The Deuteronomic Laws Pertaining to the Alien*

A. *Redactional Levels in the Law Book*

I have indicated that the book of Deuteronomy, including the legal collection, has been redacted several times. In order not to make unwarranted assumptions about the composition history of the law book, I will not adopt any one position in advance, but will see what patterns emerge from the texts pertaining to the alien, and whether it is possible to distinguish levels of redaction on that basis.

The alien is often mentioned in conjunction with other people, and these lists of people are a clue not only to the meaning and audience of the law, but also to authorship. A particularly clear example occurs in the lists found in Deut. 5.14; 16.11, 14. These extensive lists are very similar, and the minor differences that do occur can be explained on the basis of content, dependence on prior texts, and style. For example, the Sabbath command (Deut. 5.14) is the only one of the three which includes animals in its list. This can be explained on the basis of its dependence on Exod. 20.10, and because the Sabbath is primarily a taboo day. The inclusion of the phrase, 'who is in your gates', following the mention of the Levite in Deut. 16.11, and its omission in Deut. 16.14, and the difference between the widow described as 'in your midst' in Deut. 16.11, and 'in your gates' in Deut. 16.14, can be

1. Nicholson, *Deuteronomy and Tradition*, pp. 94, 101.

explained as a matter of style. Finally, the inclusion of the Levite, widow and orphan in Deut. 16.11, 14 and its omission in Deut. 5.14 is due on the one hand to Deut. 5.14's dependence on Exodus 20, and on the other hand, to the spirit of generosity which was an essential aspect of the celebration of the Feasts of Weeks and Booths, according to the author of Deut. 16.11, 14.[1] This leaves us with a basic list including, 'you, and your son and your daughter and your manservant and your maidservant and the alien', in that order, in Deut. 5.14; 16.11, 14.

Because of the similar cultic content and the similarity of style, I will conclude that these laws have a common redactor, and should be studied together. Other laws which have parts of the extensive lists of Deut. 5.14; 16.11, 14, and which have to do with cultic matters are found in Deut. 14.29 and Deut. 26.12, 13.

The spirit of generosity which directed the formulation of some of the cultic laws also resulted in the formation of many laws concerning matters of charity. In these laws the mention of the alien, orphan and widow, always in that order, is a typical feature (Deut. 24.19, 20, 21). This list of three dependent members of society is also found in many of the cultic laws (Deut. 14.29; 16.11, 14; 26.12). There also they are always mentioned together, and always in the same order, suggesting that the laws were formulated by the same hand.

In addition to the lists of people which indicates the concerns and style of a particular redactor, we find that there are motivation clauses attached to these laws which are also typical. In the laws pertaining to the alien we find that the admonition to remember the time of slavery occurs in Deut. 5.15; 16.12; 24.18, 22.[2] In all these texts the wording is identical: וזכרת כי־עבד היית בארץ מצרים. A second typical motivating clause in the laws pertaining to the alien occurs in Deut. 14.29; 16.15; 24.19.[3] Here the wording is not quite identical, but close enough to conclude that it derives from a single hand: יברכך יהוה אלהיך בכל מעשה ידיך. This is additional evidence that I have isolated a particular level of redaction.

1. I am making a series of undemonstrated assertions here in order to organize the material. Later, when I discuss these references in more detail I will examine their dependence on prior material, and the meaning of the laws in more detail.

2. It also occurs in Deut. 15.15, but the prohibition here does not involve the alien.

3. It also occurs in Deut. 15.10 and 23.21, in laws unrelated to the alien.

This redactor also prefers to designate the widow, Levite and alien as being 'in your gates' (בשעריך), or 'in your midst' (בקרבך). This descriptive phrase occurs in Deut. 5.14; 14.21, 29; 16.11, 14; 24.14 (not quite parallel); 26.11, 12 (not quite parallel); and 31.12. In Deut. 24.14 the phrase 'in your land' occurs before 'in your gate', and in Deut. 26.12 the conjunction אשר is omitted. By way of indicating that this is evidence of one level of redaction, we note that in Deut. 29.10 the alien is described very differently as, 'the alien in your camp who chops your wood and carries your water'.

The alien is sometimes described using the suffix 'his', or 'your' (Deut. 1.16; 5.15; 24.14; 29.10; 31.12). However, because of its infrequency, it does not seem to be a distinguishing feature of this redactor.

References to the alien which seem to derive from the same hand on the basis of these stylistic features are Deut. 5.14; 14.21, 29; 16.11, 14; 24.17, 19, 20, 21. Deuteronomy 26.11, 12, 13 seem closely tied to them, but do contain some differences, and Deut. 24.14 seems to be inseparable from the group of laws dealing with justice and charity in Deuteronomy 24.

These laws can be subdivided according to content into laws regulating cultic matters and laws requiring charity and justice. Although the latter category may seem to include two distinct categories, we will see that the author's way of thinking combines them. The widow, orphan and the poor are allowed to glean because the harvest belongs to the Lord, and because he allows the landowner to go over the field only once, and allows the widow, orphan and poor to go over it the second time. They, in fact, have as much right to their harvest as the landowner does to his. Because the laws do not distinguish between matters of charity and justice, I will not either.

The other references which pertain to the alien in Deuteronomy include Deut. 1.16; 10.18, 19; 23.7; 28.43, 44; 29.10 and 31.12. None of these are in the law book itself except for Deut. 23.7. The alien is not referred to in the law itself, but only in the motivating clause attached to the law. However, because this law is in a series which delineates the limits of the assembly of the Lord, it is important for our discussion concerning the identity of the Israelites and the subsequent identity of the alien.

The references in Deut. 29.10 and 31.12 also merit study since they include the alien as a participant in a covenant making ceremony.

Furthermore, these two texts seem to be related in that both verses contain lists including men, women, children, Levites and aliens (although not identical in order or phraseology).

The other references to the alien will not be studied extensively since they do not directly contribute to our understanding of the legal status of the alien.

I will proceed by first studying the group of laws which are stylistically related and which we have attributed to a single redactor.[1] I will subdivide this group of laws according to content, into laws regulating cultic matters[2] and laws requiring justice and charity.[3] Then I will study the group of laws which regulate membership in the assembly (Deut. 23.1-8), and in which the alien is mentioned in a motivating clause (Deut. 23.7). Finally, I will examine the two references which place the alien in the context of a covenant making ceremony (Deut. 29.10; 31.12).

B. *Laws Attributed to a Single Redactor*
Laws regulating cultic matters

> a. You shall not eat anything that dies of itself: you may give it to aliens residing in your towns, for them to eat, or you may sell it to a foreigner. For you are a people holy to the LORD your God (Deut. 14.21a).

The references to the alien in Deut. 14.21, and 29 both come at the end of a paragraph of laws dealing with one subject. Deuteronomy 14.3-21 regulates dietary practices and Deut. 14.22-29 regulates the giving of the tithe. McConville argues that the redactor has intentionally tied these two paragraphs together.[4] The implications of the call to be holy are worked out in regard to eating and tithing. In both paragraphs there are laws that have to do with food, and both paragraphs end with a call to be charitable to the alien. Deuteronomy 14.1-21 contains two calls to be holy. The first explains the regulations regarding mourning, and the second, the dietary laws distin-

1. The exception here are the references in Deut. 26.11, 12, 13 which are closely related to Deut. 14.22, 29 but which show signs of being latter additions.

2. Deut. 5.14; 14.21, 29; 16.11, 14; and 26.11, 12, 13.

3. Deut. 24.14, 17, 19, 20, 21.

4. J.G. McConville, *Law and Theology in Deuteronomy*, pp. 78-81. He also points to the use of the verb אכל to demonstrate that the author has intentionally linked these laws together.

guishing between clean and unclean animals. Linking the demand for holiness and food laws is not peculiar to Deuteronomy. Leviticus 11.45 explains that the Israelites must distinguish between clean and unclean as a result of their character as a holy people. Exodus 22.31 also brings together instructions not to eat a carcass with a call to holiness.

The law which concerns the alien in the first half of the chapter (Deut. 14.21) commands the Israelites not to eat anything that is already dead. They are allowed to give it to an alien living in their town or they may sell it to a foreigner.

The reason that the Israelites are not allowed to eat anything found dead is because it has not been properly slaughtered and had its blood drained (Deut. 12.16). We are not to presume that the animal has died from an illness which would render the meat inedible. The meat is unfit for the Israelites only because they are bound by the food laws. The meat is edible for those who do not belong to God's chosen people. According to this law, the alien and the foreigner do not belong. The food laws effectively separate all Israelites from all non-Israelites. Without a doubt, the alien referred to here is a non-Israelite. An impoverished dependent Israelite must still obey the food laws. We notice that the meat may not be given to the widow or the fatherless, but only to the alien.

The alien in this law is distinguished not only from the Israelite, but also from the foreigner. Whereas the Israelites are instructed to be charitable to the alien, they are allowed to sell meat to the foreigner. The difference between the alien and foreigner that emerges here is an economic one. The alien needs economic support; the foreigner has means and is expected to pay for what he gets. Both are the same, however, in that the food laws do not apply to them.

This is not the only place in Deuteronomy where there is legislation pertaining to the foreigner, although it is the only place where the three categories of Israelite, alien and foreigner occur together. Elsewhere in the legal corpus in Deuteronomy the foreigner is contrasted only with the native Israelite. In Deut. 15.3 and Deut. 23.21 the law requires the Israelites to be generous to their fellow Israelites, but not to foreigners. In the former law, the Israelites must cancel the debts of their fellow Israelites every seven years, but not those of foreigners. Similarly, in the latter law, Israelites may not charge their own people interest when lending them food, or money, but they may charge a foreigner interest. In the last reference, Deut. 17.15, the Israelite is instructed not to appoint a foreigner king.

In these laws an exclusive notion of peoplehood emerges which has been noted in essays on the theology of Deuteronomy. They have been cited by Weber as examples of the dualism of in-group and out-group morality.[1] At the same time, Deuteronomy is often applauded for its humanitarian concern.[2] What we see in the laws of Deut. 14.21 is the interplay of a nationalistic faith which is opposed to everything that is not of Yahweh, and a faith concerned for marginal groups. It resolves a possible conflict by distinguishing between classes of foreigners. There are foreigners who have sufficient economic strength to engage in business relations with the Israelites, and there are foreigners who are vulnerable. The former are treated differently from the native Israelite both in cultic matters and economic matters. The poor foreigner, the גר, is excluded from obeying the food laws, but included among those who receive generous treatment. In this way the tension between requiring humanitarian concern and being nationalistic is resolved.

The peculiar character of Deuteronomy's laws on eating an animal found dead will become clearer when we compare them with similar laws in Exodus and Leviticus. The closest parallel in the Covenant Code occurs in Exod. 22.31. Here the call to be a holy people functions as a motivating clause in a law forbidding eating the meat of an animal torn apart. The meat is to be given to the dogs.

Leviticus contains several laws dealing with eating meat which has not been properly slaughtered. In Lev. 22.8 the law prohibits eating both meat found dead and meat from an animal which has been torn apart—thus bringing together the concerns of the Covenant Code and the Deuteronomic law. However, instead of addressing this law to all Israelites, only the priests are forbidden from eating this meat. Elsewhere, in Lev. 17.15, the law again includes both kinds of dead meat, but now prohibits both the alien and Israelite from eating it. In contrast to the law in Deuteronomy, the alien in this law is incorporated into the cultic community of Israel. The law in Lev. 7.22 addresses all Israelites, but the law concerns only the fat of such animals. It allows the Israelites to use the fat for anything other than food, while the fat of domestic animals must be offered to the Lord.

1. Weber, *Ancient Judaism*, p. 343.
2. Mayes, *Deuteronomy*, pp. 55-59.

The relationship between these laws is complex. It is not possible to explain the differences between them solely in terms of a history of the cult, as Driver seeks to do.[1] I hope to demonstrate in the next chapter that the author of Leviticus has different concerns from Deuteronomy *vis-à-vis* the alien, and for this reason has given the alien a different status. In addition, it is important to realize that if the laws in Deuteronomy and Leviticus are intended to reform the cultus, they will not directly reflect prevailing customs.

> b. Every third year you shall bring out the full tithe of your produce for that year, and store it within your towns; the Levites, because they have no allotment or inheritance with you, as well as the resident aliens, the orphans, and the widows in your towns, may come and eat their fill so that the LORD your God may bless you in all the work that you undertake (Deut. 14.28, 29).
>
> Then you, together with the Levites and the aliens who reside among you, shall celebrate with all the bounty that the LORD your God has given to you and to your house (Deut. 26.11).
>
> When you have finished paying all the tithe of your produce in the third year (which is the year of the tithe), giving it to the Levites, the aliens, the orphans and the widows, so that they may eat their fill within your towns, then you shall say before the LORD your God: 'I have removed the sacred portion from the house, and I have given it to the Levites, the resident aliens, the orphans, and the widows, in accordance with your entire commandments (Deut. 26.12, 13).

Deuteronomy 14.22-29 and Deut. 26.12-15 contain laws regulating the giving of the tithe. In both places a portion of the tithe is to be given over to those without land of their own. The list of people who are to receive the tithe in the third year is almost identical in the three places where it occurs: Deut. 14.29; 26.12, 13. It includes the Levite, the alien, the fatherless and the widow—in that order. The only difference between the lists is that the one in Deut. 14.29 is more expansive. The Levite and widow are described there, and simply listed in Deut. 26.12, 13. Because these two sections of law dealing with the tithe include the alien in the same way, I will examine them together.

In order to evaluate these references to the alien, we need to understand the tithe laws in their various contexts. The tithe law in Deuteronomy 14 falls into two paragraphs—the first dealing with the

1. Driver, *Deuteronomy*, p. 165.

yearly tithe, and the second with the triennial tithe. It is this latter tithe that is to be stored in the towns and distributed. In Deuteronomy 26 we again have two paragraphs—the first (Deut. 26.1-11) dealing with offering up the first fruits, and the second (Deut. 26.12-15) with the triennial tithe. The alien is included among those who rejoice at the giving of the first fruits (Deut. 26.11), and among those who receive some of the tithe (Deut. 26.12).

In Deuteronomy 14 the connection between the two paragraphs is clear. The first paragraph reforms the law of tithing in such a way as to allow bringing the tithe to a central sanctuary.[1] This ends with an admonition not to neglect the Levite. The second paragraph then reads as an addendum which legislates more precisely for the care of the Levites and other landless groups. This tithe, commentators agree, should not be seen as an additional tithe. Its intention is to put the tithe of the third year to a different use. This last paragraph again demonstrates the concern of the Deuteronomic law to create a system of support for those who are vulnerable.

The repetition of the law of the triennial tithe in connection with laws dealing with first fruits in Deuteronomy 26 is puzzling. Mayes suggests that the two sections, Deut. 26.1-11, 12-17, have been brought together by the post-exilic redactor. His concern was to provide a historical-theological foundation for an agricultural custom which the Israelites had taken over from the Canaanites.[2] If that is the case, it is worth noting that this redactor was content to leave the Feast of Weeks and Tabernacles (Deut. 16.9-17) without any historical-theological foundation. It is also true that the ceremony of first fruits has not been dealt with previously in this law code, and it seems more likely that a later editor sought to rectify this omission. Interestingly, when he legislates for the ritual, he does so in a different way from his predecessors. In this chapter alone we are told what the participants are to say (Deut. 26.3b-10, 13b-15). In the ceremony of the first fruits, it is these words which establish the historical-theological foundation. In the giving over of the triennial tithe, the words spoken indicate that the tithe was considered a holy portion.

We can conclude on the basis of the preceding evidence that Deut. 26.1-15 was written later than Deuteronomy 14. It instructs the Israelites concerning the ceremony of the first fruits, and it expands

1. Mayes, *Deuteronomy*, p. 246.
2. Mayes, *Deuteronomy*, p. 332.

and clarifies the nature of the triennial tithe. That it has the tithe laws of Deuteronomy 14 in mind is clear from the repetition of the list of recipients. The same people are included, in the same order.

I now need to examine the relationship of these tithe laws to others in the Pentateuch.[1] It is clear that the special concerns of the authors of Deuteronomy are in evidence in these formulations of the tithing law.[2] Firstly, there is a strong didactic interest in formulating the tithe law. In Deut. 14.23 the rationale given is, 'so that you may learn to fear the Lord your God always', and in Deut. 26.13, the Israelite is to say that he has not turned aside nor forgotten any of the commands. This accords with the overall thrust of the book. Deuteronomy is cast as a speech of Moses recollecting and teaching in preparation for life in the promised land. The Israelite is instructed not only to do certain things, but to remember and understand.

Secondly, the tithe laws and the ceremony of first fruits also illustrate the eating theme. Elsewhere in Deuteronomy (Deuteronomy 16), eating goes hand in hand with rejoicing before the Lord. It serves, in the cultic sphere of life, to remind the Israelite that God has brought them to a land of plenty. Eating the tithe is a feature of Deuteronomy's tithe law which is not found in the Priestly laws. Although this can be considered a conflict between the two, it is also possible that the laws are complementary. Because it is doubtful that the entire tithe could be eaten as a festal meal, it has been proposed

1. McConville, in *Law and Theology*, pp. 68-78, has surveyed the research on this topic and formulated a position which is in opposition to the Wellhausian hypothesis that Deuteronomy is in irreconcilable conflict with the tithe law of P (Num. 18.8-9, Lev. 27.30-31), and that Deuteronomy predates P. Rather, he proposes that they are in essential agreement, and that Deuteronomy's tithe laws were written after the laws found in Num. 18. He seeks to demonstrate that Deut. 10.9, which explains that the Levites have no inheritance, that the Lord is their inheritance, 'as the Lord your God told them', is referring to another statement in the Old Testament, which he claims can only be Num. 18.20. If this is the case, then Deuteronomy is written after the tithe laws of P, and in response to them. He claims that the differences between the laws are best explained in terms of the peculiar interests of the different legal collections, and because neither group of laws presents a complete picture of the institution of the tithe.

2. I am relying on the analysis of McConville, *Law and Theology*, pp. 78-86 in this discussion.

that some was eaten, and most handed over to the priests at the sanctuary.[1]

Connected with rejoicing at the generosity of the Lord, is the call for the Israelite to respond with generosity. This act of charity in turn will move God to continue his generous treatment of the Israelites (Deut. 14.29b; 26.15). In these instances, rejoicing because of the blessings of God involves sharing the gifts of God with the Levite, the poor and the alien.

This association is more pronounced in the laws concerning the first fruits in Deuteronomy 26 than in the laws of the tithe. In Deut. 14.26 the Israelite and his household will eat and rejoice in the sanctuary, and then later we learn that a portion of the tithe will be given to the Levite, the widow, orphan and alien, so that they also may eat and be satisfied (Deut. 14.29). The rejoicing and sharing are juxtaposed in the text, but are not necessarily both in evidence at the festal meal. However, in the legislation dealing with offering up the first fruits, this is clearly the intent. The first fruits are presented at the temple, and this is followed by rejoicing with the members of the household as well as with the Levite and the alien (Deut. 26.11).

Two peculiarities of the tithe law and first fruits law, namely, the festal meal and the inclusion of the alien as a guest, can be explained in terms of the theology of Deuteronomy. Both of these aspects are absent from Num. 18.8-32 and Lev. 27.30-33. However, rejoicing and generosity are not the prime concerns of the author(s) of the Priestly legislation. Numbers 18.8-24, for example, deals with the status of the tribe of Levi over against the other tribes. This interest has tended to focus the laws on their rights. On this basis, McConville argues that the differing presentations of the institutions of tithing and first fruits are best explained in terms of the theology of the code in which they are found, rather than by reconstructing a history of the cult.[2] However, it may also be a case of both/and. The differences in emphases found in the Priestly and Deuteronomic laws may be due both to differing historical situations and differing theologies. In fact, differing historical situations often do result in new theological paradigms. In that case, it would be possible to use the laws as evidence of the development of the cultus.

Finally, we need to notice that the lists of people participating in the

1. McConville, *Law and Theology*, p. 77, and Mayes, *Deuteronomy*, p. 245.

2. McConville, *Law and Theology*, pp. 68-78.

ceremony for giving the tithes differs from those participating when the first fruits are presented. The intention of the triennial tithe to help the Levite and marginal groups is clearly brought out by the expansive list which is found in Deut. 14.29 and Deut. 26.12, 13. However, Deut. 26.11 lists only 'you, and the Levite and the alien in your midst' (אתה והלוי והגר אשר בקרבך). This is interesting because it is not what we would expect. It is a ceremony similar to the Feast of Weeks and Tabernacles, which also have an extensive list including the needy members of society (Deut. 16.9-15). The closest parallel to this abbreviated list occurs in Deut. 29.11, in which Moses is addressing all who are participating in the covenant making ceremony, and in Josh. 8.35. These lists are intended to be inclusive of the different classes of society. In all these lists the alien is described as living in their midst, using the preposition קרב. This evidence, although not extensive enough on its own, may suggest that these passages come from one hand, and that this editor is not so taken up with humanitarian concerns as the author of the legal corpus. I will investigate this more thoroughly when I examine the references found in Deut. 29.11; 31.12.

> c. Rejoice before the LORD your God—you and your sons and your daughters, your male and female slaves, the Levite resident in your towns, as well as the strangers, the orphans, and the widows who are among you—at the place which the LORD your God will choose as a dwelling for his name (Deut. 16.11).
>
> Rejoice in your festival, you and your sons and your daughters, your male and female slaves, as well as the Levites, the strangers, the orphans, and the widows resident in your towns (Deut. 16.14).

The next two references to the alien occur in the context of the laws pertaining to the pilgrimage feasts (Deut. 16.1-17). This section is a unit which is clearly summarized in Deut. 16.16, 17.

It will be helpful to this study of how the status of the alien changes through time to compare these instructions for the three yearly pilgrimage festivals to others found in Exod. 23.14-18 and Lev. 23.1-44. The relationship between these laws has been the focus of much study. I would refer the reader to the discussion of scholarship on the issue by McConville.[1]

1. McConville, *Law and Theology*, pp. 100-10. He argues against the prevalent view that the regulations in D are to be dated between those in JE and P. The sequence JE, D, P is part of the larger Wellhausian hypothesis which traces a

In all the codes, these feasts are designated as pilgrimage feasts (Deut. 16.11, 15, 16; Lev. 23.17, 34; Exod. 23.14, 15, 16). Furthermore, the summary of the three feasts in Deut. 16.16 agrees with Exod. 23.17 in requiring that the feasts be attended by all the men. In Leviticus, on the other hand, the law is addressed to all Israelites (Lev. 23.1, 9, 23, 33, 42). The relationship between Exodus and Deuteronomy is so close here as to suggest literary dependence. I would suggest that Deuteronomy is dependent on Exodus because when it specifies that the feasts be attended by all males (Deut. 16.16), it is contradicting the lists of participants which had been given in Deut. 16.11, 14.

The collections also differ regarding the naming of the feasts. Exodus 23.16 refers to the Feast of Harvest (הקציר), Deut. 16.10 has Weeks (שבעות), while Leviticus 23 does not give the feast a name. Exod. 23.16 refers to the Feast of Ingathering (האסף), while Deut. 16.13 and Lev. 23.34 both have Booths (הסכת). The name differences do not seem significant in terms of the meaning, nor for determining the relationship between the codes.

I have already noted that the dating given in Deuteronomy for the Feast of Weeks and Tabernacles is not as precise as that given in Leviticus, although it is more precise than the dating given in Exodus. However, it seems correct to conclude that this evidence is insufficient to signify the priority of one or another. The reference in Hos. 12.9 to the Feast of Booths indicates the antiquity of the festival.

The difference which concerns me most is the list of participants found in Deuteronomy and omitted in other collections. In both Exodus and Leviticus the participants of all three feasts are the same—Exodus specifying all the men, and Leviticus specifying Israelites. Deuteronomy alone makes a point to include a lengthy list of participants for just these two festivals (Deut. 16.11, 14). Clearly the law in Deuteronomy is making a distinction between Passover on

development in the ritual laws from simplicity to greater and greater elaborateness. For example, one of the reasons that the laws in Leviticus are dated later than those in Deuteronomy is that they are much more precise when giving the date for the Feast of Weeks (compare Lev. 23.15-16 with Deut. 16.9). Yet it can be shown that Deuteronomy tends to be non-technical in its legislation, and Leviticus quite precise. Since these facets of the legislation can be explained in terms of the characteristics of the law collections in which they are found, this aspect cannot be used as evidence for a historical progression.

the one hand, and the Feasts of Weeks and Booths on the other, which is not being made in the other law codes. The list of participants for the Feasts of Weeks and Booths includes aliens, widows, orphans, Levites, slaves, sons and daughters, while there is no mention of them in the Passover legislation.

This is not the only difference between the legislation concerning Passover and the other two feasts in Deuteronomy. The regulations concerning the Feasts of Weeks and Booths are quite similar in that they employ the same terminology, and exhibit similar formal characteristics. In both, the Israelites are to celebrate (ועשית חג) and rejoice (שמחת). In the Feast of Weeks they are told once to celebrate (Deut. 16.10), and in the Feast of Booths, twice (Deut. 16.13, 15). Similarly, in the Feast of Weeks they are instructed once to rejoice (Deut. 16.11), and in the Feast of Booths, twice (Deut. 16.14, 15).

The instructions concerning the feasts contain the same formal elements, though not in the same order. The instructions for the Feast of Weeks include:

a. the date (16.10);
b. an instruction to celebrate by giving (16.10);
c. an instruction to rejoice with participants listed (16.11); and
d. a motivation clause (16.12).

The instructions for the Feast of Booths contain:

a. an instruction to celebrate plus date (16.13);
b. an instruction to rejoice with participants listed (16.14);
c. an instruction to celebrate plus date (16.15a); and
d. a motivation clause (16.15b).

The list of participants for both feasts is strictly parallel, the only difference being that in Deut. 16.11 the Levites are described as, 'those living in your towns', while in Deut. 16.14 there is no modifying phrase. The participants for both include, 'you, your son, your daughter, your menservants, your maidservants, the Levite, the alien, the fatherless and the widow'.

These similarities demonstrate that the author understood these two feasts to have essentially the same meaning. They are primarily occasions of celebration for the harvest given by the Lord. As the Lord has been generous with the Israelites, they are to respond with joy and generosity. These feasts are presented in such a way as to bring out

Deuteronomy's themes of blessing (16.10, 15), rejoicing (16.11, 15), concern for the vulnerable (16.11, 14) and to contrast their life in the promised land with their life in Egypt (16.12).[1]

In order to gain greater insight into the status of aliens, it is not enough to note that they are included as participants at these feasts. We also need to note that they, and the other dependants, are not included in the Passover regulations. The absence of the list of participants is not the only difference between the Feasts of Weeks and Booths on the one hand and the Passover on the other. The terminology of celebrating and rejoicing is also absent. Instead, the Israelite is to observe the month of Abid (16.1) and keep the Passover (16.1) by sacrificing, eating, holding an assembly and ceasing from work. There are many motivation clauses attached to these instructions, and they all involve tying the Passover ritual to the events of the Exodus. The month in which the Passover is celebrated is determined by the month in which they left Egypt (16.1); they must eat unleavened bread because they left in haste (16.3). The motivation for all these ordinances is summed up in Deut. 16.3b, 'so that all the days of your life you may remember the time of your departure from Egypt'.

The reason for the omission of the list of participants lies in the significance of the Exodus event in the theology of Deuteronomy. The Exodus is the event in which God delivered them and made them his own people. It was the act whereby they gained their identity as his chosen people—demarcated from all other peoples. For this reason, the festival which remembers their founding history is not characterized as an occasion of joy and celebration. It is an occasion for observing, keeping, remembering, and holding assemblies. Because of its nature, it is not appropriate to invite those who do not share their common history, i.e. aliens. Nor is it appropriate to make a point of including everyone. The expansive list of participants was part and parcel of the spirit of generosity which the author saw as characteristic of the Feasts of Weeks and Booths.

Hence, the inclusion of the alien, and others, at the Feasts, and the silence concerning these participants in the Passover regulations is to be explained by the author's presentation of the meaning of these occasions. When celebrating the abundant gifts received from the Lord, it is appropriate to respond with rejoicing and generosity

1. McConville, *Law and Theology*, p. 111.

expressed by including all members of society. However, when remembering the event by which God created the Israelites as a people separate from others, then generosity is not at the heart of the occasion. These people may still have been present, but it was not in keeping with the meaning of Passover to explicitly name them.

> d. Observe the sabbath day and keep it holy, as the LORD your God commanded you. Six days you shall labor, and do all your work. But the seventh is a sabbath to the LORD your God; you shall not do any work—you, or your son, or your daughter, or your male or female slave, or your ox, or your donkey, or any of your livestock, or the resident alien in your towns, so that your male and female slaves may rest as well as you. Remember that you were a slave in the land of Egypt and the LORD your God brought you out from there with a mighty hand and an outstretched arm; therefore the LORD your God commanded you to keep the sabbath day (Deut. 5.12-15).

The final cultic law in which the alien is mentioned is the Sabbath command (Deut. 5.12-15) of the Decalogue of Deuteronomy. I would refer the reader to the general discussion on the form and dating of the Decalogue found in the discussion of Exodus 20, since the same applies here. I will be limiting my discussion to the Decalogue's present position in Deuteronomy, and the significance of the Sabbath command for our study of the alien.

The Decalogue is found in the hortatory introduction of the stipulations (Deut. 5.1–11.32). As Mayes notes, this section contains the statement of basic principles which in many treaty forms precedes the detailed stipulations.[1] The Decalogue suits this purpose very well by stating in apodictic form a series of prohibitions basic to societal harmony.[2]

1. Mayes, *Deuteronomy*, p. 160.

2. Unlike Deut. 1–4, which Mayes claims was not composed as a preface to the law, Deut. 5–11, apart from some interpolations, is described by him as the work of the deuteronomistic pre-exilic author who composed it as an introduction to the law code. In the original composition, the laws were presented as being given by Moses on the eve of their entry into the promised land. The editor inserted this account of a covenant making ceremony at Mt Horeb for the purpose of enhancing the authority attached to the laws of Deut. 12–26. Although Mayes does not credit the deuteronomistic editor with composing the Decalogue, he does claim that he placed it in its present position, and by means of expansions and substitutions integrated it to his purpose. See Mayes, *Deuteronomy*, pp. 161-65.

The Sabbath command here has several marked differences from the command given in Exodus 20. Several have already been noted. Here I wish only to note that the reason given for allowing the entire household a day of rest is simply kindness (Deut. 5.14); it is not tied to creation as in Exodus 20. Although only the male and female slave are mentioned in the clause stating the rationale, it seems clear that they represent the entire list of dependants mentioned earlier in the command. This motivation is in accord with what we have seen elsewhere in the laws. Specifically, the long list of participants is reminiscent of the lists in the Feasts of Weeks and Tabernacles legislation (Deut. 16.9-15). Indeed, the spirit of generosity which we noted there is dominant here also. In fact, by stipulating that not only people, but also animals must rest, it is carried still further.[1]

In addition, Israelites are to remember their own time of slavery in Egypt, and God's deliverance (Deut. 5.15). This is characteristic of the pedagogic interest of the laws. This particular motivation is also found in Deut. 24.18. In both these instances, the law presupposes that the Israelites are in a position of power akin to God. The admonition then is appropriate, for it calls upon them to remember how God used his might for their benefit, and instructs them to do likewise to others.

As for the aliens, they are dependent members of an extended household. In the hierarchy, they follow all the family members, the servants and even the animals; yet they are included. The law, as far as aliens are concerned, requires that the Israelites be generous to the strangers that have been taken in. The Israelites are instructed not to take advantage of their vulnerability by making them work on the Sabbath. It is a surprisingly egalitarian law.

Laws requiring social justice

a. You shall not withhold the wages of poor and needy laborers, whether other Israelites or aliens who reside in your land in one of your towns (Deut. 24.14).

You shall not deprive a resident alien or an orphan of justice; you shall not take a widow's garment in pledge (Deut. 24.17).

When you reap your harvest in your field, and forget a sheaf in the field, you shall not go back to get it; it shall be left for the alien, the orphan and the widow, so that the LORD your God may bless you in all your undertakings (Deut. 24.19).

1. Driver, *Deuteronomy*, p. 85.

> When you beat your olive trees, do not strip what is left; it shall be for the alien, the orphan, and the widow (Deut. 24.20).

> When you gather the grapes of your vineyard, do not glean what is left; it shall be for the alien, the orphan, and the widow. Remember that you were a slave in the land of Egypt; therefore I am command you to do this (Deut. 24.21, 22).

Deuteronomy is well-known for its humanitarian concern for the marginalized. This tells us not only about the book's vision for the people of God, but also about the existence of a well-to-do upper class and an often impoverished lower class. The rise of the monarchy brought with it a hierarchical social structure. It created a royal family, a national cult, a patrician class centered in the cities, and a semi-free artisan and peasant class.[1] The economic policies of the monarchy drew the wealth from the land, and made the life of the lower class more precarious. It is to this new socioeconomic reality that the laws concerning justice and charity are addressed.

In Deuteronomy 24 there are five references to the alien, in vv. 14, 17, 19, 20, 21. It may seem that the concerns of the alien dominate, and that is true to some extent. These references are found in a section of the law code, Deut. 24.5–25.4, which has been characterized by its concern for the needy. However, contained within this collection are laws which do not conform to that concern, such as Deut. 24.16. It is therefore more appropriate to describe this group of laws as a miscellaneous collection which begins in Deut. 23.15 and continues to Deut. 25.19. The order of the laws found here is not logical. Instead, these laws are brought together by a common subject (Deut. 24.1-4, 5), or by a catchword connection (Deut. 24.15, 16).[2] It is also miscellaneous with respect to the forms employed. There are apodictic commands, but these are often followed by motivating clauses (Deut. 24.14, 17), and there are also casuistically formulated laws which are followed by motivation clauses using the personal mode of address (Deut. 24.1-4).

Most of the laws appear to be ancient, and many have parallels in the Book of the Covenant. The hand of the author is noticeable mostly in the organization of the chapter, and in the motivation clauses which have been attached to the laws.

The first reference, found in Deut. 24.14, protects the hired man, whether he is a fellow Israelite or an alien. The law stipulates in v. 14

1. Frick, *The City in Ancient Israel*, p. 205.
2. Mayes, *Deuteronomy*, p. 323.

that the Israelites are not to oppress the hired man (שכיר),[1] and then continues in v. 15 to specify the sort of oppression. The law requires that the employer not withhold wages: the laborers are to be paid on a daily basis.

The author has connected this law to the preceding one in a number of ways. As the cloak is to be returned to the borrower before sunset in v. 13, so the wages are to be paid before sunset in v. 15. The motivation clauses attached to these laws also show that the author saw them as related. The motivation clause for the lender in vv. 10-13 states that the borrower will thank him, and that it will be considered a righteous act. The motivation clause of v. 15 makes the same point by stating it negatively. The employer must pay his laborers daily, lest they cry out against him and he be guilty of sin. Together, these laws protect the dignity of the poor, and also prevent them becoming further impoverished. They further Deuteronomy's goal of creating an economic system which supports those on the fringes—those who have no land of their own.

The alien referred to in this law holds the socioeconomic position of the hired man. This is the only law in Deuteronomy which deals with the hired man. The word occurs in one other place in Deuteronomy (Deut. 15.18), but there it is part of the motivation attached to a law dealing with slaves. What we know of the hired man, we know from this verse—he is economically vulnerable. For us it is significant that aliens fall into this category as well. Here, as in other references in Deuteronomy, the alien is classed with the weak members of society. Again, in accord with what we have seen elsewhere, the alien and landless Israelite are to receive the same generous treatment. The law recognizes an ethnic distinction between them, but in legislating generous treatment, it treats their socioeconomic status as more important than their ethnic identity.

The closest parallel to this law in the other Pentateuchal law codes occurs in Lev. 19.13b. There are verbal similarities between the two laws. In Lev. 19.13a the verb תעשק is used, but there it refers to the neighbor. In Lev. 19.13b the hired man (שכיר) is protected in the same way as in Deut. 24.14. However, the wording of the prohibition is not parallel to that found in Deuteronomy, and thus it is not possible to determine a literary relationship between them.

1. The NRSV makes explicit what sort of oppression is being referred to in its translation of 'oppress' in v. 14 as 'withhold the wages'.

For our purposes, it is sufficient to notice that the author of Deuteronomy's law made a point to include the alien in a law protecting the day laborer. It is interesting to note that the motivation clause found in Deut. 24.15 assumes that not only the Israelite, but also the alien can cry out to the Lord, and that the Lord will hold the Israelite guilty of sin for not being just to the alien. In the laws in Exodus, it is only the widows, the fatherless and the poor Israelites' cries which are heard by God (Exod. 22.22-27). In allowing both Israelite and alien to appeal to the Lord for vindication, the line dividing the two has become quite fine in this law.

The last four references to the alien in this chapter are clustered together in Deut. 24.17-21. These laws all deal with the same three classes of dependent people: aliens, the fatherless and widows. The question arises as to whether the grouping of alien, fatherless and widow is unique to Deuteronomy. The Covenant Code does not mention them together in one law, but in two successive laws (Exod. 22.21, 22). The Priestly laws also do not group these classes of people together. However, the widow, fatherless and alien are found together in Ps. 94.6, and Jer. 22.3. Although it is not correct to conclude that the theme of justice for the socially weak is unique to Deuteronomy, or even to the Israelite legal traditions, the consistent use of the terms 'widow, fatherless and alien' is typical of Deuteronomy.[1]

Lohfink has noticed that this grouping is not a grouping of the poor. Although in the Priestly law that alien is twice grouped with the poor (Lev. 19.10; 23.22), in Deuteronomy that never occurs. He clearly demonstrates that Deuteronomy has changed the semantic field. The poor are a group distinct from the widow, orphan and alien. The laws dealing with the poor are concerned only with indebtedness. They seek to return those Israelites who are losing or have lost their land to ownership through laws regulating the sabbath year and debt servitude. These laws are preventing landed Israelites from becoming destitute. The laws dealing with the alien, widow and orphan (and sometimes slaves and Levites) have a different thrust. The laws are providing for the economic maintenance of groups of people who have no land. If that system worked, members of these groups would not be poor.[2] These laws demonstrate the concern of the author(s) for

1. Deut. 14.29; 16.11, 14; 24.17, 19, 20, 21; 26.12, 13; 27.19.

2. Lohfink, 'The Option for the Poor', pp. 14-16. He presented the following table to demonstrate that the laws dealing with the poor have a different group of

marginalized members of society. Social justice for all is of paramount importance for the law collection.

The group of laws pertaining to the alien in Deuteronomy 24 falls into two paragraphs; vv. 17 and 18 form the first, and vv. 19-22 the second. They have been bound together in two ways. First, the motivating clause at the end of each paragraph is almost identical. The wording is parallel—the only difference being that v. 18 includes the phrase, 'and the Lord your God redeemed you from there', while v. 22 does not. Also, the inclusion of the orphan in v. 17 seems to be a later addition so that this law, as well as those following, would refer to the same three classes. As it stands, its inclusion disturbs what would otherwise be the parallelism of the law, and the lack of a conjunction preceding it makes it grammatically clumsy.[1]

The motivating clauses attached to these laws elucidate the theology of the author. As I noted earlier, laws requiring generosity to the needy are not easily enforced. If the law is to be obeyed, it is because the Israelites have been convinced that this is their duty, rather than because they fear punishment. Therefore the motivating clause becomes a very important part of these laws. Incidentally, the same motivating clause that occurs twice here is also found in Deut. 15.15, where it follows a law requiring generosity to the released slave.

people in mind from the laws dealing with the widow, stranger and orphan.

			Alien	Widow	Orphan
Deut.	14.29	Tithe	x	x	x
	16.11	Weeks	x	x	x
	16.14	Booths	x	x	x
	24.19	Harvest	x	x	x
	24.20	Harvest	x	x	x
	24.21	Harvest	x	x	x
	26.11	Tithe	x		
	26.12f.	Tithe	x	x	x

Poor and needy

Deut. 15.1-6	Fallow year: no exaction of debts
15.7-11	Loans without interest
15.12-18	Fallow year: liberation of slaves
24.10-13	Pledge of a poor person
24.14-15	Daily pay for a poor day-laborer

1. Mayes, *Deuteronomy*, p. 326.

This motivating clause gives two reasons for generosity to the needy. First, Israelites are to remember their own slavery and God's deliverance (Deut. 24.18, 22), and second, because God will bless the work of the Israelites if they are generous (Deut. 24.19). In both cases Israelites are to imitate God's prior action. As God was kind to the enslaved Israelites, and freed them, so now Israelites are to be kind to those in need. The relationship of Israelites to the vulnerable is analogous to God's relationship to them when they were in Egypt. Now the Israelites have some power, and can use that power to benefit others.

The same principle applies to the fruit of the land. The land and its harvests are the gifts of God to the Israelites.[1] As God was generous to the Israelites, giving them a bountiful harvest, so now Israelites are to imitate God's generosity. If they obey this command, God will continue to be generous to them. In both cases the Israelites are not to see themselves as having rights *vis-à-vis* the land or others. Their present status as free landholders, ready to harvest a crop, is seen as the result of an act of God's grace; their continuing status as such is also seen as dependent on God's grace. Being generous to others is part of the response to God's prior act. It is the required obedience which is inseparable from God's blessing both before and after. Because of this theology of land which underlies that laws dealing with fringe groups, it is more appropriate to designate them as laws advocating social justice than laws advocating charity.

The prohibition concerning the alien in Deut. 24.17 requires that the alien be given justice. There is no exact parallel to this law in the Book of the Covenant, and yet it is the logical outcome of the laws which prohibit oppressing the alien (Exod. 22.22; 23.9). Exodus 23.9, in particular, can be seen as requiring legal justice for the alien. It is the last of a series dealing mainly with justice in the courts (Exod. 23.1-9); hence its inclusion here probably makes the oppression referred to legal oppression. Deuteronomy 24.17 makes this explicit. The alien as well as the Israelite is to be granted justice at the village gate.

The alien and the Israelite are granted equal rights before the law and yet it is clear that they do not have the same social standing. Because the law is addressed to the Israelite, it is only the Israelite who is responsible under the law. The alien cannot enforce the law, but is dependent upon the Israelite to uphold the law.

1. See McConville, *Law and Theology*, pp. 11-17, for a presentation on the theology of giving in Deuteronomy.

The laws of Deut. 24.19-22 give the alien, the fatherless and the widow (mentioned three times in the same order) the right to their own grain, olive and grape harvest. The farmer is not to go back over the field, orchard or vineyard a second time, because the harvest remaining belongs to the alien, the fatherless and the widow. This way of formulating the injunction indicates again that the land and its produce are God's, and thus it is he who dispenses harvesting rights.

Aliens mentioned here have the same socioeconomic status that we have encountered elsewhere. They are vulnerable, landless and dependent on the Israelite landholder for their welfare. It is significant that Levites have not been included in the list of those who have the right to glean. They were part of the group that benefitted from the giving of first fruits and tithes (Deut. 14.29; 26.11, 12, 13) and participated in the Feasts of Weeks and Tabernacles (Deut. 16.11, 12, 14). Their inclusion in those laws and their exclusion here help us to delineate their status over against the alien, widow and fatherless. That they are included in only the cultic affairs indicates that they are paid cultic personnel. I agree with McConville that the tithes and first fruits are the dues owed to the Levite.[1] They need these dues because they are landless and cannot produce their own harvest.

Laws regulating gleaning occur elsewhere in the Pentateuch in Lev. 19.9-10; 23.22. These laws are substantially the same as those in Deuteronomy. In Lev. 19.9-10, the harvest of the olive orchard is not referred to, although the harvest of field and vineyard are mentioned. In addition, Lev. 19.9-10 includes an injunction not to harvest to the edges of the field, while Deut. 24.19-22 prohibits going over a field a second time. Similarly, Lev. 23.22 instructs the Israelite not to pick up the fallen grapes as well as not harvesting a second time. Clearly, the principle and intent behind the laws is the same, but different instances are mentioned to elucidate it.

The people for whom the gleanings are left are also substantially the same in Deuteronomy's and Leviticus's laws. Leviticus refers to the alien and the poor in both formulations of the law (Lev. 19.9-10; 23.22).[2] Although it may seem that Deuteronomy is innovating in relation to the laws of the Book of the Covenant, which has no laws regarding gleaning, it is in basic agreement with the laws of Leviticus.

1. McConville, *Law and Theology*, pp. 68-78.

2. The significance of the differing terminology of the Deuteronomic and Priestly laws has been dealt with above.

Rather than seeing either Deuteronomy or the Priestly laws as being innovative, it is more likely that the custom is ancient. What was first practiced as a social convention has been inscribed in law by both the Deuteronomistic and Priestly writers.

C. *Laws Regulating Membership in the Assembly*

Deut. 23.1-8 contains a series of prohibitions which delineate who is excluded from the assembly of the Lord (קהל יהוה). This phrase is also found in Mic. 2.5, where it also seems to designate the cultic community. The assembly includes fully enfranchised male citizens who are eligible for cultic participation and also for military service.[1] Although we could expect to learn a great deal about the status of the alien by studying what excludes people from full membership, this passage raises more questions than it answers.

There are five prohibitions in this series, all in apodictic style. However, the first three have the form, 'no...may enter' (Deut. 23.1, 2, 3), while the last two use the form, 'Do not abhor...' (Deut. 23.7). In addition, the criteria by which people are excluded are quite different, as well as the type of people excluded. The first two prohibitions exclude an Israelite on the basis of a physical deformity or being the offspring of an improper marriage (ממזר). This has been interpreted as referring to children of an incestuous marriage or a marriage between an Israelite and non-Israelite.[2] The last three exclude people, in varying degrees, and for various reasons, who are not Israelites. The exclusion of the Israelites, it seems clear, has to do with cultic impurity as this has been described elsewhere in Deuteronomy. But the exclusion of the last three groups of people is rationalized on the basis of past events. Based on the variety of forms found, and the heterogeneous content, some commentators have concluded that this

1. Mayes, *Deuteronomy*, p. 316.

2. The issue is significant for my study, but the evidence is too meager to substantiate any thesis. On the basis of the use of ממזר in Zech. 9.6, it could refer to the son of a marriage between an Israelite and a non-Israelite. However, if a connection is made between this law and the preceding law in Deut. 23.1 (ET 22.30) and the subsequent mention of the Ammonites and Moabites, then it refers to the son of an incestuous marriage. See Mayes, *Deuteronomy*, p. 316, for a discussion of the options.

series is not an original unit.[1] These prohibitions have been brought together because they all result in exclusion from the assembly.

The reasons given in the text for the exclusion of the Ammonite, Moabite, Edomite and Egyptian (Deut. 23.3-8) are not accepted at face value by most commentators. Von Rad claims that the determining factor for excluding anyone is cultic, and not political or historical. Therefore, he concludes that the initial reason was cultic, and that arguments based on salvation history which we find here are later additions.[2] However, what the cultic reason was is not discernible, nor is it understandable why the Edomites and Egyptians receive better treatment than the Ammonites and Moabites.

Mayes, however, arrives at some more tangible conclusions. He suggests the prohibitions arose in the border sanctuaries at Mizpah and Beersheba, where the issue of foreigners worshiping Yahweh would arise. Furthermore, he suggests that calling an Edomite a brother might refer to the fact that there was a treaty made between the Israelites and Edomites during the reign of David (2 Sam. 8.13, 14.).[3]

Carmichael, on the other hand, finds the historical explanation in the text entirely acceptable, and expands upon it. He claims, for example, that because Esau was friendly to Jacob when he returned from Laban (Gen. 33), that the Edomites are now given special treatment.[4] However, his explanation is not based on a critical use of the texts, and is therefore unconvincing.

The reference to the alien occurs in the motivating clause attached to the prohibition not to abhor an Egyptian. The reason given is that 'you (singular) were an alien in his country' (Deut. 23.7). Commentators have wondered at this reason because it seems to overlook the fact that the Israelites endured great hardship during their sojourn in Egypt.[5] For this reason Mayes suggests that the 'you' may not be referring to the entire people of Israel, but only to several individuals who had left Beersheba to live as aliens in Egypt for a time, and were

1. Mayes, *Deuteronomy*, p. 316.

2. G. von Rad, *Deuteronomy: A Commentary* (trans. D. Barton; OTL; Philadelphia: Westminster Press, 1966), p. 146.

3. Mayes, *Deuteronomy*, p. 317.

4. C.M. Carmichael, *The Laws of Deuteronomy* (Ithaca: Cornell University Press, 1974), p. 176.

5. Mayes, *Deuteronomy*, p. 318; Carmichael, *The Laws of Deuteronomy*, p. 176.

well-treated.[1] However, elsewhere in the law, it is always the people of Israel who are addressed and referred to. It seems highly unlikely, therefore, that this phrase should refer only to individual Israelites. Instead, I would suggest that the motivation given for the inclusion of the Egyptian after three generations indicates that the Israelites felt an obligation to the Egyptians. Whether or not the Egyptians always treated them well, they had allowed the Israelites to live as aliens, for a long time, in their land. The rationale given indicates the strength of the notion of obligation which existed in ancient Israelite society, as well as in other oriental cultures.

All in all, this passage supports commentators' description of Deuteronomy's theology as extremely nationalistic. As Mayes notes, Deuteronomy seeks to demonstrate that the promises of land and people made to Abraham are about to be fulfilled, but makes nothing of the last promise found in Gen. 12.2-3.[2] There is no missionary zeal to be found here. This concurs with what I have already noted in the passages referring to the alien. Aliens dare to be treated with generosity, to be extended hospitality, but they are not invited to become Israelites.

In summary, we can note that this passage addresses the issue of the outsider from a different vantage point. It identifies people according to their nationality, and not according to their socioeconomic status. This is because the issue raised is whether or not they can be considered full citizens. The laws which have referred to the alien have never directly addressed this question, although I have sought to gain this information from the laws. It would seem that the particular nationality of aliens is of no import, since in all the references in the Pentateuchal laws there has never been a mention of the people to which they belonged or the locale from which they came. The only significant thing about the alien's nationality was that it was not Israelite. The reason that this information is not important to the laws is that the legislation deals only with the alien as an isolated individual or family. This is not to say that the term alien can only refer to individuals and not to groups, but that the legal corpora do not concern themselves with these alien tribes.[3]

1. Mayes, *Deuteronomy*, p. 318.
2. Mayes, *Deuteronomy*, p. 56.
3. Weber, *Ancient Judaism*, pp. 32-42, distinguishes between the individual alien who needs to be taken in to the 'father's house' as a guest, and a tribe of

D. *The Alien as a Participant in a Covenant Ceremony*

> a. You stand assembled today, all of you, before the LORD your God; the leaders of your tribes, your elders, and your officials, all the men of Israel, your children, your women, and the aliens who are in your camp, both those who cut your wood and those who draw your water (Deut. 29.9, 10 [ET 10, 11]).

In Deut. 29.10 the alien is mentioned as one of several who together confirm the covenant made first with their forebears, and renewed in the present. This list intends to be inclusive of all elements of society. The members are listed hierarchically, beginning with the leaders and chief men, elders and officials, all the other men of Israel, and concluding with the children, wives and aliens. We have not encountered this type of list before. We have had lists of dependent members which have been quite extensive (Deut. 5.15), but this is the only list in Deuteronomy which attempts to enumerate all elements of society. A shorter list of similar type is found in Deut. 31.12, Josh. 8.30-35, and Josh. 24.1, in which covenant making ceremonies are described. The lists found in these texts are not strictly parallel,[1] but all function in the same way in a narrative describing a covenant making ceremony.

The list of participants mentioned in Deut. 29.10-15 is in the context of a new speech of Moses—the third in the book, which is made on the occasion of ratifying a covenant in Moab.[2] This discourse begins in Deut. 29.2 and continues to the end of Deuteronomy 30.

foreigners who are in a clientele relationship to the Israelites. This sort of distinction, he claims, existed only in pre-exilic times when the social structure was basically tribal.

1. Lists of participants in:

Deut. 29.9-10	Josh. 8.33	Josh. 8.35	Josh. 24.1
ראשיכם	כל־ישראל	כל־קהל ישראל	זקני ישראל
שבטיכם	זקניו	הנשים	לראשיו
זקניכם	שטרים	הטף	לשפטיו
שטריכם	כגר	הגר	לשטריו
כל איש ישראל	כאזרח		
טפכם			
נשיכם			
גרך			

2. Von Rad, *Deuteronomy*, p. 178, notes that nowhere else in the Old Testament is a covenant in Moab distinguished from the covenant at Sinai.

This speech is clearly separate from the legal material in Deuteronomy, but seems to presuppose it.[1] Although, now in the context of a speech, Deut. 29.10-15 is unlike what precedes it. It is not a homily, but gives the impression of being an official record; an accurate naming of the parties present at the making a covenant.[2] The distinctiveness of Deut. 29.10-15 is borne out in other ways. The alien in this list is qualified by the phrase, 'in the midst of your camp'. The word 'camp' (מחניך) is not typical of Deuteronomy, occurring elsewhere only in Deut. 2.14, 15.[3] We have already noted above that the preposition בקרב following 'alien' is not typical of the way the alien is described in the legal corpus of Deuteronomy. Furthermore, the aliens are described as 'hewers of wood and drawers of water'. This is the only time in the Pentateuch that they are described in this way.

Although there are few connections between the terminology connected with the alien in Deuteronomy 29 and the alien in the legal corpus of Deuteronomy, there are several striking similarities between this account of aliens being participants in a covenant ceremony and the covenant with the Gibeonites in Joshua 9. Firstly, the Gibeonites are described three times there as 'hewers of wood and drawers of water' (Josh. 9.21, 23, 27).[4] Furthermore, the Gibeonites

1. Mayes, *Deuteronomy*, pp. 367-68, argues that this chapter is connected with other speeches in Deuteronomy. Its author is also responsible for Deut. 4. It is an exhortation from the hand of the second deuteronomistic editor addressed to those in exile. Its purpose is to explain their present situation and to provide a basis of hope for the future. J.A. Soggin, *Joshua* (trans. R.W. Wilson; Philadelphia: Westminster Press, 1972), pp. 240-41, makes different connections. He argues that the deuteronomistic historian is responsible for Josh. 8.3-35; 24.25-27, and that these are dependent on Deut. 11.26-32; 27.1-26. He attributes Deut. 1–4 to this author as well, and claims that these passages which are dealing with a covenant making ceremony are not the creation of the deuteronomic historian, but reflect an ancient covenant making ceremony. The erection of the plastered stones and the mention of these rituals taking place outside of Jerusalem indicate to him that these passages are historically reliable.

2. Von Rad, *Deuteronomy*, p. 178. The list of participants in Josh. 8.30-35 also seems out of place in its present context. Here the break with what precedes and follows is even more abrupt, and the placing of these verses after Josh. 9.2 in the LXX indicates that the problem is an ancient one, according to Soggin, *Joshua*, p. 240.

3. According to Driver, *Deuteronomy*, p. 322, it is often found in JE and especially P.

4. These four occurrences of this phrase are the only four in the Old Testament.

come to the Israelites in their 'camp' at Gilgal (Josh. 9.6). Finally, Joshua 9 narrates that the Gibeonites are incorporated into the people of Israel by means of a disparity treaty. These similarities seem to be intentional, the result of redactional activity.[1] Mayes argues that one of the goals of the redactor of Deuteronomy 29 was to cast the Gibeonites as aliens, and thereby bring them into a closer relationship with the Israelites. This was important, because in Joshua 9 the Gibeonites are connected with temple service, and the Deuteronomist is concerned that foreigners should not be involved in the sanctuary. By means of the connections we have noted, he makes it clear that the Gibeonites are not foreigners, but are aliens.[2]

My discussion of the redactional intent of Deuteronomy 29 and Joshua 9 should not obscure the conclusion that at the base of Joshua 9 lies a narrative which describes what seems to be an actual covenant by which the Gibeonites were incorporated into the tribes of Israel. From this we can learn that it was possible, by means of a disparity treaty, to incorporate a tribe that was ethnically dissimilar into the tribes of Israel. The fact that it was a disparity treaty implies that the status of the Gibeonites was on a different legal footing to that of the Israelites, and this is further verified by 2 Sam. 21.1-6.[3]

1. See the article by A.D.H. Mayes, 'Deuteronomy 29, Joshua 9, and the Place of the Gibeonites in Israel', in *Das Deuteronomium* (ed. N. Lohfink; Leuven: Leuven University Press, 1985), pp. 321-22, for a discussion of other points of similarity between these two accounts.

2. Mayes, 'Deuteronomy 29, Joshua 9 and the Place of the Gibeonites in Israel', pp. 323-25, understands that the Priestly redactor, whom he sees as responsible for the insertion of Josh. 9.18-21, had a similar concern. He solved his problem by relating the Gibeonites to the congregation of Israel rather than to the sanctuary. He further argues that the Chronicler continues this tradition. He notes that in 1 Chron. 22.2 David gathers the aliens to prepare stones for the temple, and in 2 Chron. 2.16, 17 Solomon takes a census of the aliens and puts them to forced labor. This stands in the tradition of Deut. 29 and Josh. 9 rather than 1 Kgs 9.20, in which Solomon employs all the people who were left of the Amorites, Hittites, Perizzites, Hivites and Jebusites. In these passages also, the aliens are laborers on the temple, but not servants of the sanctuary.

3. See Blenkinsopp, 'Are There Traces of the Gibeonite Covenant in Deuteronomy?', pp. 211-13. This conflicts with the reconstruction of A. Cody, *A History of Old Testament Priesthood* (Rome: Pontifical Biblical Institute, 1969), pp. 55-56, on the position of the Gibeonites in Israelite society. He describes ancient Israelite society as being similar to Bedouin society in that there existed a three-tiered hierarchy. The full-blooded members of the tribe were at the top, the aliens who are

I have gone quite far on the basis of a single reference. Yet it is clear that the alien referred to here is quite different from the alien mentioned in the legal material. These aliens are one of several parties about to enter into a covenant relationship with Yahweh. The גר referred to here is not the vulnerable individual or family who came without connections into a strange place, and needed the protection of an Israelite household. Instead, the aliens referred to here are a group of people, the Gibeonites, who have entered into a legal relationship with Israel and hence with Israel's God. They are second-class citizens, being mentioned with the wives and children, and yet they are involved in a legally binding relationship.

> b. Assemble the people, men, women, and children, as well as the aliens residing in your towns, so that they may hear and learn to fear the LORD your God, and to observe diligently all the words of this law (Deut. 31.12).

Deuteronomy 31.12 occurs in what is generally designated as an appendix. The hortatory addresses of Moses are now finished, and the book concludes by resuming the narrative of the Pentateuch. Joshua is instituted as the new leader (Deut. 31.1-8), and provision is made for the regular reading of the law (Deut. 31.9-13). The purpose is both to describe the events leading up to the death of Moses, thereby rounding off the Pentateuch, and to fit these events into the larger deuteronomistic history.[1]

The reference to the alien that occurs in this chapter is reminiscent of what we have just encountered in Deut. 29.10. Moses is giving instructions providing for the reading of the law during the Feast of Booths at the end of every seven years. Part of the instructions includes a list of those who should hear the law (Deut. 31.9-11). This

ethnically similar but not tribal members came next, and lastly came the slaves and captives, who were often not of the same race. He concludes on the basis of this analogy and Josh. 9 that the Gibeonites belonged to the lowest class—citing as proof their jobs as hewers of wood and carriers of water. Blenkinsopp notes that they were of Hurrian stock (p. 211) at the same time presenting them as having the status of aliens. It seems that the evidence of Josh. 9 coupled with Deut. 29 supports the defining of their status as aliens. First, they are not captured or bought, but enter into a covenant agreement, and secondly, the epitaph 'hewers of wood and drawers of water' cannot be taken to indicate their slave status, since it is applied to aliens in Deut. 29.

1. Von Rad, *Deuteronomy*, p. 188; Mayes, *Deuteronomy*, p. 372.

list also intends to be all-inclusive. It simply begins with the people, and then goes on to enumerate precisely who is included in that term: 'the men, women, children and aliens living in your gates' (וגרך אשר בשעריך). This is similar to other lists in which the alien, although at the bottom of the hierarchy, is still included.

However, the phrase by which the alien is described is dissimilar to anything encountered in previous passages connected with covenant ceremonies. Here we find the phrase, 'which is in your gates'. This occurs elsewhere in Deuteronomy, in the Decalogue and in Deut. 14.21. In the latter, the alien is distinguished from both the foreigner and Israelite alike. Can we draw any conclusions from this fact? Can we conclude that these passages are related, and that the same understanding of alien occurs in each one? It would seem that this phrase alone cannot establish dependence, and that in meaning it is similar enough to the phrase, 'in your midst', that it can be connected with Deut. 29.11 and Josh. 8.30-35. Not only the members of the list, but also the description of the ceremony, are very similar in these three passages. The aliens referred to here, then, correspond to the aliens, who like the Gibeonites, are related to the Israelites by means of a suzerainty treaty which places them in the inferior position of a vassal. They are obliged to observe the law of Moses because it is the law of the land in which they are residing. As permanent residents they are bound to know that law, and to pay homage to the God who stands behind it.

3. *Conclusion*

I would very briefly like to pull together the main lines which have emerged from this examination of the references to the alien in the book of Deuteronomy.

In the level of redaction which was isolated, which included most of the references in the legal corpus, we saw that the author was writing to well-to-do landowners. He was concerned that they remember from whence they came and on whom they needed to rely. He treated their economic prosperity as a threat to their required humility before God. He sought to counter this tendency to self-sufficiency by reminding them of their past slavery; and of their dependence on God for a bountiful harvest. He limited their ambitions by emphasizing the need for sabbath rest, and sabbath years. The requirement to rejoice and hold feasts also served to restrict their utilitarianism. He believed that they themselves were not ultimately responsible for their prosperity, and that they would be in the position of the widow, fatherless and alien if tragedy befell them.

These concerns were very evident in the laws referring to the alien. The care taken by the author in legislating feasts which were characterized by joy and generosity necessitated the inclusion of the alien, as well as other marginal groups. In what could be seen as a contradiction, the Israelites were promised prosperity if they were generous to those who were landless. The redactor was seeking to instil the virtue of generosity by reminding the Israelites of God's gracious treatment of them in the past, and his anticipated generosity in the future.

Going hand in hand with the concern to undercut the pride of the success-oriented is the notion that the Israelites are a people separated from all other peoples by their relationship to Yahweh. The implications of this exclusivity are worked out in the legislation pertaining to the Passover, and also in the law prohibiting the Israelite from eating meat found dead, while allowing the alien and foreigner to eat it. The morality that holds for the Israelite does not hold for outsiders. The duality of insider/outsider ethics was evident especially in the economic relations with the foreigner (Deut. 15.3; 23.21). The exclusive relationship which the Israelites had with God meant that no way was open for aliens to become members of the Israelite community. They were accorded generous treatment, unlike foreigners, but they were never given the option of becoming Israelites

There are many connections with the Book of the Covenant and the Priestly laws in the laws requiring social justice for the alien. However, the laws in Deuteronomy were distinguished by the consistent way in which they mentioned the alien, widow and fatherless together, and in the great number of laws which were enacted for their benefit. Together these laws created a permanent support system for these groups which would prevent them from becoming poor. In this concern, its character as a reform document is surely evident.

In the many instances of similar laws in the Book of the Covenant and the Priestly Code, it was seen that the differences could be explained in terms of the theologies of the respective law codes. This emphasized the difficulty of using these laws to trace a history of the cult, and also the history of the status of the alien. For example, the fact that the laws in Deuteronomy consistently treat the alien as a non-

Israelite does not mean that in actuality Israelites travelling outside their tribe or city would not be considered aliens. It only means that the legislation is dealing only with foreign individuals who found their way into Israelite territory.

In this body of material aliens are consistently characterized as people who are needy and who are non-Israelites. They are defined according to their socioeconomic status and ethnic identity. This, as I have shown, is related to the Israelites' definition of themselves. Israelites defined themselves in terms of their past history, i.e. in terms of what God had done for them. This had many implications for how they were to live in the promised land. As far as aliens were concerned, it meant that they should be accorded generous treatment, as the Israelites had been granted generous treatment by their God. The Israelites were required to echo God's character in their dealings with others. In addition, God's choosing them to be his own people was understood to be an exclusive act. God had chosen them and not others. This resulted in their standing in a special relationship to God and to each other. Because their identity was forged by an act in the past which could not be repeated, and which separated them from all other people, there was no way for non-Israelites to become Israelites. Aliens were considered non-Israelites, and there was no way that this status could be changed.

In addition, we saw that the aliens dealt with by the laws were individuals, who, although non-Israelites, were not identified according to their nationality. Because they were dealt with in isolation from their ethnic group, they were only described negatively as a non-Israelite, and not positively as an Edomite, Moabite, Ammonite, etc.

However, the final references to the alien which were examined seemed to be speaking of a different person in a different position. Here the alien was party to a covenant renewal ceremony. Because of the many connections with the Gibeonites, I have concluded that these references may have been to groups of non-Israelites who were allowed to enter into a covenant relationship, albeit in an inferior position, with Yahweh.

Chapter 5

THE PRIESTLY LAWS

Of the thirty-four references to the alien in the Priestly legislation,[1] some are virtual repetitions of laws we have met previously, and some bring us to new frontiers. This is due to the existence of a living legal tradition in ancient Israel, a tradition which continually re-applied and reformulated the laws. The laws concerning the alien can be seen as one example of this dynamic of Israel's faith. By means of the tools of historical and literary criticism, I will attempt to reconstruct the stages in this process, and the situations to which the laws were responding.

1. *Introductory Matters*

In this study what has been called the Holiness Code and Priestly legislation will be treated together.[2] There are several reasons for this. First, it is not clear that the Holiness Code ever existed as a separate document,[3] nor is it clear from the text that a distinct collection has

1. Exod. 12.19, 48, 49; Lev. 16.29; 17.8, 10, 12, 13, 15; 18.26; 19.10, 33, 34; 20.2; 22.18; 23.22; 24.16, 22; 25.23, 35, 47; Num. 9.14; 15.14, 15, 16, 26, 29, 30; 19.10; 35.15.

2. The Holiness Code (Lev. 17–26) was first isolated and named by A. Klostermann in 1877. He saw its distinguishing characteristic in the demands for holiness and purity. He claimed that it was at one time an independent law collection which was incorporated into the P source. Although there is no superscription to indicate its beginning, ch. 17 was deemed to be the beginning because of internal consistency with what followed, and because it broke with what preceded; the ending was said to be clearly indicated in Lev. 26.46. See Boecker, *Law and the Administration of Justice*, p. 127; and Fohrer, *Introduction to the Old Testament*, p. 137, for a summary of Klostermann's position.

3. R. Rendtorff, *The Old Testament: An Introduction* (trans. J. Bowden; Philadelphia: Fortress Press, 1986), p. 145, points to the lack of any internal order,

been incorporated.[1] In addition, even those who argue for the existence of the Holiness Code as an independent document at one time, claim that it was thoroughly edited when it was incorporated into the Priestly laws.[2] However, this process of incorporating and reworking existing laws is not seen to be unique to the laws of the Holiness Code, but can be said of many laws in the Priestly Corpus. For these reasons I will not treat the so-called Holiness Code separately, but will include it in my discussion of the Priestly laws.

A. *Date of Priestly Laws*

I now need to indicate what I understand the date, provenance and authorship of the Priestly legislation to be. Introductory matters associated with the P document are among the most disputed in Old Testament scholarship, and most of the discussion has focused on the narrative material. I shall not attempt to justify my position exhaustively, but briefly state what my starting point will be on those areas pertaining to this discussion.[3]

to the uneven stress on holiness and to the fact that this stress is not unique to the Holiness Code. Fohrer, *Introduction to the Old Testament*, p. 138, points out what seem to be separate collections within the Holiness Code. The differing subjects, forms and repetitions suggest to him that we have several individual collections which were at one time autonomous. None of these arguments alone decisively demonstrates that the Holiness Code did not exist as an independent document at one time. In fact, most of these statements could also be applied to the Covenant Code. However, the decisive difference is that the Covenant Code has a clear beginning and end in the text, whereas the Holiness Code does not.

1. J. Milgrom, 'Leviticus', in *IDBSup* (Nashville: Abingdon Press, 1976), pp. 541-45, argues that Lev. 17 is not an opening chapter since it is connected thematically and verbally with what precedes it. Cf. G.J. Wenham (*The Book of Leviticus* [Grand Rapids: Eerdmans, 1979], p. 7).

2. Fohrer, *Introduction to the Old Testament*, pp. 138-42.

3. One area which need not concern us is whether or not P was initially a narrative source into which the laws were inserted at a later date, or whether P was ever an independent document. P.R. Ackroyd, *Exile and Restoration* (Philadelphia: Westminster Press, 1968), p. 91; S.E. McEvenue, *The Narrative Style of the Priestly Writer* (Rome: Biblical Institute Press, 1971), p. 8, and J. Blenkinsopp, 'The Structure of P', *CBQ* 38 (1976), p. 275, argue that it was first an account of the founding events into which the laws were inserted at a later stage. F.M. Cross, 'The Priestly Work', in *Canaanite Myth and Hebrew Epic* (Cambridge, MA: Harvard University Press, 1973), pp. 293-94, concludes that P is a tradent, but not an independent narrative.

One reason that P is often dated to the exilic or early post-exilic period is the position which Aaron and his family occupy in the Priestly law. Their status there corresponds to their position in Ezekiel and Chronicles, rather than in the early sources.[1]

Arguments on the basis of language also place P in the time of Ezekiel and Deutero-Isaiah.[2] There are, of course, dissenting views from this position. The school of Kaufmann argues for a pre-exilic date on the basis of language, among other evidence.[3] The situation is made complex because P does use archaic terms, such as forms of the root שכן in order to denote the covenantal presence of God in the tabernacle. However, Cross argues that the author(s) does this intentionally, giving the words a precise, technical meaning.[4] Because P is multi-layered, it is in fact difficult to date. Various laws do come from pre-exilic times, but these may not be used to date the final redaction of P.

1. N.K. Gottwald, *The Hebrew Bible: A Socio-Literary Introduction* (Philadelphia: Fortress Press, 1985), p. 207; Cross, 'The Priestly Work', p. 324. J.G. Gammie (*Holiness in Israel* [Minneapolis: Fortress Press, 1989], pp. 9-70), discusses the variations in the Priestly understanding of holiness, and traces the differing conceptions of the status of Levites in the Priestly laws, Ezekiel and the Chronicler's work.

2. R.J. Thompson, *Moses and the Law in a Century of Criticism since Graf,* (VTSup, 19; Leiden: Brill, 1970), p. 164; Cross, 'The Priestly Work', p. 324.

3. See Kaufmann's major work, *The Religion of Israel* (London: Allen and Unwin, 1961), pp. 175-200. One of the pillars in Kaufmann's dating of P prior to D is his claim that P is a constitution of worship at the high places and does not have the interest in cult centralization that is so dominant in D.M. Haran, who also accepts a pre-exilic date for P, does not agree with Kaufmann regarding cult centralization. See his discussion in 'Behind the Scenes of History: Determining the Date of the Priestly Source', *JBL* 100 (1981), p. 326. Haran argues that P is later than and responds to JE, but has no connection with D since it preceded D. He understands P to be a private document of the priests until it was published by Ezra. A linguistic argument for the pre-exilic dating of P has been advanced by A. Hurvitz, in 'The Evidence of Language in Dating the Priestly Code', *RB* 81 (1974), pp. 24-57, but his results have not gained much credence because he does not address the issue of P being a multi-layered document. See Thompson's assessment in *Moses and the Law*, p. 164, and D. Smith, *The Religion of the Landless* (Bloomington: Meyer Stone Books, 1989), pp. 139, 149.

4. Cross, 'The Priestly Work', pp. 299-300.

The law and Ezra. Many scholars since Wellhausen have also connected some form of P with the mission of Ezra. Wellhausen postulated that Ezra brought the entire Pentateuch with him from Babylon, and that it was unknown before that time.[1] Shaver has discussed this position, and the difficulties inherent in it at length.[2] He demonstrates that the phrase 'the law of God which is in your hand' (Ezra 7.14), should not be taken to mean that Ezra had physical possession of the entire law. Shaver notes that this phrase is used elsewhere in the Chronicler's history (1 Chron. 24.19; 2 Chron. 33.8; 34.14) with a clearly non-literal meaning.[3] Instead, he claims that the passage intends with these words to convey Ezra's skill, dedication and authority in interpreting the law. In addition, there is no evidence to suggest that the law was new.[4] The mandate of Ezra to appoint judges who know the law, and to teach those who do not know it (Ezra 7.25), presupposes that the law was already in existence in Jerusalem. This in turn coheres well with the intent of the Persian court to allow subject people to live according to their own traditional laws, rather than imposing a new law on them.[5]

What, then, can be said of the law which Ezra interpreted and enforced? Does it have any bearing on the attempt to date the Priestly laws? Shaver's dissertation demonstrates that the author of Chronicles and Ezra–Nehemiah understood the Torah to be authoritative, but that his Torah was not identical with the canonical Pentateuch. When the author(s) of Ezra, Nehemiah and Chronicles refers to the law, he draws from the Priestly or Deuteronomic laws, as well as from laws extant only in Ezekiel, and to laws not found in canonical Scripture, and in some instances, he combines laws found in different sources.[6]

1. Wellhausen, *Prolegomena to the History of Ancient Israel*, pp. 405-408.

2. J. Shaver, *Torah and the Chronicler's History Work* (unpublished PhD dissertation, University of Notre Dame, 1983), pp. 2-6.

3. Shaver, *Torah and the Chronicler's History Work*, p. 106; H.G.M. Williamson, *Ezra, Nehemiah* (Word Biblical Commentary, 16; Waco, TX: Word Books, 1985), p. 101.

4. This is the conclusion of Williamson, *Ezra, Nehemiah*, p. xxxix. He goes on to add that it is a law whose demands could not be simply applied to the restoration situation, but had to be constantly reinterpreted.

5. Shaver, *Torah and the Chronicler's History Work*, p. 44.

6. Shaver, *Torah and the Chronicler's History Work*, pp. 183-87. Smith, *Palestinian Parties and Politics*, p. 123, notes that Ezra's law could not be the present Pentateuch since it did not provide for the Day of Atonement. J.G. Vink, 'The Date

Hence we can conclude that at the time of Ezra, much of the Priestly law was extant, but not that the Pentateuch was complete, nor that it had achieved canonical status.[1]

The law and the community at Elephantine. Yet another issue which bears on the dating of P concerns the relationship, if any, between the Priestly laws and the Jewish community at Elephantine.[2] Of particular significance is a letter from Hananiah containing a command from King Darius, to Yedoniah and the colleagues at the garrison. It instructs them when and how to observe the Feast of Unleavened Bread. Unfortunately, the text is badly preserved, and there are many gaps. One of these, Cowley and others have claimed, contained the word 'Passover'.[3] For this reason it is called the Pascal letter.

Here, it is argued, we have a situation in Egypt which is analogous to the situation in Palestine at the time of Ezra. The Persian court is

and Origin of the Priestly Code in the Old Testament', *OTS* (1969), p. 30, concludes that Ezra did not observe *Yom Kippur* because the people were already overwhelmed with sorrow at the reading of the new law. This is not a convincing argument, especially in the light of the evidence that the law of Ezra was not a completely new law. Nor is Vink's discussion of the opposing view convincing. He claims that if *Yom Kippur* was not celebrated because it was not part of Ezra's law, that then we must conclude that there is no connection between Ezra and the Priestly Code (p. 29). Such an either/or conclusion is not warranted in light of the evidence presented by Shaver. The Priestly Code was utilized by Ezra, but it had not reached its final form, nor achieved canonical authority.

1. Shaver points to the Chronicler's use of Num. 28.16-25, which he understands to be the latest stratum of P, as evidence that the Priestly laws were almost complete. See *Torah and the Chronicler's History Work*, p. 157. J. Blenkinsopp, *Ezra–Nehemiah: A Commentary* (OTL; Philadelphia: Westminster Press, 1988), pp. 155, 157, suggests that the basic content of Ezra's law was Deut. 12–26 and the cultic legislation of P, as well as other traditions which did not achieve canonical status.

2. See the Introduction to A. Cowley's *Aramaic Papyri of the Fifth Century BC* (Osnabruck: Otto Zeller, 1967 [repr. 1923 edn]), and B. Porten, 'The Jews in Egypt', in *The Cambridge History of Judaism*, I (ed. W.D. Davies and L. Finkelstein; Cambridge: Cambridge University Press, 1984), pp. 372-400, for an overall description of this community based on the documents and the archaeological finds.

3. See Document 21, and the discussion of it, in Cowley, *Aramaic Papyri*, pp. 61-64, and B. Porten, *Archives from Elephantine* (Berkeley: University of California Press, 1968), pp. 131-33.

intervening directly in the cultic affairs of the community, and is using its authority to enforce the observance of a local feast. Cazelles lists other interventions of the Persian court which involved financing and building temples, recovering and preserving ancient texts, giving instructions concerning liturgy and clergy, in order to demonstrate that this was a consistent pattern in the Persian empire.[1]

Do the obvious similarities between activities in Egypt and Palestine point only to the fact that they both occur within the reign of the Persian kings, or are there closer connections? Grelot argues that there are literary connections between the Pascal letter and certain laws in the P document.[2] He examines contacts with both Deuteronomic and Priestly laws on the Passover, and concludes that whereas the relationships to the former are vague and infrequent, the connections with the Priestly laws occur often and are quite striking.[3] He concludes, on this basis, that 419 BC constitutes a *terminus post quem* for the compilation of the priestly legislation, and for the redaction of the laws inserted at the final stage.[4] His case is not convincing because of the state of the Pascal papyrus, and the paucity of the evidence.

Porten also connects the Pascal letter with the canonization of the Torah. He argues that the occasion for Hananiah's letter to the garrison was the canonization of the Torah and its proclamation at Jerusalem. Under these circumstances, a letter was sent to Elephantine to remind them of the proper procedure. Porten ties this action in with the political situation as well. Because the Jews at Elephantine had remained loyal during the disturbances which followed the death of Artaxerxes I, Darius II now rewarded their loyalty by guaranteeing their right to celebrate the passover.[5] Again, the evidence is so slim that although this reconstruction is possible, it is not compelling. It is

1. Cazelles, 'La mission d'Esdras', p. 125. This is further substantiated in J. Blenkinsopp's 'The Mission of Udjahorresnet and those of Ezra and Nehemiah', *JBL* 106 (1987), pp. 409-21. Udjahorresnet uses his position to convince Cambyses to restore the sanctuary of Sais. This involved expelling foreigners, cleansing the sanctuary, restoring the clergy and the rituals. This was all backed by the Persian court.

2. P. Grelot, 'Etudes sur le "papyrus pascal" d'Elefantiné', *VT* 4 (1954), pp. 349-85.

3. Grelot, 'Etudes sur le "papyrus pascal" d'Elefantiné', p. 367.

4. Grelot, 'La dernière étape de la rédaction sacerdotale', VT 6 (1956), p. 174.

5. Porten, *Archives from Elephantine*, pp. 132-33.

interesting to note that the arguments of Porten and Grelot, when combined, are circular. Grelot argues from the similarities between the Pascal letter and the Priestly laws to a date for canonization, and Porten argues on the basis of canonization for a connection between the Torah and the Pascal letter.

The law and Ezekiel. Finally, the references to aliens found in Ezekiel will be considered to see how they contribute to a discussion of the date and historical context of the Priestly laws. Of the five references,[1] the two in Ezekiel 22 reflect the traditional image of aliens as dependent, vulnerable people. Ezekiel 22.7 groups them with the fatherless and widow; and Ezek. 22.29 with the poor and needy. They cannot help us date the priestly references. However, the references in Ezek. 14.7 and 47.22, 23 are very illuminating.

In Ezek. 14.1-11 we have a unit framed by a narrative introduction and concluding formula.[2] The addressees of this law are the house of Israel (v. 6), which is repeated and expanded in v. 7 by the addition of 'and from the alien who resides in Israel' (ומהגר אשר־יגור בישראל). This phrase occurs, with minor variations, in Lev. 17.3, 8, 10, 13; 20.2; 22.18.[3] This similarity points to the close contact that exists between the author(s) of Ezekiel and the Priestly laws.

The content of the laws pertaining to the alien in Ezek. 14.7 is also very close to the content of the laws in the Priestly legislation. The aliens as well as the Israelites are threatened with being cut off, being made an example and a by-word if they set up idols in their hearts. The significance of this legislation is ambiguous. It might be taken to mean that aliens are to be included in the cult. Zimmerli, however, suggests that Ezekiel is here using a fixed expression from pre-exilic times because of the phrase 'residing in Israel'. At that time, the phrase could have had a literal meaning.[4] He claims that because it had become stereotyped, we cannot read much into it. However, when we look closely at the laws pertaining to aliens, we will notice that many do in fact provide for their cultic inclusion, as an equal, to the Israelites. The phrase, 'residing in Israel' need not refer to the land of

1. Ezek. 14.7; 22.7, 29; 47.22, 23.

2. W. Zimmerli, *Ezekiel I* (trans. R.E. Clements; Philadelphia: Fortress Press, 1979), p. 302.

3. This is noted by Zimmerli in *Ezekiel I*, p. 303.

4. Zimmerli, *Ezekiel I*, p. 303.

Israel, but could refer to the people of Israel, as in 2 Chron. 15.9.

The reference to the alien in Ezek. 47.22, 23 is also very closely related to the Priestly legislation. This is the only place, outside of the Priestly laws, where the alien is juxtaposed with the native (אזרח). In this passage, the aliens are allocated land in the midst of the tribe where they have settled. Both Zimmerli and Eichrodt describe these verses as secondary additions.[1] Zimmerli gives two reasons for this conclusion. First, the verses are only loosely linked by והיה, and secondly, if vv. 22 and 23 were omitted, there would be no lacuna in the text. He does not discuss its relation to the Priestly legislation, but only notes that the texts reflect a post-monarchy situation. He claims, citing no evidence, that aliens did not own land in pre-exilic Israel. It is significant that this is an addition to a vision which is set in the exile.

The many connections in content and phraseology between this addition and Priestly laws dealing with aliens help us to date them to the same time-period. There are especially close connections between these verses and the laws dealing with the alien in Leviticus 25. There, in the laws regulating the year of Jubilee, the alien as well as his extended family is mentioned, and the issue concerns land ownership. Tentatively, we will suppose that this addition derives from the same time-period and situation—the restoration community dealing with land distribution.

The thesis that many of the laws which pertain to alien are to be dated to the restoration community is further strengthened by Isa. 14.1.[2] In this verse, which looks to the time after the exile, the prophet describes the Lord's compassion, and promises that the Lord will settle them in their own land. At that time, the text continues, the alien will join them (ונלוה הגר עליהם). This verb in the niphal is used elsewhere to describe joining oneself to a wife (Gen. 29.34); joining one's fellow tribesmen (Num. 18.2-4); foreigners joining themselves to the Lord (Isa. 56.3); and eunuchs joining themselves to the Lord (Isa. 56.6).[3] These references indicate that in the exilic restoration

1. W. Eichrodt, *Ezekiel: A Commentary* (trans. C. Quin; Philadelphia: Westminster Press, 1970), p. 592; Zimmerli, *Ezekiel II* (trans. J.D. Martin; Hermeneia; Philadelphia: Fortress Press, 1983), p. 526.

2. This text is dated to the exilic or post-exilic period by J. Blenkinsopp, *A History of Prophecy in Israel* (Philadelphia: Westminster Press, 1983), p. 222.

3. Isaiah 56 is traditionally dated to the post-exilic period.

community the possibility existed of non-Israelites (as defined by those who had been in exile) becoming incorporated into the people of God.

We have arrived at an exilic/post-exilic date for the Priestly laws on the basis of language, historical context and connections with other biblical texts. I have noted that the formation of the Priestly legislation spanned many centuries, and hence the dating of individual laws is complex. The evidence suggests that the final phase of editing and consolidation occurred in the Persian period in response to the policy of the empire to allow people to live according to their own religion and customs.

Authorship and provenance. I wish briefly to explore the social setting of the exile and restoration period in concluding this introductory section. The laws pertaining to the alien as well as the bulk of the Priestly legislation are illuminated when they are understood as a creative response to the crisis brought about by the exile, and the subsequent reuniting of the returnees with those who had remained in Judah. The exile was a crisis of mammoth proportions for the Jews. It involved coming to grips with being defeated, with losing their homeland to pagan conquerors, with being deported, with losing their identity as citizens, with being a minority people who were dominated by their conquerors. In exile they survived by fashioning 'mobile identities' through a variety of survival strategies. They redefined themselves, and became an ethnic minority, and a confessional community. When they returned, they had to become integrated with a group who claimed the same religious heritage, but had not undergone the profound ideological and sociological transformation as the group that had survived the Babylonian exile.[1]

The laws pertaining to the alien, as well as the entire priestly corpus were edited and revised during this period, and certainly many of the concerns and emphases of the laws can be understood as a creative response to this new situation. For example, in order for any deported people to maintain their separate identity, they must address the issue of self-identification, and create patterns to preserve it. Smith analyses the Priestly laws, with their emphasis on clean and unclean, contamination, order and separation, as a reflection of the anxieties about the

1. See Smith, *Religion of the Landless*, for a social study of this period, as well as a comparative study of the survival strategies of other refugees who have maintained their distinct identities.

survival of this group, as well as a strategy for its survival. The rituals and laws prescribed by the Priestly laws functioned as an effective mechanism for maintaining boundaries which separated the Jews from foreigners. By insisting on the requirement of purity, and claiming that purity is lost upon contact with the unclean and can be restored through ritual, the Priestly laws helped to preserve the distinct identity of the Jews.[1]

Because purity can be restored and acquired through ritual, these boundaries do not necessarily preclude a movement of people across them. This will become very significant in my study of the new status of the alien. For the first time, the possibility will exist of an outsider acquiring insider status. Smith's analysis is helpful in holding together what has often been perceived as a contradiction in the Priestly legislation. We will see that the laws which require equal treatment for the alien are consistent both with the insistence on purity and on the integration of outsiders.[2] Furthermore, the concern to incorporate the alien is part of the universalism of the P document, according to Blenkinsopp. In addition to pointing out that the Pentateuch came to be accepted by both Jews and Samaritans, he notes that P confers a divine blessing on all humankind (Gen. 1.26-28) and also extends the first covenant and promises to all humanity (Gen. 9.8-17).[3]

M. Smith has suggested a sequence of events in the post-exilic period which would explain chronologically the two emphases of separation and integration. He points to Ezra and to the fact that Ezra did not even consider the possibility that aliens, among whom Smith includes the foreign wives, could become purified and be granted the status of proselytes, as evidence that much of the legislation of P, especially the laws referring to the alien, had not yet been formulated. He characterizes the time from Zerubbabel to Nehemiah as a time dominated by the question of purity to the extent that it could not envision incorporating the impure. He claims that the author of Isa. 56.1-8, writing when Nehemiah was governor, introduced the notion that outsiders could join the holy people. Smith concludes that his

1. Smith, *Religion of the Landless*, pp. 10, 80, 81, 140-43. Other strategies for survival include structural adaptation (changes in leadership and authority patterns) and the creation of a new folk literature which features the hero story.

2. Cazelles, 'La mission d'Esdras', p. 131, and Smith, *Palestinian Parties and Politics*, pp. 173-75.

3. Blenkinsopp, 'Yahweh and other Deities', p. 365.

prophecy was fulfilled much later in the legislation of P found in Exod. 12.43-50, Num. 9.14, 15.1-31, 19.10, 35.15, Deut 29.10 and Josh. 20.9.[1] Although there is development within the Priestly laws, Smith's reconstruction does not adequately take into account the social dynamics of the exilic post-exilic communities. This will be discussed in more detail as individual laws are considered.

In conclusion, I understand the Priestly legislation as a body of law which was revised by the priests in exile in response to the crisis that the Jews experienced. In exile, the Jews could no longer identify themselves as a nation. Membership of this community was no longer synonymous with being a citizen under a king. The chosen people were now a defeated minority people in a foreign land.[2] They had become aliens themselves in the land of Babylon. The nature of the community, the basis of authority, the form of worship of Yahweh, all had to be reformulated. Furthermore, when this group returned to their homeland, they then faced new challenges in terms of self-identity, ownership of land, participation and membership in the cultic community. The laws in the P corpus articulate one of the responses of Israel's faith to this crisis.

2. *The Priestly Laws Pertaining to the Alien*

I am now in a position to turn to the pertinent Priestly laws, and investigate the legal status of the alien. Examining the thirty-four references to the alien in the order in which they appear in the canonical text does not seem helpful. For example, there are references, such as the one in Num. 9.14, which are clearly connected to the provisions of Exod. 12.48, 49. Then there are laws, such as the laws of gleaning in Lev. 19.10 and Lev. 23.22, which are almost identical in form and content. For these reasons, it is appropriate to group the laws according to their form and content. It would, of course, be ideal if the laws could be arranged in the order in which they were composed and integrated into the P legislation. Although I cannot do that now, I do hope to be able to indicate that some of the laws preceded others.

It is of significance for organizing this discussion, that aliens are

1. Smith, *Palestinian Parties and Politics*, pp. 179-82.

2. See Fishbane's description of the social results of the exile on the community in *Biblical Interpretation*, pp. 264-65.

always mentioned with another member of society in the Priestly legislation. They are mentioned together with the poor,[1] the temporary resident,[2] the native,[3] and the Israelite.[4] Within the group in which they are juxtaposed with the native, we can note a further distinction. Only in the Passover legislation of Exodus 12 and Numbers 9 is the phrase 'native of the land' (אזרח הארץ) used to describe the native. Because these verses are distinguished both by content and terminology, they will be treated separately from the larger group in which alien and native are mentioned together.

The laws in which the alien is grouped with the temporary resident (תושב), are also distinguished by their content. They are laws dealing mostly with the Sabbatical Year, and the Year of Jubilee (Lev. 25.6, 23, 35, 45). Only Num. 35.15, which designates the cities of refuge in the promised land, and groups the alien together with the Israelite and temporary resident, is an exception. These laws are similar in content in that they deal with civil matters as opposed to cultic matters, and because they all present Israelite society as a hierarchy, with the same members in the same positions.

However, distinguishing between the alien juxtaposed with the 'sons of Israel' (בני־ישראל) and with the 'house of Israel' (בית ישראל), is not warranted. In similar contexts, these phrases appear to be interchangeable (Lev. 17.8, 10, 13; 20.2; 22.18). In addition, there seems to be no distinction between the use of the term 'Israelite' and 'native'. This is verified by noting that in a series of related commands, the Israelite is described as either a son of Israel, from the house of Israel, or a native (Lev. 17.8, 10, 12, 13, 15). The import of the laws in which the native and alien, or Israelite and alien, are mentioned together is likewise the same. In all cases, the law is requiring equal treatment for both groups.

These considerations lead me to organize the references to the alien into four groups:

1. laws which juxtapose the alien with the poor;[5]

1. Lev. 19.10; 23.22.
2. Lev. 25.6, 23, 35, 45; Num. 35.15.
3. Exod. 12.19, 49; Lev. 16.29; 17.15; 18.26; 19.33, 34; 24.16, 22; Num. 15.13, 14, 29, 30.
4. Lev. 17.8, 9, 10, 12, 13; 20.2; 22.18; Num. 15.26, 29; 19.10.
5. Lev. 19.10; 23.22.

2. laws in which the alien is considered along with the temporary resident;[1]
3. laws which set the alien alongside the native of the land;[2] and
4. laws which treat the alien as equal with the native or the Israelite.[3]

I will also include in this final group Num. 15.15, 16, since, from the context, it is clear that the alien is being juxtaposed with the native.

A. *The Alien and the Poor*

> You shall not strip your vineyard bare, or gather the fallen grapes of your vineyard; you shall leave them for the poor and the alien: I am the LORD your God (Lev. 19.10).

> When you reap the harvest of your land, you shall not reap to the very edges of your field, or gather the gleanings of your harvest; you shall leave them for the poor and for the alien: I am the LORD your God (Lev. 23.22).

Leviticus 19.10 and 23.22 are among the few laws in the Priestly legislation which require the Israelites to be charitable. In other places in this collection the poor are taken into account, and allowances are made for them, but they are not generally the object of charity. For example, Lev. 12.8 makes it possible for the poor to bring sacrifices in that it allows a woman to bring doves or pigeons if she cannot afford a lamb. However, Lev. 19.10 and Lev. 23.22 require the Israelites to be more than just. They are required to be generous.

The paucity of laws protecting the poor in the Priestly laws is in striking contrast to the great concern shown for them in the Deuteronomic laws. It causes Smith to claim that the Priestly laws were written by an aristocratic class, which, apart from a few instances in the Holiness Code, had no interest in the under-privileged.[4] I would like to qualify these remarks somewhat by noting that the Priestly laws, as all other ancient Near Eastern compilations, are not comprehensive. The fact that laws providing for the widow and the fatherless are non-existent does not necessarily mean that the authors of the law

1. Lev. 25.6, 23, 35, 45; Num. 35.15.
2. Exod. 12.19, 48, 49; Num. 9.14.
3. Lev. 16.29; 17.8, 9, 10, 12, 13, 15; 18.26; 19.33, 34; 20.2; 22.18; 24.16, 22; Num. 15.13, 14, 26, 29, 30; 19.10.
4. Smith, *Palestinian Parties and Politics*, p. 175.

code were unmoved by the plight of those less fortunate. It means that it was not their primary concern, and not the area that they perceived as needing reform. It is tempting to suppose that they were aware of the Deuteronomic laws, knew that social concerns were of paramount importance, and hence did not require further attention. However, there is not sufficient evidence to support that premise. I cannot concur with Friedman, who argues that not only did the Priestly authors know of the laws of Deuteronomy, but that they were writing in response to them.[1]

The two paragraphs which deal with the regulations for gleaning (Lev. 19.9, 10; 23.22) although separated by several chapters, are almost identical in wording. Both begin with a temporal clause using the second person plural form of address. The law itself is formulated in the apodeictic style and is stated negatively first. It prohibits the Israelites from harvesting to the very edges of the field, or going over the vineyard a second time. The law in Lev. 23.22 abridges the law in Lev. 19.9, 10 by omitting the reference to the grape harvest. Wenham explains this as appropriate, since it follows the laws for Pentecost (Lev. 23.15-21), and grapes ripen later in the year.[2] After stating the law in negative terms, it is restated in positive terms. Here again the two laws are identical in their wording, speaking first of the poor, then the alien, and in both instances using the second person singular form of address. This is then followed by a motivating clause common to the Holiness Code, 'I am the Lord your God', formulated in the second person plural.

The conclusions which have been drawn from this mixing of second person singular and second person plural are varied. Noth understands that the second person plural forms are secondary to the second person singular forms in Lev. 19.9, 10; and that Lev. 23.22 is altogether a secondary addition, being out of place in the calendar of feasts. The alternating of second person singular and second person plural in this verse are explained as wholesale copying of the law in

1. R.E. Friedman, *The Exile and Biblical Narrative: The Formation of the Deuteronomic and Priestly Works* (HSM; Missoula, MT: Scholars Press, 1981), pp. 77-102. He claims that the P corpus was written in two stages. P1 is pre-exilic and was written as an alternative to JE and D; P2 is exilic and is concerned to organize and elaborate the existing traditions. He reckons that Lev. 17–26 is pre-exilic.

2. Wenham, *The Book of Leviticus*, p. 305.

Lev. 19.9, 10.[1] Wenham finds more coherence in the organization of the chapters, and is better able to account for the placement of these laws. He suggests that in both chapters the laws requiring sacrifices which provided for the needs of the priests (Lev. 19.5-8; 23.17-21) are followed by laws providing for the weaker members of society (Lev. 19.9, 10; 23.22).[2] We have already seen this sort of arrangement in Deuteronomy. There, the laws for celebrating Pentecost and Sukkoth (Deut. 16.9-15) and for tithing (Deut. 14.22-29) included provision for the poor.

Wenham explains the final phrase, 'I am the Lord your God', which occurs at the end of both verses, as a device of the redactor to divide the laws into paragraphs. In ch. 19 it occurs sixteen times, and in ch. 23 it occurs twice.[3] If this phrase was inserted later by the redactor, it would explain why it does not agree in number with the preceding singular verbs.

On the basis of style and content these laws are clearly of ancient origin. Although I am not convinced by Noth that leaving the gleanings for the poor has replaced the pre-Israelite, primitive custom of leaving the remains for the fertility spirit,[4] this tradition is long-standing. The content of these laws is basically the same as the laws on gleaning in Deut. 24.19-22. The intent of both is charity. The recipients are the widow, fatherless and alien in Deuteronomy, and the poor and alien in Leviticus. In both lists, the alien is classed with the socially and economically weak. On the basis of these two laws, the identity of the alien as a non-Israelite is not obvious.

In the Deuteronomic law we saw that the laws on gleaning, together with all the laws dealing with the widow and orphan, were not requiring charity, but establishing a support system which would ensure that vulnerable, landless members of society would not be poor. The poor were a distinct group of land-owning Israelites who had become debt-ridden. In the Priestly laws, the distinction that Deuteronomy made between the alien, widow and orphan on the one hand and the poor on the other is not maintained. Poor is once again a term referring to all those who are economically at risk. This law collection is not concerned with creating a society in which poverty

1. Noth, *Leviticus*, p. 172.
2. Wenham, *The Book of Leviticus*, p. 141.
3. Wenham, *The Book of Leviticus*, pp. 262, 300.
4. Noth, *Leviticus*, p. 141.

does not exist, hence the refinements of Deuteronomy's laws have been dropped.

The motivation clause attached to these laws is typical of many laws in the Priestly collection. The frequent occurrence of some form of the phrase, 'I am the Lord your God' (sixteen times in ch. 19), and the lack of most other explanatory phrases, or motivating clauses, again sets the Priestly laws off from the Deuteronomic. The Israelites are motivated to obey the laws in Leviticus not because they understand the reason for the law, nor out of gratitude, but because the law derives from the Lord, their God. This phrase is an appeal to authority. It is because God said so that the law is to be obeyed.

This type of motivation is more at home in an authoritarian, hierarchical community than in an egalitarian, democratic one. It is such a community, and such a world, that we meet in these laws. People as well as animals are hierarchically ordered. The order is based on purity and holiness as defined by these laws. The priest is the most holy, and can come the closest to God, while the infirm, the foreign and the female are furthest from God.[1]

In conclusion, the aliens we meet in this legislation appear to be the same as those we have met elsewhere. They are defined in socioeconomic terms. However, the concerns of this law collection are quite different from those of the Deuteronomic law. Although the Israelite is required to be charitable in both law codes, the manner in which the Israelite is approached, and the motivation for obedience are quite distinct.

B. *The Alien and the Temporary Resident.*

> The land shall not be sold in perpetuity, for the land is mine; with me you are but aliens (גרים) and tenants (תושבים) (Lev. 25.23).[2]
>
> If any of your kin fall into difficulty and become dependent on you, you shall support them; they shall live with you as though resident aliens (Lev. 25.35).[3]

1. See Wenham's discussion on holiness in the introduction to his *The Book of Leviticus*, pp. 18-25.

2. What is translated here as 'tenant', I shall consistently translate as 'temporary resident'.

3. The last phrase is more precisely translated 'as resident aliens and temporary residents, they shall live among you'.

> If resident aliens among you prosper, and if any of your kin fall into difficulty with one of them and sell themselves to an alien, or to a branch of the alien's family, after they have sold themselves they shall have the right of redemption; one of their brothers may redeem them (Lev. 25.47, 48).[1]

> These six cities shall be for refuge for the people of Israel, and for resident or transitory alien among them, so that anyone who kills any person without intent may flee there (Num. 35.15).

Four times in the Priestly legislation, the alien is juxtaposed with the temporary resident (תושב). This is a new association, for neither in the Covenant Code nor in the Deuteronomic laws was the alien classed with the temporary resident. The significance of this association needs to be investigated.

The identity of the temporary resident. The word תושב occurs fourteen times in the Old Testament.[2] The vast majority of these occurrences are in the P document. Of those outside P, 1 Kgs 17.1 is textually disputed, and may or may not be referring to Elijah as a temporary resident. In 1 Chron. 29.15, Ps. 39.13 (ET 12) and Gen. 23.4, the temporary resident is juxtaposed with the alien, and it is clear that the two have the same meaning. In Gen. 23.4 Abraham refers to himself as a גר, and תושב when approaching the Hittites in order to purchase the cave of Machpelah. In 1 Chron. 29.15 and Ps. 39.13, the speaker is describing himself as a alien and temporary resident as were his fathers before him.

However, we should not presume that תושב in the Priestly legislation has an identical meaning to גר. In order to appreciate the nuances associated with the word תושב, we need to take note of the laws pertaining to him. Firstly, there are several places in the Priestly legislation where laws regulate eating holy food (Exod. 12.43-47; Lev. 22.10-13; 25.6). In all three cases, the temporary resident and hired worker (שכיר) are mentioned together, and there is no discernible difference between them. Furthermore, in none of these laws is the alien mentioned along with other dependent people, i.e. slaves,

1. More precisely, Lev. 25.47 would read, 'If an alien or temporary resident with you becomes rich, and your brother beside him becomes poor and sells himself to the alien or temporary resident with you, or to a member of the alien's family'.

2. In Gen. 23.4; Exod. 12.45; Lev. 22.10; 25.6, 23, 35, 40, 45, 47; Num. 35.15; 1 Kgs 17.1; 1 Chron. 29.15; Ps. 39.13.

maidservants, manservants, daughters. I will look at these references in some detail since, although the alien is not mentioned, the laws are specifying the limits of membership in the community, and hence are very instructive in revealing the rationale behind inclusion or exclusion.

The first references to the temporary resident occur in a paragraph (Exod. 12.43-49) which regulates who may or may not participate in the Passover, and is generally included in the P corpus.[1] This particular verse is extremely instructive since it legislates for four different classes of people: the foreigner (בן־נכר), the slave (עבד איש מקנת־כסף), the temporary resident (תושב), and the hired worker (שכיר). The law prohibits the foreigner, the temporary resident and the hired worker from eating the Passover meal. Slaves are allowed to eat the meal after they have been circumcised.

We meet these same classes of people in similar legislation in Lev. 22.10-13. Here the regulations delineate who may eat the priest's food. In both cases we are dealing with food that is considered holy, and in both cases the same groups of people are referred to, although the nomenclature is not identical. The foreigner is designated as זר (Lev. 22.10), and the slave is referred to as a person bought with money or born in his household. The temporary resident and hired worker are included in the legislation, and the status of the priest's daughter is also considered. The content of these two laws is almost the same. In both, the foreigner, the temporary resident and the hired worker may not eat the priest's food, whereas the slave may eat it. Here it should be noted that nothing is said about whether or not the slave is circumcised. The law only stipulates that both slaves bought and slaves born into the household are included in the legislation.

We need to stop at this juncture and inquire about the need for such legislation. I would suggest that it is only because the foreigner, slave, temporary resident and hired worker are members of the household that the issue arises. If the temporary resident and hired worker lived and ate apart from the priest's residence, there would be no need for this legislation. The fact that this law is needed to delineate who may

1. Smith, *Palestinian Parties and Politics*, p. 181, attributes this passage to the second last stage of redaction. Noth, *Leviticus*, p. 8, also contends that the passage is late, being composed in the post-exilic community. Vink, *The Date and Origin of the Priestly Code in the Old Testament*, p. 97, also claims that these regulations date from the time of Ezra, whom he places at the beginning of the fourth century BC.

or may not eat the holy food presupposes that the priest's household could include this variety of people. Similarly, the Passover legislation suggests that the households of Israelites could include slaves, hired workers, foreigners and temporary residents. The legislation arose in response to this sort of familial situation.

There is another occurrence where the members of a household are listed in connection with food, although not in connection with a meal. In the legislation concerning the Sabbatical Year, the law states that whatever the land produces in the sabbath year will be food for the Israelite as well as for his manservant, maidservant, hired worker and temporary resident living with him (Lev. 25.6). Here again we have the temporary resident and hired worker listed together with other dependants. There is no one who is prohibited from harvesting the crop, leading us to conclude that this food was not considered holy.

I will also mention Lev. 25.40 at this point, since here also the temporary resident and hired worker are mentioned together.[1] In this verse the Israelites are called upon to be kind to their fellow Israelites in distress, as they are accustomed to being kind to the תושב and שכיר. In all these references, the temporary resident and the hired worker seem to have the same social status—they are dependent on and associated with a household, but are not included in the same way as the slaves seem to be.

The Alien and the Laws of Jubilee. I will continue my investigation of the meaning of alien and temporary resident by examining the references to them in the laws which regulate the Sabbatical Year and the Year of Jubilee (Lev. 25). This chapter has occasioned much controversy on historical-critical issues, and composition history.[2] I will

1. These references are very similar to those in Exod. 12.43-47 and Lev. 22.10-13. Taken together they reflect a common social situation.

2. See, for example, R. North's *Sociology of the Biblical Jubilee* (Rome: Pontifical Biblical Institute, 1954) in which he concludes that the kernel of the chapter, containing the laws pertaining to the jubilee, is ancient. He argues that the institution of the Year of Jubilee presupposes a simple, agrarian economy, such as would exist in the time of the occupation or during Ezra's period. He concludes that the time of the occupation is the more likely date of composition since at that time the people of Israel were united, buoyed up by success. In such an optimistic age, legislation restricting wealthy land owners would be more likely to arise (pp. 191-212, 204-205). This assessment of the economy and the morale of the Israelites, and its relation to the formation of the law seems too facile. More helpful was the paper

briefly indicate my point of departure for those areas which are relevant to this discussion. Firstly, it seems clear that the laws regulating the Year of Jubilee are not ancient, but a late addition. The tradition of the Sabbatical Year is found in previous legislation (Exod. 23.10-11), but not that of Jubilee. In addition, H.T.C. Sun demonstrates that the language of the Jubilee laws is late.[1] Furthermore, there are no references to the Year of Jubilee in pre-exilic literature, whereas there are close parallels between this legislation and the reforms of Nehemiah. Finally, Sun suggests that the fifty-year cycle of the Year of Jubilee is to be connected to the fifty years in exile. These laws are best explained as justifying the re-appropriation of the land of Judah by the returning exile in the early years of the restoration.[2]

The references to the alien and temporary resident occur in the concluding paragraphs of the chapter (Lev. 25.35-53). These laws do not deal with the institution of the Sabbatical Year or Year of Jubilee, but seek to ensure that the Israelite does not become destitute. It stipulates certain safeguards that would prevent the rich from taking advantage of the poor.

The form of these laws fits Patrick's category of primary law.[3] In this type of casuistic law, the protasis describes a legal relationship, and the apodosis describes the terms of the relationship. Patrick notes that primary law developed in the direction of personally addressed commandments, and this is certainly evident in Leviticus 25, where the impersonal and personal form of address fluctuates. For example, Lev. 25.35 is impersonal, vv. 36,37 are personal, vv. 39-42 are impersonal, v. 43 is personal, vv. 44-46 are personal, vv. 47-53a are impersonal, v. 53b is personal.

These paragraphs are not a compositional unity, and the references to the alien and temporary resident reflect this. Leviticus 25.35 and v. 40 make the same point, but the phraseology is quite different. In

presented by H.T.C. Sun at the Nov. 1990 Annual Meeting of the SBL, 'The Structure, Composition and Date of Lev. 25.1-55'.

1. The phrase, 'a sabbath to the LORD', he argues, is found elsewhere (Exod. 31.15; 35.2; Lev. 23.3) only in a late level of redaction. See his paper, 'The Structure, Composition and Date of Lev. 25.1-55'.

2. H.T.C. Sun, 'The Structure, Composition and Date of Lev. 25.1-55', pp. 26, 27. This is also argued in Baruch Levine's recent commentary, *Leviticus* (JPS Torah Commentary; Philadelphia: Jewish Publication Society, 1989), pp. 272-74.

3. See Patrick, *Old Testament Law*, p. 23 for a description of the form of primary law, a sub-group of casuistic law.

v. 35 the Israelite is to treat his poor brother as an alien or temporary worker, while in v. 40 the poor brother is to be treated as a hired worker or temporary resident. Leviticus 25.44, 45 allows the Israelites to procure slaves from foreigners or temporary residents, and in v. 46, Israelites are ensured the right of redemption if they are forced into debt servitude to an alien or a temporary resident or a member of the alien's clan. The reason for this differing terminology is not obvious. On the basis of content, v. 35 and v. 40 could be expected to list identical classes, as well as v. 45 and v. 46.

What sort of conclusion can we draw from this varied terminology? Can we assume, for example that because the alien is not mentioned in Lev. 25.44-48, the Israelites were not allowed to enslave them? I would suggest that interpretation would be reading more into the text than is warranted. Since the terms גר, תושב, and שכיר seem interchangeable, we cannot assume that they had discrete connotations, and that the omission of aliens in the law regarding acquiring slaves (Lev. 25.44, 45) means that they have a different status from the temporary resident and hired worker.

In the following verses (vv. 47-51), it is made clear that the alien is a non-Israelite. 'One of your brothers' is set over against the temporary resident and the alien. This is exclusive language, and draws the line between insiders and outsiders quite distinctly. In opposition to outsiders, the Israelites are not allowed to become enslaved. In the matter of slavery, the Israelite is set over against all the groups mentioned so far—the foreigner, the hired worker, temporary resident and alien.[1] Here there are no shades of grey. The Israelites have special status, according to this law collection, because they were delivered by God out of Egypt (Lev. 25.42).

In reconstructing the historical situation to which this text responds, it is important to keep in mind that these laws are written from the vantage point of the Israelites. It is they who declare that the alien is not on a par with Israelites, even though the content of the laws make it clear that this alien is not transient, but is a permanent resident. The text (Lev. 25.47) speaks of the Israelite who sells himself to the alien or to a member of the alien's clan (לעקר משפחת גר). The law envisions the alien as economically secure, even wealthy, and in the

1. Smith, *Palestinian Parties and Politics*, p. 277, concurs that whereas the alien may not be included in the temporary residents of v. 45, he is certainly not included among the brothers of vv. 47-54.

land for several generations. If the Jubilee laws are set in the historical context of the restoration community, then it is possible that the aliens are the Judeans who remained in the land, and were not considered true Israelites by the returnees. If that is the case, then the 'aliens' might well consider themselves 'Israelites', while the returnees would not.

What conclusions can be drawn regarding the status of the alien and temporary resident on the basis of the references in Leviticus 25? Do these verses support Smith's conclusions that, as the term גר came to take on new meaning in the Priestly legislation, the word תושב was used to designate 'resident alien' in the traditional sense of a vulnerable, dependent person?[1] In order to substantiate this thesis, it would have to be demonstrated that those passages in which תושב has the same connotations as גר used to have are contemporary or later than passages in which גר has taken on the new meaning of proselyte. However, that does not seem to be true. The references to the temporary resident which have been examined (and I have looked at all but one), seem to be contemporary with references to the alien which do not treat him as an equal, i.e. as a proselyte. Hence, rather than concluding that תושב came to take on new meaning, I would suggest that at this level of redaction the terms תושב, גר and שכיר are more or less synonymous. The Priestly writer uses them interchangeably in this chapter. The occurrences of תושב in places where the Covenant Code and Deuteronomy may have used גר is to be understood as a Priestly preference for this word. Therefore, although it is true that גר does develop in meaning, there is no evidence that תושב came to replace it in its traditional meaning.

The alien and the cities of refuge. As has been indicated, the only reference to the alien and temporary resident outside of Leviticus 25 is found in Num. 35.15, and it is only here that the pair does not function as a hendiadys. Numbers 35.9-34 deals with the problem of blood guilt. The land of Canaan must be purified from the shedding of innocent blood, because it is a holy land, and bloodshed pollutes it (Num. 35.33, 34). The laws instruct the Israelites on how to preserve the land's purity.[2] Part of the provision includes the setting up of

1. Smith, *Palestinian Parties and Politics*, p. 182.

2. See Wenham, *The Book of Leviticus*, p. 235, for a discussion of blood as both a powerful means of atonement and a powerful contaminant.

cities of refuge. In Num. 35.15 it is stipulated that for the sons of Israel, the aliens and the temporary residents, there will be six cities of refuge. From the context it is clear that all bloodshed pollutes the land—not only bloodshed caused by the Israelites. Thus it is necessary that the law should deal with all blood guilt. In this context, the listing of three groups, the Israelite, the temporary resident and the alien, would be in the interests of being all-inclusive. The redactor is not strengthening his case by saying the same thing twice, but making sure that all the free agents in the land are included. I would suggest that slaves are not mentioned here because legally they are treated as members of the Israelite's family, and not free to act on their own behalf.

Because the three terms refer to three different classes of people, it is possible that here גר refers to proselytes and not strangers. What we see happening, then, is not that תושב came to be used to designate alien in the traditional sense, but that תושב retained its traditional meaning as temporary resident while גר came to take on new meaning.

What is being commanded here is carried out in Joshua 20. There are verbal similarities between the two which supports the thesis that Joshua 20 as well as Numbers 15 derives from the Priestly hand. In Josh. 20.9, the cities of refuge are set aside for the sons of Israel and the aliens residing among them.[1] Because of the connections between this passage and the one in Joshua 20, a late date has been suggested. Noth claims the laws providing for the cities of refuge in Numbers 15 is part of the redactional unification of the Pentateuch narrative and the deuteronomic historical work.[2] The late date of this passage supports the conclusion that the alien and temporary resident mentioned here are two distinct classes of people.

C. *The Alien and the Native of the Land*

> For seven days no leaven shall be found in your houses; for whoever eats what is leavened shall be cut off from the congregation of Israel, whether an alien or a native of the land (Exod. 12.19).
>
> If an alien who resides with you wants to celebrate the passover to the LORD, all his males shall be circumcised; then he may come near to cele

1. Smith, *Palestinian Parties and Politics*, pp. 181-82, seems to have made an error when he states that in both Num. 35.15 and Josh. 20.9 the גר and תושב are granted the protection of cities of refuge. The תושב is not mentioned in Josh. 20.9.
2. Noth, *Leviticus*, p. 253.

> brate it; he shall be regarded as a native of the land. But no uncircumcised person shall eat of it; there shall be one law for the native and for the alien who resides among you (Exod. 12.48-49).

> Any alien residing among you who wishes to keep the passover to the LORD shall do so according to the statute of the passover and according to its regulation; you shall have one statute for both the resident alien and the native (Num. 9.14).

These three references to the alien are grouped together because they are the only three which mention the alien in connection with the Feasts of the Passover and Unleavened Bread, and because they are the only three which associate the alien with the native of the land (אזרח הארץ). I will deal with Exod. 12.48-49 first because the other two references presuppose it.

Exodus 12.48-49 is of paramount importance to this study since it opens to the alien the option of moving from outsider status to insider status, and because it describes a ritual which accomplishes that change. The verses are found in P's conclusion to the legislation on observing the Passover (Exod. 12.43-50). I have already dealt with some of these regulations as they illuminated the status of the temporary resident.

These Passover laws stipulate that the feast is to be celebrated in the home. It is not to be a pilgrimage feast. It is not pertinent to this discussion whether this is to be understood as a return to an earlier custom, but would refer the reader to de Vaux's and McConville's discussions of the history of the development of the Feasts of Passover and Unleavened Bread.[1] However, it is significant that the Priestly laws, responding to the crisis of the exile and restoration period insist that this ceremony, which remembers the creation of Israel as a separate people, can be celebrated at home. This custom allows the Israelites to carry on this tradition, which is so crucial to their self-identity, no matter where they reside. As such it is typical of what D. Smith has described as 'strategies for survival' of refugee communities.

These laws agree that the option to join requires that the alien be circumcised. It is clear that the ritual of circumcision is functioning as baptism did in the early church. It is the visible sign of membership in

1. R. de Vaux, *Ancient Israel: Its Life and Institutions*, pp. 484-92; and McConville, *Law and Theology in Deuteronomy*, pp. 100-10.

a cultic community. It is important to note that this was not the only possible option presented in the Old Testament. Isaiah 56.1-8 speaks of keeping the Sabbath as the distinguishing mark of membership in the congregation, and does not mention circumcision. J.D. Gammie suggests that circumcision became the sign of membership in the exilic community because in that historical situation it did serve to distinguish the Israelites. Not only Israelites, but also Egyptians, Edomites, Ammonites and Moabites (Jer. 9.25,26) practiced circumcision, hence in pre-exilic Israel this custom did not function to separate them from non-Israelites. Because the Babylonians did not practice circumcision, the ritual took on a new function. It could then become an effective sign of membership in the Israelite community.[1]

In the Priestly writings, circumcision is the means to 'ritual ethnicity'. Circumcision is the sign of the covenant made with Abraham which established him and his descendants as God's chosen people (Gen. 17). Furthermore, many scholars have noted that the P document stresses the promises to the Patriarchs, and does not contain its own version of the Sinaitic covenant.[2] Ackroyd explains this emphasis on the promises to the patriarchs, and the subsequent description of the Sinaitic covenant as a fulfillment of these promises on the basis of the exilic situation. As their only hope for the future lay in an act of grace, the authors portrayed their past as acts of grace which accomplished the promises made to Abraham.[3] The sign of this covenant which brought the people of Israel into existence, and on which the hope of their continued existence as a people was based, was circumcision. The account in Genesis 17, which is widely acknowledged to be from the Priestly hand,[4] promises Abraham and his descendants that the land of Canaan shall be theirs, and that the Lord will be their God. Abraham, and his descendants, and all male members of their households (whether sons or slaves) must be circumcised. Circumcision is the sign, for all time, of the covenant. Any male who is not circumcised is not a member of the community. He is cut off

1. Gammie, *Holiness in Israel*, p. 24.

2. Ackroyd, *Exile and Restoration*, pp. 95-96; and Cross, *Canaanite Myth and Hebrew Epic*, p. 318.

3. Ackroyd, *Exile and Restoration*, pp. 95-96.

4. See Gottwald, *The Hebrew Bible: A Socio-Literary Introduction*, pp. 471-72. He describes Gen. 17 as one of the three perpetual covenants with which P divides the history of Israel into distinct periods.

(ונכרתה הנפש ההוא מעמיה, Gen. 17.14). Circumcision functions in this passage as a sign of membership in the community. For this reason, we can conclude that when the alien is circumcised, he is considered a member of the community.

We need also to consider the significance, if any, of the fact that the alien is juxtaposed in Exod. 12.48, 49 with the native of the land. As has been noted, it is only in connection with the Passover legislation that the native is qualified in this way. Elsewhere the term 'native' stands alone, except for Ezek. 47.22 where the native is described as a native of the sons of Israel (אזרח בבני ישראל). On the basis of this phrase, Friedman dates this passage (Exod. 12.48, 49) to the pre-exilic period, arguing that only in that historical context does the term have a literal meaning. It is unlikely, he claims, that an exilic writer would have designated the Israelites in this way.[1] Although there is an immediate appeal to his argument, there are weighty considerations which go against a pre-exilic dating. The most persuasive is that in the exilic and post-exilic periods, circumcision became a sign of membership. This became necessary because the nature of the community changed from being a national community to being a faith community. There is no need for a visible sign of membership in a national community, but there is such a need in a cultic community.[2]

The reference to the native of the land could also be used to indicate a very late date, although I have not found this argued. This phrase could be construed to support Smith's thesis that these passages are among the latest in the Pentateuch. At that time, the returned exiles (בני־הגולה) would have been in the land for several generations. The juxtaposition of the native-born with the alien would again have a literal meaning. If we understand these verses to arise in the same historical context as the Laws of Jubilee, then we could understand them as part of the strategy to allow the returnees to re-appropriate their land. This phrase emphasizes that they are the 'natives of the land', and hence have a claim to ownership. At the same time, the law is allowing the alien (perhaps to be identified with those who had remained in the land) to become equal members of the confessional community. The evidence is only suggestive and not conclusive, but it is clear that issues of membership in the cultic community and land

1. Friedman, *The Exile and Biblical Narrative*, p. 105.

2. See Smith's discussion of membership in the post-exilic cult community in *Palestinian Parties and Politics*, pp. 108-11.

rights were tied together in the restoration period.[1]

The next law, Num. 9.14, comes at the end of a section dealing with the problem of celebrating the Passover when one is ritually unclean because of contact with a dead body (Num. 9.6). Fishbane discusses this passage as an example of the text explicitly acknowledging that the legal norms available to the judge are insufficient. In Num. 9.6-14, the older, incomplete law, is distinguished from a new *ad hoc* ruling.[2] It is one of the four instances in the wilderness wanderings when cases are brought to Moses who cannot adjudicate them (Lev. 24.10-23; Num. 9.6-14; 15.32-36; 27.1-11). These cases are then referred to God, who gives an oracular adjudication.

In the context of the preceding decision, the law in Num. 9.14 is giving the alien the right to defer the celebration of the Passover if unclean or on a journey. It presupposes that the alien has been circumcised, and requires of him adherence to all the rules and regulations that apply to the native-born.[3]

There are several interesting features in the preceding part of the legislation which are pertinent to our discussion of the self-identification of the Israelites, and the limits of membership. The law stipulates that those who fail to celebrate the Passover when they are ceremonially clean and not on a journey, must be 'cut off' from the community (Num. 9.13). This is the same phrase that was used in connection with the rite of circumcision in Gen. 17.14. This phrase also occurs with slight variation in Exod. 12.15 (there they are 'cut off' from the assembly of Israel), Lev. 7.21 and Lev. 23.29. Grelot concludes that this punishment (being cut off) is to be understood socially. It is not referring to physical death, but being dead to the members of the community, i.e. being ostracized. Being cut off in this way also means being cultically cut off, i.e. being cut off from communion with God.[4]

He also claims that these five passages are later additions, and

1. See Blenkinsopp's discussion of the social context of the restoration community in his commentary, *Ezra–Nehemiah*, pp. 67-70.

2. Fishbane, *Biblical Interpretation in Ancient Israel*, p. 97.

3. Smith, *Palestinian Parties and Politics*, p. 181; Fishbane, *Biblical Interpretation in Ancient Israel*, p. 103; and Rendtorff, *Die Gesetze in der Priesterschrift*, p. 59, all agree that the alien referred to here must be circumcised, and for that reason claim that this passage is dependent on Exod. 12.48, 49.

4. Grelot, 'La dernière étape de la rédaction sacerdotale', p. 177.

belong to the last stage of the redaction of the Pentateuch. According to him, these passages derive from the post-exilic age when the nature of the Israelite community underwent profound changes. The community of Israel is dispersed, and the real need arises to distinguish Israelites from their non-Israelite neighbors. Boundaries between these two groups are maintained in part by establishing procedures which enforce the boundaries. These passages, which require that an offender be cut off, are effectively instituting excommunication. Excommunication formulas occur after legislation regulating circumcision, sabbath observance, unleavened bread and the Noachite commands (Exod. 12.15-20; Lev. 17.19b-21; the liturgical calendar in Lev. 23; Num. 9.6-14). Observance of these commands, according to Grelot, is practicable in the dispersion as well as in Palestine because they do not require the temple or priests, hence they would be fitting laws to distinguish the Israelite community.[1] His thesis is very attractive, but made less convincing by noting that Lev. 7.20, 21, which Grelot classes as a Noachite command, connects excommunication with the fellowship offering, a ritual which could only be carried out in Palestine, However, he is surely correct in his interpretation of the phrase 'he shall be cut off from the people'. That this refers to excommunication suggests that these laws derive from the time when the nation was a confessional community.

Grelot also claims that Num. 9.14 is an addition to the case handled in Num. 9.6-13.[2] The impersonal form of Num. 9.6-13 breaks in v. 14, and the issue is concluded satisfactorily in v. 13. He postulates that this addition, along with the many other laws which require equality between the alien and native are among the latest in the Pentateuch. These passages are dated to the time of Ezra; connecting them with Ezra's mission of unifying the Samarians and Israelites under the Persian government. This coheres with our understanding that the Priestly laws respond to the crisis of the exile by maintaining boundaries based on purity. As D. Smith points out, when this group returned from exile, they came into conflict with the Judeans who had remained in the land. Their customs, theology and self-identification was very different from those Israelites who had not experienced life in exile. The conflict is resolved by not only maintaining boundaries, but allowing movement across them. Hence, in its final version the

1. Grelot, 'La dernière étape de la rédaction sacerdotale', p. 181.
2. Grelot, 'La dernière étape de la rédaction sacerdotale', p. 174.

Priestly legislation insists on purity as a way of separating Israel from foreigners while also being integrationist in allowing aliens to become purified and acquire membership in the cultic community.

The final law in this section, Exod. 12.19, also presupposes that the alien is circumcised, and hence, is also dependent on Exod. 12.48, 49. This verse is part of a paragraph which deals with the Feast of Unleavened Bread (Exod. 12.17-20), following other instructions dealing with the Passover. It is here, in Exod. 12.6, that we encounter the phrase, 'the whole congregation of Israel' (כל קהל עדת־ישׂראל). Noth claims that here, we have for the first time the people of Israel designated as a cult community.[1] Exodus 12.15, 19 contain further evidence that this legislation is addressed to a community which identifies itself cultically, for it contains the excommunication formula in connection with the failure to observe the feast of Unleavened Bread.

In Exod. 12.19, 20 we find two ways of referring to the Israelites which appear contradictory. First, in Exod. 12.19 they are referred to as natives of the land, a phrase which Noth interprets to mean native of the land of Palestine, and which identifies the Israelites in terms of their residence in the holy land.[2] If the identification with the land is the key aspect of being an Israelite, as v. 19 would seem to imply, then we would expect that once out of the land, the Israelites would lose their identification, and not be obliged to follow the law. But this is not the case. Exodus 12.20 makes it clear that this law is applicable no matter where the Israelite resides. Perhaps the description of the Israelite as 'native of the land' derives from the time of the restoration community and reflects the claims of the returnees to be 'natives' and hence have a legitimate claim to the land.

Exodus 12.20 is a verse which Grelot dates very late. It is one of several verses which give directives which are to be obeyed 'in any place where you live' (see also Exod. 35.3; Lev. 3.17; 7.26; 23.3, 31). This phrase is interpreted as referring to the situation of the dispersion. The laws which add this stipulation are laws which could be observed outside of Palestine—the Sabbath laws, prohibition on eating blood, and Passover legislation. Only its occurrence in Num. 35.29, where it follows the legislation on cities of refuge, does not fit in with

1. Noth, *Exodus: A Commentary*, p. 95.
2. Noth, *Exodus: A Commentary*, p. 97.

this hypothesis.[1] These indications strengthen the case for an exilic or post-exilic date for these laws. Before this time there would be no need to address the issue of the Jews as a dispersed people.

In conclusion, we have seen that these three references to the alien treat aliens in an entirely new way. Their former status as socially vulnerable and isolated individuals who depended on charity is not discernible. Aliens here are people whose social and economic status is either not mentioned, or who are patriarchs of their own household (Exod. 12.48). These aliens are given the option of becoming Israelites. Once they have been circumcised, they are allowed to participate in the Passover. Because of the significance of circumcision as a ritual which distinguishes Israelites from non-Israelites, a circumcised alien is in effect, an Israelite. This would also seem to be the implication of the law in Num. 9.14, which begins by applying the laws of the Passover to the alien in the same way that it has been applied to the Israelites, and then follows this by a statement of principle which applies all laws pertaining to the Israelite to the alien as well.

D. *The Alien and the Israelite*

Because there are so many laws in this category,[2] I will cite only one as a typical example.

> An alien who lives with you, or who takes up permanent residence among you, and wishes to offer an offering by fire, a pleasing odor to the LORD, shall do as you do. As for the assembly, there shall be for both you and the resident alien a single statute, a perpetual statute throughout your generations; you and the alien shall be alike before the LORD. You and the alien who resides with you shall have the same law and the same ordinance (Num. 15.14-16).

The majority of the references to the alien are included in this last group because in all cases the law calls for equality between the alien and Israelite. The Israelite is variously called 'a son of Israel' (six times), 'from the house of Israel' (three times), 'a native' (six times), or 'a native of the sons of Israel' (once). Since these different appellations seem to be interchangeable, I am grouping them together.

1. Grelot, 'La dernière étape de la rédaction sacerdotale', p. 179.
2. Lev. 16.29; 17.8, 10, 12, 13, 15; 18.26; 19.33, 34; 20.2; 22.18; 24.16, 22; Num. 15.14, 15, 16, 26, 29, 30; 19.10.

The 'native' in the Priestly laws. Before I begin to study the individual references, it is appropriate to look more closely at P's preference for the term 'native' (אזרח). It is not a common word, occurring only seventeen times in the Old Testament. It is also a word which is almost exclusive to the Priestly laws. Outside of the P legislation it occurs in Ezek. 47.22, Josh. 8.33, and Ps. 37.35. This is strong evidence for a late date for these laws which designate the Israelite as a 'native'. If they existed prior to being incorporated by P, they have at least been re-formulated by the Priestly author(s).

The strong preference for this term in P, and its complete absence in Deuteronomic law and the Covenant Code also suggest that it is significant in understanding P's theology and anthropology. Before we can discuss its significance, we need to be clear on what its meaning is, i.e. native to the land or to the people. I would propose that the term means 'native of the land', and that its significance is linked to P's notion of the sanctity of the land. It is the belief in the land as a holy place, a land set apart for God, which would lead to the designation of the Israelites as natives, i.e. drawing attention to their relationship to the land. A corollary of this belief is that the land must be kept pure; that it is kept pure by right behavior, and that all who reside in the land are responsible for keeping it pure. There is no room in this way of thinking for a plurality of religions or legal systems.

Milgrom points out that only in the Holiness Source, as defined by him, i.e. Leviticus 18–20, is the sanctity of the land proclaimed, with the result that both Israelite and resident aliens are to obey the laws.[1] I dispute the exclusivity of this notion to Leviticus 18–20 (see, for example, Lev. 22.24), but do agree that the clearest statement on the sanctity of the land and the necessity to keep it holy is found in Lev. 18.24-28. The land, in this passage, is personified and given the ability to vomit out its inhabitants if they become repulsive. This metaphor is part of a warning which makes it clear that all in the land are responsible for keeping the land pure. This is the primary reason, I would suggest, that the law is to apply to the alien as well as to the native.

The theology of the land also plays a role in the blessings and curses found in Leviticus 26. In the context of a curse which threatens the Israelites with being exiled, the text offers hope to those who are in exile. Their hope is based on God remembering his covenant with

1. Milgrom, 'Leviticus', p. 544.

Abraham, Isaac and Jacob, and also remembering the land (Lev. 26.42). The promise to remember the land seems to have gone unnoticed by commentators.[1] I am not surprised that in the P document, hope is based on God's remembering his promise to the patriarchs, which included the promise of the land, but it is significant that God also remembers the land. The land is clearly much more than the place where the chosen people happened to live. It is a land separated from other lands for God.

These two things—hope for the future based on God's remembering the land, and the nature of these laws as a charter for the returning exiles in order to prevent them from repeating their history—explain the prominence of the land theology, and the concomitant designation of God's people as natives. This theology makes sense also as a part of the returnees claim to the land of Judah. Although those who had remained might dispute their claims, this terminology, written from the vantage point of the returnees, affirms that they have a rightful claim to their inheritance.

Leviticus 16.29. I now turn to the individual references, beginning with Lev. 16.29. It occurs in a paragraph (Lev. 16.29-32) which fixes the date of the Day of Atonement, and which gives instructions to the laity. Noth claims that this paragraph is a later addition on the basis of its position at the end of the chapter.[2] The wording in this paragraph is similar to that in the Holiness Code (Exod. 23.27-32a) which regulates the Day of Atonement. However, only in the legislation of Lev. 16.29-31 is the alien mentioned.

The law requires that the alien ceases from all work in the same way as the native. It should be noted that this is not the first time that the alien is included in a sabbath. The laws for the sabbath (Exod. 20.10 and Deut. 5.14) also stipulated that the alien cease from working. In the rest of the paragraph, the law gives the reason for this sabbath: 'atonement will be made for you'. Does the 'you' in these verses include the alien? I would suggest that grammatically, the 'you' does not include the alien. When he is designated as 'the one in your midst', (Lev. 16.29), then it seems that the 'you' refers only to the natives. However, it also seems likely that this is too individualized a

1. For example, Wenham, in his commentary, *Leviticus*, pp. 31-32, notices the promises to the patriarchs, but does not comment on the mention of the land.

2. Noth, *Leviticus*, p. 126.

reading of the text. The Day of Atonement cleanses the Israelites as a people, cleanses their temple, and cleanses the land. By virtue of being associated with the people of Israel, and living in the land, the alien would also be involved in being cleansed.

Leviticus 18.26. The next reference to the alien, Lev. 18.26, has already been mentioned as a clear example of the thinking which necessitated treating the alien equally. This chapter is self-contained; delineating unlawful sexual relations. It contains a series of laws formulated in the apodictic style, using the second person singular form of address (Lev. 18.7-18). These laws are framed by an introductory section (Lev. 18.2b-5) and closing section (Lev. 18.24-30), which Noth claims are secondary additions since they use the second person plural form of address.[1] The theme of this opening and closing section are similar. The Israelites are to be distinguished from both the Canaanites and Egyptians by their sexual morality. The laws are rationalized in several additional ways: they come from God (Lev. 18.4); they lead to life (Lev. 18.5); the land will not tolerate sexual immorality (Lev. 18.25, 27, 28); the Israelites will become defiled (Lev. 18.30); and be cut off from the community (Lev. 18.29) if they are disobedient. The aliens are addressed in the closing section as an integral part of the community. In what seems to be an addition, both the privileges and requirements of citizens are applied to them. This closing frame treats them as insiders—people who have crossed over the boundary.

Leviticus 19.33, 34. The laws in Lev. 19.33, 34 come at the end of a relatively self-contained chapter containing laws formulated on the whole in the apodictic style, fluctuating between the second person singular and second person plural form of address. The content of these laws ranges widely, and there seems to be no significant arrangement.[2] Leviticus 19.33, 34 stand out in the chapter because they are formulated casuistically, and are an example of primary law. In the apodosis, the relationship is indicated, and in the protasis, the terms of the relationship are spelled out. In this relationship, the Israelite is the native and the alien is a guest in his land. The law

1. Noth, *Leviticus*, p. 134.

2. See Noth's introductory remarks on this chapter in his commentary, *Leviticus*, p. 138.

demands that the Israelite not oppress the alien. The verb used here, תונו from ינה, is the same used in Exod. 22.20 (ET 21), and the reason given in Lev. 19.34 is also the same as that given in Exod. 22.20. The Israelites are to be kind because they remember that they were also aliens, and dependent on the charity of others. The similarity in terminology and motivation suggests that Lev. 19.33, 34 is related to Exod. 22.20. It also suggests that the oppression referred to here is socioeconomic oppression. The demand to treat the alien as native-born, in this context, is not referring to cultic equality, but is speaking of justice at the gate, being paid fair wages, not making immoral demands of the alien or his family, and so on. This law, using the terminology peculiar to P, is making the same demands as the related laws in the Covenant Code.

However, the law in Leviticus goes further than the Covenant Code when it demands that the Israelite love the alien. As Wenham has noted, the great command to love the neighbor is extended here to include aliens. The almost identical phraseology of Lev. 19.18 and v. 34 and the fact that the laws come at the end of sections closed with the phrase, 'keep my rules' (Lev. 19.19, 37), suggests to him that this is an intentional balancing.[1]

Leviticus 20.2. The reference in Lev. 20.2 concerns the Israelites or aliens who give one of their children to Molech. This chapter is again a self-contained unit, separated from the preceding unit by the heading in v. 1. The laws in this chapter are similar in content to the laws in ch. 18, but the form is different. Whereas the laws in ch. 18 were cast in the apodictic style, these are generally casuistic. Chapter 20 looks at these offenses from the point of view of capital crimes.[2]

In contrast to the law in Lev. 18.26, the inclusion of the alien does not make the verse grammatically clumsy, or destroy the form, and it is reinforced by the punishment which involves the 'people of the land'. It does not seem to be an addition.

The law in Lev. 20.2 is prohibiting the giving of children to Molech. Because of the explanation given in vv. 3-5, this is understood as meaning that the children are being given over in worship. It is a law against an idolatrous cult, which Heider concludes was Canaanite in origin; well established by the time of Ahaz, and prac-

1. Wenham, *Leviticus*, p. 273.
2. Noth, *Leviticus*, p. 146.

ticed in Jerusalem until the fall of the city in 587–6 BC.[1] The basic law given in Lev. 20.2 includes aliens twice. It names them among those who may not give their children over to Molech, and it also involves them in punishing the guilty. The translations are not faithful to the Hebrew here, when they render עם הארץ as 'the community'. The use of the phrase 'people of the land' is significant. It, along with the inclusion of the alien, and the involvement of all in the punishment, indicates that this crime is understood as a crime which defiles the land and endangers all. All must obey the law, and all in the land must be involved in the punishment as a way of showing communal abhorrence. The type of thinking evident in this law, and in the law requiring equal justice for aliens is consistent with the land theology we have noticed already in the Priestly legislation.

Leviticus 22.18. The reference in Lev. 22.18 is less clearly integral to the text. Grammatically, the alien's inclusion appears as an afterthought. In Lev. 22.18a, the law is addressed to Aaron, his sons and all the Israelites. Then, in Lev. 22.18b, the alien is added to the addressees. This inclusion is textually disputed, for the Septuagint translates הגר as a qal participle with the definite article, rather than as the noun with the definite article.

The law prohibits the Israelite and the alien from presenting blemished animals as free-will or fellowship offerings. This is not the only place in the Holiness Code where the alien is allowed to bring sacrifices. Leviticus 17.8 also includes the alien in its legislation on offering sacrifices. Does their inclusion here indicate that they have been given the privileges of full members? Smith claims it does not. He theorizes that in the Holiness Code we see aliens required to submit to purity laws and civil laws in order to keep the Israelites undefiled, but that no privileges are extended to them.[2] The fact that they are here allowed to sacrifice is considered by him to be irrelevant—so might gentiles.[3] To demonstrate that gentiles had been allowed to worship Yahweh, Smith points to the prophecies of the exilic and post-exilic period that all nations will come to worship Yahweh. He concludes that this idea would not have occurred to the prophets had

1. G.C. Heider, *The Cult of Molek* (JSOTSup, 43; Sheffield: JSOT Press, 1985), p. 405.
2. Smith, *Palestinian Parties and Politics*, p. 179.
3. Smith, *Palestinian Parties and Politics*, p. 277 n. 162.

not individual foreigners already come to worship him.[1] This argument is not persuasive, and does not address the question of whether or not the Gentile was allowed to worship before or after submitting to purification or conversion rites of some sort. It does not seem likely, given Smith's own description of the obsession for purity displayed in the Holiness Code, that gentiles would be allowed to come, in an impure state, to offer sacrifice at the temple. He may be correct that historically some foreigners did worship at temples of Yahweh, but that is not an argument which demonstrates that this law is allowing foreigners to worship.

I would suggest, rather, that the aliens spoken of here are converts,[2] and that sacrificing is one of the privileges extended to them. Hence, I would also disagree with the sharp distinction that Smith makes between the Holiness Code and the Priestly legislation. He hypothesizes that only much later, after the promulgation of the Holiness Code, were gentiles allowed the privilege of purification.[3]

I would also point out that the law prohibiting animals with damaged testicles being presented as offerings is extended to prohibit castration in the entire land (Lev. 22.24). The purity of the land as well as the temple must be maintained by disallowing a practice which destroys the life-giving capabilities of male animals.

Leviticus 24.16, 22. Leviticus 24.16 and 24.22 will be considered together because they both occur in the passage dealing with the foreigner who blasphemes against the name of God (Lev. 24.10-23). This pericope is another example of Moses seeking the will of the Lord in order to settle a case because the existing law is inadequate. The reasons why the law is insufficient are not explicitly stated, but Fishbane suggests that the mixed parentage of the offender would have raised the question as to whether the law of Exod. 22.27 was applicable. An additional issue concerns the punishment for blaspheming, since the law in Exodus 22 does not specify any punishment.[4] The

1. Smith, *Palestinian Parties and Politics*, p. 93.

2. In this context, I am using it to refer to someone who has joined the cultic community of the returnees. It does not necessarily mean that they were originally non-Israelites, but that they have changed membership from one cultic community to another.

3. Smith, *Palestinian Parties and Politics*, pp. 179-80.

4. Fishbane, *Biblical Interpretation*, p. 101.

verdict given here allows foreigners to blaspheme the name of their own god without any consequences, but blaspheming the name of the Lord is punishable by death by the whole assembly (כל־העדה, Lev. 24.16).

The two references to aliens seem to be integral to this passage, in terms of grammar and content. They are mentioned first in Lev. 24.16, the legal statement which decides the case. Their inclusion makes perfect sense, for the person of mixed parentage might well be considered to have the legal status of the alien. The case seems to assume that the son of an Israelite woman and Egyptian man is not an Israelite—otherwise the case would not present a problem.[1]

In the second part of the pericope, Lev. 24.17-24, we have a series of laws which spell out the principles of justice which govern biblical law. Wenham has pointed out that this series is arranged in a concentric pattern.

A resident alien and native Israelite (v. 16)
B take a man's life (v. 17)
C take an animals's life (v. 18)
D whatever he did, must be done to him (v. 19)
D1 whatever. . . must be done to him (v. 20)
C1 kill an animal (v. 21a)
B1 kill a man (v. 21b)
A1 resident alien and native Israelite (v. 22)[2]

This palistrophe reinforces the point that the same penalty must be applied to the native and to the alien, and that the punishment must match the offense.

Leviticus 17.8, 10, 12, 13, 15. The laws in Leviticus 17 are addressed to the laity, and regulate the slaughtering of domestic animals (Lev. 17.3-7); prohibit sacrifices offered outside of the tabernacle (Lev. 17.8, 9); prohibit the eating of blood (Lev. 17.10-12); regulate the slaughtering of game (Lev. 17.13, 14); and the eating of an animal found dead (Lev. 17.15, 16). The first four paragraphs begin in the same way by stating the addressee. In the first paragraph, the law is addressed to the Israelite, and in the second, third and fourth, to the Israelite and the alien. In the fifth paragraph, the Israelite and alien are both mentioned, but the form is quite different from the preceding

1. Noth, *Leviticus*, p. 179.
2. Wenham, *Leviticus*, pp. 311-12.

four. The last paragraph fits here, in terms of content, since it also regulates food; however, it differs in how it handles the matter. The alien and Israelite are allowed to eat an animal found dead, and then are required to purify themselves by a ritual cleansing. The preceding laws have simply allowed or disallowed a practice. On the basis of form and content, the law in Lev. 17.15-17 seems to be an addition.

The fact that the first four paragraphs have the same form, and differ only in that the alien is added to the addressees in the last three, also suggests that the alien is a secondary addition here. That raises the further issue as to why the alien is included in Lev. 17.8, 10, 13, and not mentioned in Lev. 17.3. This law requires that all domestic animals be killed at the temple. It effectively makes all slaughter of domestic animals sacrificial. The reason given for this law is that this requirement will prevent the Israelites from offering sacrifices to the goat idols. Can we conclude that the aliens here are non-Israelites who are being allowed to offer sacrifices to the goat idols? Wenham asserts that because the law makes specific requirements, we can assume that when the aliens are not mentioned they are allowed to follow their own customs.[1] He presumes in this reconstruction that the alien is a foreigner. This theory receives support from the pericope in Lev. 24.10-23 which allowed outsiders to curse their own god, but not the name of the Lord. However, the cases are not entirely parallel. This law prohibits sacrificing, i.e. a way of honoring another god, whereas Lev. 24.10-23 allows cursing, i.e. dishonoring another god. I am not sure that we can assume, with Wenham, that if aliens are not mentioned, we can conclude that they are allowed to pursue their traditional customs. Furthermore, I would suggest that the law concerning blood in Lev. 17.8-11 also precludes allowing anyone, either Israelite or alien, from sacrificing to idols. Leviticus 17.11 states that the life of the animal is in the blood, and that blood is a means of atonement. The corollary to this statement of principle in the text is that the blood may not be used as food. I would also expect that blood could not be used to worship another god. Hence, I would conclude that the reason for the alien's omission in the addressee in Lev. 17.3 was simply that it was not seen as a problem to the author(s), and that it testifies to the *ad hoc* character of the laws.

The legislation of Lev. 17.8-10 allows aliens to offer sacrifices at

1. Wenham, *Leviticus*, p. 244.

the Tent of Meeting, and threatens them with being cut off from their people if they do not comply. Are these aliens circumcised or not? We have already seen that Smith understands that foreigners were allowed to sacrifice, however, I disputed that on the basis of the many laws which regulated what people, priests and animals were allowed to come near to the presence of the Lord in the tabernacle. Noth agrees and claims that this alien is part of the 'cultural community', and hence subject to cultic regulations.[1]

This regulation and the following, which regulates eating blood, threatens offenders with being 'cut-off' from their people. As we have already seen, this amounts to excommunication, and according to Grelot, points to its originating at a time when Israel was a confessional community rather than a nation state.

In this chapter, the *kareth* penalty is invoked three times (Lev. 17.9, 10, 14). In the first two instances, offenders are cut off from their people; in the last they are simply cut off. I have focused on the significance of this punishment as it relates to delineating the limits of community. However it is also instructive to examine what the penalty tells us of P's understanding of the world and how to live in it. Wold has studied the occurrences of this penalty applying the insights of the anthropologist M. Douglas. He has found her understanding of pollution beliefs and their effect on structuring society especially helpful in understanding the purity laws in P.[2] Since holiness requires that individuals conform to the class to which they belong, it is necessary to keep distinct the categories of creation. The ordered society that results is kept intact by practical sanctions. Where the offense against the divinely ordained order is likely to go unpunished because of the nature of the crime, then pollution beliefs are called upon to supplement other sanctions. Wold attempts to demonstrate that the *kareth* threat is such a sanction which is used to preserve the distinction between pure and impure.[3] He does not address the issue as to whether there is a distinction between being 'cut off' and being 'cut off from his people', or, as in Lev. 17.16, 'bearing his sin'.

The law in Lev. 17.15 is significant for tracing the development of the legal status of the alien. It treats both the alien and native the same

1. Noth, *Leviticus*, p. 131.

2. D.J. Wold, 'The *Kareth* Penalty in P: Rational and Cases', in *SBL 1979 Seminar Papers*, I (ed. P.J. Achtemeier; Missoula, MT: Scholars Press, 1979), p. 1.

3. Wold, 'The *Kareth* Penalty in P', p. 2.

with regard to eating meat found dead. If they eat it, they are both rendered unclean, and must purify themselves. By not distinguishing between the alien and native, as was done in Deut 14.21, the law includes the alien in the cultic community. The reason given in Deuteronomy for prohibiting the Israelites from eating such meat was that they *are* a holy people (Deut 14.21). Fishbane contrasts this with P's laws warning that if they (the Israelite and alien) eat ripped carrion, they will *become* impure. He also points out that the similar law in the Covenant Code forbids eating meat found dead because 'You *shall be* a holy people to me' (Exod. 22.30). There are differing notions of holiness evident in these laws, he concludes. In the Covenant Code and Priestly laws, the status of holiness is conditional; it must be attained; whereas in Deuteronomic laws, it is unconditional, and provides the basis for right behavior.[1]

Numbers 19.10. In Num. 19.10 the alien is included at the end of instructions which tell the Israelites how to make purifying water. In this legislation, which is reminiscent of Lev. 17.16, the alien and the Israelite are involved in burning the heifer, gathering up the ashes, and putting them in a ceremonially clean place outside the camp. All of this activity renders them unclean, and in Num. 19.10 they are instructed on how to make themselves clean again.

Commentators have noted that this is a ritual without parallel in the Old Testament. It involves killing an animal, outside the camp (not in the gate of the temple, in the presence of God), manipulating some of the blood, and then burning the carcass, including the remaining blood. Noth decides that this chapter is an addition, having no reference to the surrounding material.[2] He suggests that it is inserted here before the narrative is resumed, making this section of Numbers a legal dumping ground. Wenham sees more significance in its position here. He notes that according to Numbers, there are three important social divisions in Israel: priests, Levites and laity. Numbers 18 dealt with the responsibilities and privileges of the first two groups, and this chapter deals with the third group.[3] In this chapter, the Israelites are instructed on how to purify themselves after contact with death. As we have seen before, God's holiness is opposed to death and illness. This

1. Fishbane, *Biblical Interpretation in Ancient Israel*, pp. 122-23.
2. Noth, *Leviticus*, p. 139.
3. Wenham, *Leviticus*, pp. 145-46.

necessitated not castrating animals in Lev. 22.24, and here it requires purification rituals after being in contact with a corpse.

The phrase involving the alien has been understood by some commentators to be the beginning of the next section rather than the closing of the previous.[1] The introductory phrase of Lev. 16.29 is similar, but not identical to this phrase. On the basis of content, the inclusion of aliens in a law regarding contact with a corpse makes more sense than their inclusion in a law providing for the making of cleansing water. In either case, it is clear that in these verses the alien is cultically integrated into Israel.

Numbers 15.13-16, 26, 29, 30. The laws dealing with the alien in Numbers 15 also indicate that the alien has become a full member of the community. The position and arrangement of these laws is an anomaly—even Wenham cannot account for their placement here.[2] This chapter is organized into three paragraphs, each beginning with the heading, 'The Lord said to Moses, "Say to the people of Israel"', moving on to mention the land, and followed by a command to do something. The chapter then closes with a formula recalling Israel's deliverance from Egypt and her call to holiness.[3]

The first cluster of references to the alien, in Num. 15.13-16 seem to have the legal status of the alien as its primary focus. However, Fishbane notes that the mention of the alien is secondary. The law is first stated in terms applying only to the native.[4] He claims this is more often evident in the Priestly legislation. The alien is mentioned as a legal afterthought. Although it is an addition, it is the first addition where the status of the alien is the main concern. This statement is the first which attempts to articulate in a comprehensive way the alien's legal status.

The law in Num. 15.13-16 involves the offering made by fire as an aroma pleasing to the Lord. We have seen that the alien was included in Lev. 17.8 in the bringing of a burnt offering. It does not seem possible to argue any dependence of one on the other, for they do not employ similar vocabulary or form. Whereas the law in Lev. 17.8 was ambiguous as to whether the alien was cultically integrated into

1. Noth, *Leviticus*, p. 141.
2. Noth, *Leviticus*, p. 114; Wenham, *Leviticus*, p. 126.
3. Wenham, *Leviticus*, p. 126.
4. Fishbane, *Biblical Interpretation in Ancient Israel*, p. 191.

the community, this law specifies that the alien and Israelite are the same before the Lord. There is to be one law for both. This statement seems to require a comprehensive interpretation. It begins by specifying that this one law is applicable to both alien and native (Num. 15.14), but then expands that to a general principle applicable to all rules for all time (Num. 15.15, 16). At this point, the legal status of aliens is on a par with Israelites. They are fully integrated, legally, into the community of Israel.

In the following section (Num. 15.22-30), aliens are again mentioned in Num. 15.26, 29, 30. This passage concerns the matter of unintentional and intentional sin. As Fishbane indicates, this law is related to Lev. 4.13-31. The nature of the relationship has long been debated, but he concludes that Numbers 15 is an expansion of Leviticus 4.[1] The law on intentional sin in Num. 15.30-31 is seen as a still later addition. This law is distinctive in that the *kareth* penalty has been expanded to include the willful transgression of all laws. This reflects, Fishbane argues, a new attitude to the law and its observance in that it raises all commands to the same level of significance.[2]

Fishbane also notes that this expansion is not introduced into the text by ascribing these laws to Moses or Yahweh, as in Num. 15.1-2a, 17-18a. Num. 15.22-31 does not ascribe the law to God or Moses, since it speaks of both in the third person. Instead, according to the text, the speaker is a preacher of the law as given to Moses. It is the beginning, Fishbane claims, of a new stage in exegesis in which human exegesis is allowed to change the divine revelation and adapt it to new circumstances. It is the beginning of a new form, the exegetical legal discourse.[3] Because of the equal status given to the alien, and because of the new manner of reforming the legal tradition, it is clear that it represents a late stage in the redaction of the Pentateuch.

The law on intentional sin is also instructive in attempting to understand the situation which the law code addressed. Such a law is not intended to be applied at the village gate by a court of elders. The law seems to be one that is unenforceable. It is written not so much because in practice it was found to be necessary, but because it fills a theoretical loophole. It seeks to make the statement that intentional sins cannot be atoned for but result in excommunication. In order to

1. Fishbane, *Biblical Interpretation in Ancient Israel*, p. 190.
2. Fishbane, *Biblical Interpretation in Ancient Israel*, pp. 190-92.
3. Fishbane, *Biblical Interpretation in Ancient Israel*, p. 194.

make this point consistently, the principle has been applied to all the laws.

E. *The Identity of the Alien in the Post-Exilic Community*

I have argued that the term גר came to take on a new meaning in the post-exilic community on the basis of the laws which require equal treatment for the Israelite and the alien. This involved a major shift in how the alien was defined—from a social definition to a cultic definition. In order to make my presentation more persuasive I need first to combat Cazelles' thesis, which argues to a very different conclusion, and then I will consider other biblical and extra-biblical evidence that the possibility of conversion existed in the restoration community.

Cazelles has concluded that the laws requiring equal treatment for the alien are the work of a late redactor of the Priestly laws. However, he draws some quite different conclusions regarding the date of this redaction, the situation which it addresses and the identity of the alien and native-born.[1] It is this last point which concerns me now. He argues that quite a radical shift in meaning has taken place for the term גר. He identifies the native-born with the indigenous population in Judah, and the alien with the Jews returning from Babylon.[2] Cazelles argues extensively for his description of Ezra's mission as being one of reconciliation, but does not argue his identification of the alien and the native-born. Once having dated the origins of these laws to the time of Ezra, and assumed their relevance to the situation existing in Judah, he concludes that אזרח means 'native to the land' (those who did not go into exile), and גר means 'alien to the land' (those who had returned from Babylon).

However, there are good reasons for supposing that this shift in meaning has not occurred. Such a shift presupposes that the people of Israel are defined only in terms of their residence in the land. The

1. Cazelles, 'La mission d'Esdras', pp. 116, 131, 132. He attributes the layer of redaction which includes the laws requiring equal treatment for the alien and native born to the time of Ezra (dated to the reign of Artaxerxes II: 404–358 BC). He understands that these laws fit in with Persia's concern to stabilize the province of Judah, and Ezra's concomitant task to unite the Jewish and Samarian communities in the province of Judah. I will not pursue the matter of dating here; see, however, the discussion at the beginning of this chapter.

2. Cazelles, 'La mission d'Esdras', p. 131.

corollary to this idea is that the Jews who went into exile lost their status as the chosen people. However, as Schultz points out, the various traditions in the Old Testament all present the returnees as the true Israel and are written from their vantage point.[1] According to the Chronicler, the land of Judah was left empty during the exile to enjoy its sabbaths (2 Chron. 36.17-21). Similarly, in Ezra it is the returnees who are called Judah and Benjamin, i.e. the true Israel, and it is the 'people of the land' who are the enemies (Ezra 4.1-5). When the Chronicler records celebrating the first Passover after the exile, Israelites who returned from exile together with those who had separated themselves from the unclean practices of their Gentile neighbors (Ezra 6.21) are the participants. That is, the returnees were the insiders, and it was to them that the others were joined. The Deuteronomist also claims that 'Judah' was taken into exile (2 Kgs 25.21). This is interpreted by Schultz to mean that those who were deported were the true remnant, while those who remained in the land were of no significance.[2] The prophet Jeremiah shares this assessment (Jer. 24.1-10), as do Ezekiel (Ezek. 11; 33.23-24, 27-28) and Isaiah (Isa. 43.28; 49.6; 51.3; 52.2,9). Finally, Ezek. 47.22, the only text outside the Priestly corpus to juxtapose alien and native-born and demand equal treatment for the alien, is clearly using the term native-born to refer to the Jews in exile. The reference occurs in a vision which gives instructions about allocating the promised land to both alien and native-born. In doing so, it completely disregards the people who would have been living in Palestine during the time of the exile.

We can conclude, then, that according to the various biblical traditions, the Israelites who went into exile remained Israelites, and even more, that they considered themselves the true Israelites. The laws of P are no exception to this consensus. I have already referred to the study of D. Smith which describes the Priestly laws as one of the strategies of those in exile to maintain their identity. The term 'native-born' (אזרח) must refer to the Israelites who had been in Babylon.

What information do we have from texts and archaeology which might support or refute this reconstruction? A description of the social and political organization, and the form of worship of the

1. C. Schultz, 'The Political Tensions Reflected in Ezra–Nehemiah', in *Scripture in Context* (ed. C.D. Evans, W.W. Hallo and J.B. White; Pittsburgh: The Pickwick Press, 1980), pp. 223-24.

2. Schultz, 'Ezra–Nehemiah', p. 223.

exilic/post-exilic community would certainly be helpful.

The exiles in Babylon were settled on new crown land on the outskirts of the city of Nippur. Because these were new settlements, we can suppose that the bulk of the population was Jewish, and that this was a contributing factor to their maintaining a distinct identity.[1] The mode of government in the community is difficult to discern, but it seems likely that some self-rule did occur. Ezekiel refers to the 'elders of Judah' (Ezek. 8.1; 14.1), and Ezra knew that when he needed Levites, he should inquire of Iddo, the leader of Casiphia (Ezra 8.17).

The form of worship in the exile is not clear. The fact that Ezra also acquired 220 temple servants from Casiphia has been interpreted to mean that there was a functioning temple there.[2] However, in a traditional society where the occupation of priest was inherited, 220 temple servants could probably be acquired without a temple existing. If there was a temple in Babylon, then the question of the status of outsiders who wished to join would be pressing. It is also possible that synagogue worship developed in Babylon. The absence of archaeological evidence on the existence of synagogues at this time is because there have been no attempts to uncover them, and even if there were attempts, it is likely that at its beginnings the synagogue was not bound to a distinct architectural form. It may have existed in peoples' homes, or in public buildings, and would be difficult to detect in excavations.[3]

Whatever institutional form the worship of Yahweh took on, it is clear that the Jewish community in Babylon did not lose its identity. That this was not without struggle is indicated by the Murasha tablets.[4]

1. E.J. Bickerman, 'The Babylonian Captivity', in *The Cambridge History of Judaism* (ed. W.D. Davies and L. Finkelstein; Cambridge: Cambridge University Press, 1984), I, pp. 344-46.

2. Bickerman, 'The Babylonian Captivity', p. 353, suggests that the Jews in Babylon, as the Jews in Egypt, had a temple to Yahweh. He interprets Ezek. 20.39 to indicate that the Jews had set up a temple with an image.

3. M. Smith, 'Jewish Life in the Persian Period', in *The Cambridge History of Judaism* (ed. W.D. Davies and L. Finkelstein; Cambridge: Cambridge University Press, 1984), I, p. 259, claims that the first archaeological evidence of synagogues are two Greek inscriptions from Egypt dated to 240 and 221 BC.

4. According to Bickerman ('The Babylonian Captivity', p. 344), 650 cuneiform tablets from the archives of the business house of Murasha in Nippur, written between 455 and 403 BC, have been uncovered. Jewish names occur on approximately eight per cent of the documents.

These tablets list people according to their personal names and the name of their father. What is interesting about this evidence for the religious life of the Jews is that although most of the fathers' names are compounds acknowledging Babylonian gods, these fathers, almost without exception, name their sons with Yahwistic names. The change in nomenclature begins c. 480 BC, and according to Bickerman and Smith, indicates the victory of the Yahweh-alone party. They go on to suggest that the rebuilding of the temple in Jerusalem would have been the cause of the turning point. Up to that time, many of the exiles, it is supposed, may have turned to pagan gods. Yet with the return of some Israelites, and the building of the temple, they were again convinced of the power of Yahweh, and the need to honor his name when naming their children.[1]

This evidence indicates that maintaining a distinct identity while in exile was a struggle for the Israelites. Through a variety of strategies, they eventually came to forge a self-identity involving allegiance to Yahweh as the only God in a place far removed from the promised land.

The new self-identity and communal solidarity that was forged in the crisis of the exile had social repercussions when some of those who had been in Babylon returned to their homeland. Their new customs and conventions created a separation between them and the population which had not experienced life in exile. For example, D. Smith analyses the concern for ethnic purity evidenced by Ezra and Nehemiah, both of whom came from Babylon, as a transference of what was a creative strategy for self-preservation while in exile to a community that did not need such tactics. Although there were undoubtedly economic causes for the conflict between the returnees and the indigenous population, it was also due to the separate religious and social development of the two groups.[2] The community who returned saw themselves as the 'remnant of the people' (Hag. 2.2) who were threatened by the impurity of the 'people of the land' (Ezra 4.4). It seems highly plausible that the laws granting the aliens equal rights if they purify themselves arise out of this situation in the restoration community. These laws seek both to preserve purity, and yet also

1. Bickerman, 'The Babylonian Captivity', pp. 356-57; M. Smith, 'Jewish Religious Life in the Persian Period', p. 222.

2. D. Smith, *The Religion of the Landless*, pp. 196-97.

respond to the need to include those who had remained in the land.[1]

In this reconstruction, the aliens are those Israelites, and perhaps others, who had been relocated to Judah during the years of Babylonian domination, and who joined the cultic community created by those who returned to Judah. These 'aliens' would not be converts in our sense of the word. However, later, these laws would be understood to be referring to converts, and would be used to legitimate the inclusion and equality of converts after ritual purification. The first evidence we have for the inclusion of converts among the Israelite community occurs in the Septuagint (LXX).[2] What began as a strategy for maintaining purity while at the same time allowing for the integration of 'unclean' Israelites, came in time to allow Jews to be open to receiving converts.

3. *Conclusion*

Within this body of law, a significant development in the legal status of aliens has occurred. They are not only the resident aliens who need aid, but they are also given the rights of members of the community. They are granted not only civil justice, but also the privileges of the insider on certain conditions.

When I claim that a development has occurred, I am presupposing that levels of redaction in the Priestly laws can be discerned and arranged chronologically. Although such arranging is a risky business, certain tendencies can be noted. The laws which stipulate equal treatment for the alien and Israelite are often secondary additions to the pericope in which they are found. However, the laws associating the alien with the poor and the temporary resident were mostly integral to their context. Because of this difference, I can conclude that the laws stipulating equal treatment in cultic matters are later than laws requiring charity and civil justice for the alien.

The laws requiring equal treatment speak of aliens in a new way. They have become part of the chosen people. In these contexts, the

1. See Ezra 4.19-22 for a description of the celebration of the Passover by the returned exiles and all those who had joined them and separated themselves from the pollutions of the nations of the land.

2. See the Appendix for a discussion of the evidence in the LXX for the inclusion of the alien as a proselyte in the Jewish community in Alexandria in the third century BC.

meaning of the word גר has changed quite drastically to the point that its original meaning of a socially and economically dependent person has been superceded. Here I would disagree with Smith when he asserts that גר never lost the connotation of 'resident alien' in the Old Testament.[1] In the laws requiring equal treatment for the alien, the word connotes the outsider who has become an insider in the cultic community.

We have also seen indications that the aliens who were treated as equals were not poor and dependent. This is most obvious in the Passover legislation in Exod. 12.48, 49, which presumes that they were heads of households and responsible for the behavior of dependants. They are people in a position of responsibility, whereas the slave, the temporary resident and the hired worker are not. This change in their social status coheres with my hypothesis that the term came to refer to the Israelites who had remained in the land and who joined the community of the returnees.

Since the Priestly laws are greatly concerned with maintaining purity and the proper cult, the laws which delineate the responsibilities and privileges of aliens outline their duty to preserve the purity of the land and temple. They are allowed to participate in the Feast of Unleavened Bread and the Passover (Exod. 12.19, 48, 49; Num. 9.14); are required to be sexually moral (Lev. 18.26); are given equal justice in civil law (Lev. 19.33, 34); are not allowed to be involved in the worship of Molech (Lev. 20.2); are not allowed to present blemished animals (Lev. 22.8); must not blaspheme the name of the Lord (Lev. 24.16); must observe slaughter laws (Lev. 17.8-14); must purify themselves after eating meat found dead (Lev. 17.15, 16); must observe the Sabbath connected with the Day of Atonement (Lev. 16.29); must cleanse themselves after contact with a corpse (Num. 19.10b); must follow the correct procedure when bringing an offering made by fire (Num. 15.13-16); and are bound by the law dealing with intentional and unintentional sin (Num. 15.26, 29, 30).

Unfortunately, the laws are not comprehensive, nor entirely consistent, so that we cannot account for every inclusion or exclusion of the alien in a satisfactory way. However, there is, as Douglas has pointed out, a clear system of thought which underlies these laws.[2] Of crucial

1. M. Smith, *Palestinian Parties and Politics*, p. 178.

2. See Douglas, *Purity and Danger*, pp. 48-49 for her assessment that past interpretations of the cultic laws failed because the laws were approached in a piecemeal

significance for understanding the position of the alien in these is the notion that the purity of the land must be maintained so that the presence of the holy God might reside in its midst. In order for the land to be kept pure for the Lord, all permanent members of the community were required to uphold the laws. The Israelite, alien and slave were to obey the laws, while the temporary resident and foreigner were not.

When we examine the laws which pertain to the alien in the Priestly collection, the thesis of Douglas proves illuminating. By understanding the concept of holiness, we can also understand the rationale behind these laws. For example, one obvious implication of the need to keep the land holy, i.e. separated for the Lord, is that the land belongs exclusively to Yahweh. Worship of Molech may not be allowed (Lev. 20.2), nor may the name of the Lord, the owner be blasphemed (Lev. 24.16). Further connotations of holiness also help explain the content of many laws imposed on the alien as well as the Israelite.[1] For example, the incompatibility of death and holiness explains the need for purification after contact with a corpse (Num. 19.10b) or carrion (Lev. 17.15, 16); the incompatibility of imperfection and holiness explains the prohibition of presenting blemished animals (Lev. 22.8); and the incompatibility of holiness and confusion, or holiness and double-dealing explains the laws requiring sexual morality (Lev. 18.26). Thus, the laws which bring us to new frontiers by requiring equal treatment for the alien are consistent with the larger vision present in these laws of a God who has promised his people his abiding presence in his holy land if they keep the land pure.[2]

fashion, so that the coherence that exists was not perceived, and the laws not properly understood.

1. Douglas, *Purity and Danger*, pp. 49-57. She examines the meaning of holiness by investigating laws in Deuteronomy and Leviticus. Although its root meaning is 'separated', it also connotes wholeness, completeness, perfection, life, order and integrity.

2. See the presentation by Ackroyd, *Exile and Restoration*, pp. 85-86, 90, in which he describes P's intent to make possible again the communing of a holy God with a sinful people, and also Cross's discussion of the purpose of P in 'The Priestly Work', pp. 299, 300.

Chapter 6

CONCLUSION

In this final chapter the results of my examination of the references to the alien in the Pentateuchal laws will be analysed to see what sort of development has occurred. First, the differing ways in which the legal collections have dealt with the alien will be summarized, and then the results will be used as evidence for reconstructing the historical identity of the alien through Israel's history. This twofold process is necessary, because not only does the Covenant Code treat the alien differently from the Priestly Code, but also because the historical identity of the alien in the Covenant Code is not the same as the identity of the alien in the Priestly Code.

Second, I wish to see if I can characterize the changes that have occurred. Are these changes responses to new social situations, or are they the result of a legal tradition refining older laws in order to make them more consistent, or more enforceable? Is there a process of secularization going on? Because the laws pertaining to the alien are typical of the laws in each of the collections, conclusions on the development of these laws can be generalized to describe the development of law in general in Israel.

Because these laws are part of the moral and ethical development of ancient Israel, a study of the various forms employed and the motivation clauses attached to the stipulations will help to discern the rationale proposed for right conduct. This will illuminate how the various legal collection pictured the responsible agent, how they defined moral conduct, and what the results of moral as well as immoral behavior were. On this basis, I will attempt to characterize the ethical development that has occurred in this body of literature.

1. *History of the Identity of the Alien*

In order to consider the legal material in the Pentateuch as a historical source, it is necessary to consider its genre and historical reliability. The Deuteronomic law and the Priestly legal collection can be described as reform documents. They were attempting to reformulate and reinterpret the law in order to make it pertinent to a new socio-historical situation. It was possible to conclude this because there was a prior legal collection with which to compare it. Furthermore, within the Deuteronomic and Priestly legal collections, there were additions which indicated that a redactor was changing the existing law. Because the Book of the Covenant stands at the beginning of Israel's legal tradition, it is more difficult to characterize it as a reform document. Yet there are indications that it too was written in order to change some existing customs. This was especially evident in the altar law (Exod. 20.22-26), which has been understood as a polemic against the Canaanite manner of building altars. It is appropriate therefore to characterize all the legal collections as documents which do not directly reflect prevailing social practice. The authors are attempting to reform some of the customs of their contemporaries and do this, in part, by reformulating the laws.

The laws, therefore, only indirectly reflect the status quo. They present the reader with what ought to be done. We cannot infer from these laws that the practices they describe were actually enforced. We may, however, assume that they were understandable to the reader, and most of them could have been implemented. Some laws, to be sure, are more utopian than others, and yet all reflect what would have been a possibility to the author.

Furthermore, the genre of the individual laws pertaining to the alien also suggests this indirect relation to social reality. All the laws concerning them in the pre-deuteronomic legal collections are apodictic in form. I concluded that the likely *Sitz im Leben* of this form was the cult rather than the informal court at the city gate. Its purpose was to present the Israelite with normative conduct. The Deuteronomic law in addition was typified as preached law. Both the content and parenetic style of the individual laws suggest that they were originally addressed to the people in a cultic setting with the aim of convincing them to live in a certain way. The Priestly laws also intended to create a holy people whose purity would allow the presence of God to dwell in their midst.

On the basis, then, of the genre of the legal collections as a whole, and because of the form and content of the individual laws pertaining to the alien, the intent of laws' is to reform society. When using these laws for the purpose of reconstructing the status of the alien, we must therefore be mindful of the fact that we are reading how one group of people thought the aliens ought to be treated. We cannot conclude that they were treated in that way, but only that it was within the realm of possibility.

The pre-deuteronomic laws pertaining to the alien required hospitality to the stranger who would occasionally enter the village. The Book of the Covenant specified that aliens should not be oppressed, be treated fairly in any legal disputes, and required that they share in the Sabbath rest. The Sabbath law presupposed that aliens resided with Israelites, and placed them on the same level as other dependants. In this case, the alien could have been a non-Israelite, but was also perhaps an Israelite from another tribe. For example, the Levite from Bethlehem who is looking for work informs an inquirer that he is going to sojourn (גור) where he can find a place (Judg. 17.7-13). The Book of the Covenant has been dated to the pre-monarchic period, and because Israel itself was not yet a nation state at that time, people's primary identification was with their tribe or village.

The extra-legal evidence from this time suggests that even though someone might be designated as an alien, he or she could be well integrated into society. At the beginning of David's reign we meet people who seem to be full members of the Israelite community and yet retain a distinct ethnic identity. For example, Uriah, identified as a Hittite, fought with the army and obeyed the laws requiring purity when at war (2 Sam. 11.6-13), and the son of an alien, an Amalekite, came to tell David of the death of Saul (2 Sam. 1.13). These narratives indicate that non-Israelites lived among Israelites, were loyal to Israel and its God, and participated in its social and cultic life. However, they nonetheless retained their ethnic identity as non-Israelites.

In the Deuteronomic laws the aliens are clearly and consistently treated as a non-Israelite; nor was there any opportunity given for them to become Israelites. However, they were accorded the same generous treatment that Israelite widows and orphans received. I assumed, on the basis of their being mentioned along with widows and orphans in laws requiring social justice, that aliens were economically vulnerable, and most likely landless. They relied on assistance from the well-to-do landowners. However, it is not clear that they resided within the household of the patriarch. Because they are accorded their own harvest, aliens seem to have their own household, and had to feed and clothe themselves. Only the Sabbath command, which occurs in the Decalogue and not in the main Deuteronomic legal corpus, envisioned them living in the patriarch's household. Rather than preeminently requiring hospitality, these laws would seem to be creating a system of support which would allow those on the fringes to be economically self-sufficient.

Is this portrayal of the alien during the time of the monarchy supported by other biblical references? Certainly the social changes that the institution of the monarchy ushered in created a class society. The consolidation of the kingdom under Solomon involved extensive taxation and the use of forced labor in order to support an aristocracy and carry out an ambitious building program. 1 Kings 9.15-22 speaks of Solomon's use of forced labor and indicates that the non-Israelites left in the land became slaves of the king. According to this text, the status of non-Israelites could be that of second-class citizens. The identification of these people with aliens is not obvious however, since they are designated as slaves.

Can we assume that all non-Israelites were in fact used by Solomon as forced labor? This seems difficult to accept, given the fact that non-Israelites had been an integral part of David's fighting force. It could be that groups of non-Israelites who had been conquered were conscripted as forced labor, but that the stranger from afar or the individual alien who had resided among them for a long time would not be included among Solomon's slaves. However, it does seem that beginning at this time in Israel's history the line between Israelite and non-Israelite became fixed. The identity of the Israelite as a citizen of the state had become consolidated, with the result that the outsider was someone who was not a citizen.

Whether or not the aliens were included in the cult during the time of the Monarchy cannot be answered with certainty. Clearly the Deuteronomist does not think it appropriate to include them in all the festivals. They could be participants in the Feasts of Booths and Weeks, but not at the Passover. This limited inclusion was based on his understanding that Israel had a unique relationship with Yahweh. Yahweh had intervened to deliver them from the Egyptians, and it was this non-repeatable saving act in the past which defined them.

Hence, if individuals were not heirs to this tradition, they did not belong to the chosen people, and were not subject to the food laws (Deut. 14.21) or observance of the Passover (Deut. 16.1-8). However, ancient religiosity was at odds with this way of thinking. More typical would be Ruth's confession to her mother-in-law that she would go with her to her land and adopt her people and her God as her own (Ruth 1.16, 17). Hence, according to the Deuteronomic law, aliens were identified according to their socioeconomic class and ethnic identity, and due to the latter were excluded from some cultic responsibilities. However, this is perhaps not reflective of the prevailing custom during the time of the monarchy.

Finally, I need to consider what becomes of the alien in the exilic/restoration period. The Priestly laws are our primary source of data, and they are ambiguous at best. Assigning the individual laws, subunits and levels of redaction to a particular time is problematic, and the results remain within the realm of the probable only. Nevertheless, I did note what seem to be two distinct ways of treating the alien, and was able on the basis of textual evidence to conclude that one preceded the other.

The primary level, which would seem to reflect ancient tradition, and would most likely derive from the pre-exilic period, treated the alien in what has become a traditional way. In the gleaning laws, they were classed with the poor, and Israelites were instructed to be charitable to them.

It was in what I deemed the second level of redaction of the Priestly laws, dated to the time of the restoration period, that the status of the alien changed quite drastically. First of all, I encountered legislation which allowed the alien, but not the temporary worker, hired hand or foreigner, to celebrate the Passover if he and his household were circumcised (Exod. 12.48, 49). Because of the significance of circumcision as the sign of the covenant which God made with Abraham and his heirs (Gen. 17), according to the Priestly writer, and because this stipulation ended with the general principle that the same law applied to the alien as to the native (Exod. 12.49), I concluded that according to this law, the alien could, given certain conditions, be allowed to become an Israelite.

The next challenge is to ascertain in just what way the laws have allowed the alien to become one with the Israelites. If we look at the laws which specify equal treatment, we discover that most of them deal with cultic matters, but there are also those that deal with sexual morality (Lev. 18.26). In addition, the Israelite is instructed many times to treat the alien as a native-born in all things. This even includes an admonition to love the alien which is parallel to a previous admonition to love the fellow Israelite (Lev. 19.18, 34). According to the law, the alien is given the same status as the Israelite in all things. We do not find here the dualistic morality that was evident in the Deuteronomic laws or the first level of redaction in the Priestly laws.

However, the laws regulating the Sabbath Year and Year of Jubilee, which we dated to the time of the Restoration, do treat the alien as a second-class citizen. In Leviticus 25, they were associated with other temporary residents: the תושב and the שכיר. These three groups were accorded the same treatment, and all were set over against the Israelites. The Israelite was admonished to be charitable to them, and yet they were not treated as equal in all things. When it came to slavery and charging interest on loans, the Israelite was given preferential treatment (Lev. 25.39-46). Furthermore, in the Laws of Jubilee was that the alien was someone who could be wealthy, and had resided in the land for several generations. They were treated as second-class citizens, and yet they had acquired economic stability and permanence.

When the new historical situation of Israel in exile followed by the situation of the restoration community is taken into account, then the dual emphases in the Priestly laws on purity and holiness, separateness as well as the concern to integrate the outsider, become understandable. As their self-identity changed from being a nation state to being a confessional community in exile the cult came to occupy a central place, and hence the preponderance of laws regulating the cult. This change in self-definition was crucial to their survival as a group. The Priestly laws are one of several creative tactics which achieved this. However, the second level of redaction does not derive from this historical situation. In the exilic context, according to the analysis of D. Smith, much effort would be expended in remaining separate from the foreigners. The fear of assimilation to the more wealthy, dominant, majority culture make it unlikely that laws stressing equality with the alien come from this period. Rather, it was the historical context of the restoration community and the need for the returnees to eventually incorporate those Israelites who had remained in the land, that these laws respond to. The aliens, according to this reconstruction, were those who were considered impure by the returnees, and who must go through a purity ritual before being considered members with them of the confessional community. In addition, these aliens had appropriated the land vacated by the returning Jews, and were economically secure. The laws sought to redistribute land as well as grant aliens equal rights and privileges.

The question still remains concerning the actual identity of the alien. Because, as I have indicated, the Priestly laws were aimed at reforming, we cannot assume that at this time the alien did in fact gain entry into the Israelite community in all things. In the prophetic literature there is evidence that the possibility was being promoted that 'outsiders' be allowed to join themselves to the Lord.[1] In addition, the acceptance of the Pentateuch by the Samaritans can be taken as evidence that they considered themselves included with the Israelites in this literature.

In summary, the legal status of the alien has changed dramatically over time. What began as legislation pertaining to a stranger needing hospitality and justice in the Covenant Code changed in Deuteronomy to legislation dealing with a class of vulnerable, landless people and created a system of support which gave them economic stability. It encouraged the Israelites to be just in their social dealings, but did not encourage them to allow the outsider to join the community. This was also the case for the first level of redaction in the Priestly laws. However, in the second level, in addition to the laws which treated aliens as outsiders and inferiors, there was also legislation allowed the outsider to join the community and be on equal terms with the Israelite.

Each of these legal collections was tied to a certain stage in the history of Israel. The first stage of the history of Israelite law coincided with the period of the Judges. In this era the patriarch had almost sole legal responsibility, and justice was enacted between clans of people by the elders. The second stage, reflecting the period of the monarchy, seems to have been influenced by the eighth-century prophets, and was addressed to the responsible citizens of the city. Justice was enacted at this time by a council of elders at the city gate. The period of the monarchy was also the most likely era from which the first level of redaction of the Priestly laws derived. However, I concluded that the

1. See, for example, Isa. 14.1, which speaks of aliens joining themselves to the Lord, and Isa. 56.3, 6, which speaks of eunuchs and foreigners joining themselves to the Lord. These texts are generally dated to the post-exilic period.

second level of redaction was formulated in response to the needs of the restoration period. It was addressed to a confessional community, and sometimes only to the priests in that community. It was largely concerned with matters of purity and proper cultic ritual, which the priests had the responsibility to enforce.

2. *Development of the Forms of Laws*

The forms of the laws pertaining to the alien also changed from one period to another. The pertinent laws in the Book of the Covenant are all apodictic in form, and are followed by a brief motivating clause. In Deuteronomy, most of the laws are neither clearly apodictic nor casuistic in form. Von Rad's characterization of them as 'preached law' is appropriate. There were some laws pertaining to the alien that exhibited characteristics of apodictic laws, but in all cases, what began perhaps as a brief negative prohibition has been expanded. For example, Deut. 14.21 begins with the injunction not to eat any meat found dead. This is then followed by an expansion which specifies in positive form what they are to do with the carcass—they may give it to an alien, or sell it to a foreigner. To this expansion of the stipulation is a added a clause which gives the rationale. It is because they are a holy people that this food is not fit for them. That the latter two clauses are additions is suggested by the change in person. Whereas the original prohibition is in the plural, the expansion clause and rationale are in the singular. In summary, most of the pertinent laws in Deuteronomy begin with a positive injunction, contain no penalty clause, and end with a motivating clause. For example, in Deut. 14.29 the Israelite is instructed to bring the tithe of the third year to the town to be stored for the purpose of providing food for the Levite, the alien, the fatherless and the widow. The rationale for this stipulation is so that the Lord will bless the work of their hands.

The forms of the Priestly laws are varied, and do not clearly fall into the apodictic or casuistic category. There are some laws which contain negative prohibitions, and these seem to be the more ancient laws since they all deal with civil or criminal matters, rather than cultic matters. None of them deal with the alien and native as equals, but all treat the alien as a temporary resident and second-class citizen (Lev. 19.10, 33, 34; 23.22; 25.23, 35). All but one of these employ the negative particle לא, which is typical of the apodictic form. Only Lev. 25.35 contains אל.

The bulk of the Priestly laws are positively formulated stipulations concerning cultic matters which are followed by a rationale. This priestly torah can be quite intricate. For example, Num. 15.30, 31 legislates against sinning defiantly. The basic prohibition is refined by making clear just who is being addressed. 'Anyone' is made more precise by a statement specifying that it includes both the alien and the native. It also expands on the crime by placing it in a certain category; it is to be considered as blasphemy. To the prohibition is added a penalty clause—the guilty party will be cut off from his people. To this basic law is added a rationale. The nature of the crime is again made clear—the Lord's word has been despised and his commands broken. This is then followed by a re-statement of the penalty, and a statement indicating what the result of this ultimately is the person's guilt will remain with them. Their ostracism from the community means that they have no access to the temple, and hence no access to God. They cannot carry out the ritual needed to atone for their sin, and hence they remain guilty.

3. *Development of Motivation Clauses*

Finally, the content of the motivating clauses has changed over time. I shall define a motive clause, following Gemser, as grammatically subordinate sentences in which the motivation for the commandment is given.[1] He categorizes them according to content into four groups—those of an explanatory character; those of ethical content; those which offer religious/cultic explanations; and those which offer religious/ historical explanations. I did not find his categories very helpful in documenting the different sorts of arguments and appeals used to encourage obedience, and hence have produced my own.

A. *Motivation Clauses in the Book of the Covenant*

In the Book of the Covenant, all three of the laws pertaining to the alien contain motivating clauses. The first two I shall categorize as an appeal to the past. This is the type of motivation with which Protestant

1. Gemser, 'The Importance of the Motive Clause in Old Testament Law', pp. 50-66. Motive clauses are not formally the same. He describes the variety of ways in which motive clauses are introduced on pp. 53-56.

biblical theology has been most at home. Obedience is grounded in the memory of what God has done for them in their past history as a people. Levenson describes this rationale as subsuming a community's *ethos* to its *mythos*.[1] The Israelites are told to be just and kind to aliens because they had themselves been in that position at one time in the past (Exod. 22.23; 23.9). Their time in Egypt is used to make the Israelites empathize with aliens, and on that basis to treat them well. Levenson also describes this rationale as a kind of ancient analogy to the Kantian imperative. The law is universally valid, both for the speaker and the hearer.[2] We could add that it sounds like an Old Testament version of the Golden Rule.

In the third law pertaining to the alien, the patriarch is commanded to allow the alien to rest on the Sabbath day so that he may be refreshed (Exod. 23.12). The law is backed by being connected to a goal. The goal is not defended, presumably because the patriarch himself knows how good it is to rest on the Sabbath. The command is thus based in universal human experience as well as being presented as a means to an end. One could suppose that if the purpose of the law could be better achieved in another way, or if it could be shown that following this law did not achieve the goal, that then the law would be rendered invalid. This law could be classed as teleological in that it is goal-oriented. It is attempting to arrive at the good by legislating effective behavior. Such motivation appeals to the understanding of the hearer. It presumes that if we can understand the goal of the law that we will be better able and more willing to obey it.

The Sabbath command contained in the version of the Decalogue in Exodus 20 is accompanied by a very different type of motivating clause. The Sabbath day is to be a day of rest for all because on the seventh day the Lord rested after creating the world. As God rests, so the entire household is to rest. The rationale employed here could be classified as imitating God (*imitatio Dei*). The pattern of our lives, the six days of work followed by one day of rest, causes us not only to remember that God created the world, but that he created it in a certain time frame which is now normative.[3]

1. Levenson, 'The Theologies of Commandment in Biblical Israel', pp. 18-19.

2. Levenson, 'The Theologies of Commandment in Biblical Israel', p. 27.

3. See Levenson, 'The Theologies of Commandment in Biblical Israel', pp. 31-33 for a brief presentation on the variety of ways in which the Sabbath command is motivated.

B. *Motivation Clauses in the Deuteronomic Laws*

In the Deuteronomic laws we see two of these types of motivation clauses again, as well as four new types. The reasons given for obeying the law can be categorized as follows: (1) appeal to the past; (2) appeal to humanitarian instincts; (3) promise of divine blessing; (4) appeal to a principle; (5) connection of the law to a goal; and (6) threat of penalty for disobedience.

The past that is appealed to in Deuteronomy is again their time in Egypt. Rather than describing the Israelites as aliens in Egypt, Deuteronomy prefers to describe them as slaves. This past experience is referred to in order to encourage them to identify with and be charitable to the alien as well as the widow and orphan.[1] It is put to a new use in Deut. 23.7 where it is appealed to in order to prevent the Israelite from hating the Egyptian.

The appeal to humanitarian concern is again attached to the law requiring the observance of sabbath rest for the entire household (Deut. 5.14). In addition, the requirement to pay the hired worker on a daily basis is backed by a statement which presupposes that people do care for each other. The reason given for daily payment is simply because the hired worker is poor and is counting on it. This would not be a cogent reason if we could not presume that there is such a thing as human kindness which will respond to need when need is pointed out.

A third and new reason given for obeying the law occurs in Deut. 14.29 and Deut. 24.19, 21. In these laws the Israelites are promised divine favor and blessing if they are generous to the alien, widow and orphan. According to the law, their required generosity to the socially vulnerable has been preceded by God's generosity to them, evidenced in the bountiful harvest. This motivation clause promises that obedience will also be followed by God's generosity towards them. Although the text does not make it explicit, the Israelites are being asked to imitate God in this command. As he has been generous to them in the past, and as they anticipate his generosity in the future, so they are to be generous in the present.

A fourth way in which obedience is encouraged is by backing a commandment with an argument from principle. In Deut. 14.21 compliance to the food laws is motivated by reminding the Israelites

1. See Deut. 5.14; 10.19; 16.12; 24.17, 22.

that they are a people holy to the Lord. The law is arguing from a principle. It is because of their separateness from other people that they must not eat as other people do. Eating an animal found dead is permissible for other people, but not for a people separated for God.

The fifth type of motivation clause in Deuteronomy is teleological. This occurs in both of the laws concerning the triennial tithe (Deut. 14.29; 26.12). The tithe is to be separated this year so that the Levite, the alien, the fatherless and the widow may eat and be satisfied. The purpose is to be supportive of the entire community rather than only one's immediate household. The law strives to set up a system whereby all those who for various reasons are not members of a land-owning household do not become destitute.

The sixth and final way of motivating the Israelite to obey the Deuteronomic laws is to remind them of the penalties incurred for disobedience. Deuteronomy 24.14 reminds them that if they do not pay their hired help daily, they may cry to the Lord and that then the Israelite will be guilty of sin. This is a rather nebulous penalty since it does not specify what happens as a result of being guilty of sin. However, in the larger context of the Deuteronomic legal corpus, it is made clear that disobedience brings on curses.

In these laws we see that the Israelite is appealed to in new ways. Besides encouraging empathy, appeals to reason are made by stating the purpose of the law, or the principle on which the law is based. Finally, in what is typical of covenantal stipulations, obedience is encouraged by promising blessings on those who comply and curses on those who disobey.

C. *Motivation Clauses in the Priestly Laws*

In the Priestly laws we also meet a variety of reasons given for obeying the law. Some of these we have met before, some are quite new, and some use familiar themes in new ways. The reasons given can be categorized in six groups. Obedience is encouraged by: (1) appeal to the past; (2) appeal to authority; (3) explaining the purpose of the law; (4) explaining the principle on which the law is based; (5) describing the result of disobedience; and finally, (6) basing the law in the nature of creation. Of all the laws pertaining to the alien in the Priestly legislation, only two do not contain motivating clauses—Lev. 25.47 and Num. 9.10. Both of them are statements of cultic law, which are given a rationale in the larger context of the unit, but this is not directly connected to the law. Some of the Priestly laws have several differing types of motivating clauses, and hence I have included them in several categories.

The first category of motivation clauses is quite small. There are only two references to the past in the Priestly laws we have studied. One harks back to the time when they were aliens in Egypt (Lev. 19.33, 34), and one to God's delivering them from Egypt (Lev. 25.35). These are similar in that they both derive from the Exodus tradition, but it is interesting to note that they function in very different ways. The reference in Lev. 19.33, 34 is used in what has become a typical way; it encourages the Israelite to love the alien. Their past is referred to in order to emphasize their fraternity with the alien, and on this basis to motivate kindness. However, the reference to their deliverance from Egypt in Lev. 25.38 is used to maintain the status of aliens as second-class citizens. Because the Israelites were freed from Egypt, they may not be enslaved, nor may they be charged interest on loans. However, this is not the case for the alien, or the temporary resident (Lev. 25.35-46). Because they have not been liberated by God, they can now be enslaved and can be charged interest. Hence, rather than appealing to the Exodus tradition in order to encourage empathy and kindness, it is used to back up a hierarchy in which the Israelites are allowed to treat non-Israelites in an inferior way socially and economically.[1]

The second way in which obedience is encouraged is by appealing to the authority which stands behind the law. In the laws pertaining to the alien, this appeal occurs only four times (Lev. 19.10, 34; 23.22; 24.22). These laws all end with the refrain, 'I am the Lord your God'. They are instructing the Israelite to be obedient because the laws derive from God. This appeal does not aim at increasing understanding or empathy, but respect for authority. It reminds the Israelite of their place in the scheme of things. They are subservient to God. Because the priest speaks for God in this legal collection, it also serves

1. This is both similar and dissimilar to Deuteronomy's use of the Exodus tradition. Insofar as aliens were not invited to be participants in the Passover, their deliverance from Egypt did function to keep them separate from the Israelites in cultic matters. However, this did not allow the Israelites to treat the alien in an inferior way economically. In this, Deuteronomic laws distinguished between the poor alien and the self-sufficient foreigner, and did not allow the alien to be treated any differently than the poor Israelite.

to strengthen a social hierarchy in which the priestly class is at the top, closest to God, and the rest of the Israelites are subservient to it.

The third way of encouraging obedience to the law is teleological. There are only two laws pertaining to the alien which fall into this category—Lev. 25.35 and Num. 35.15. The laws recommending kindness to fellow Israelites in need are for the purpose of allowing them to continue to live among them (Lev. 25.35), and the law setting aside cities of refuge are to allow someone who has accidentally killed another to flee to a safe place (Num. 35.15). The second rationale is not as strong as the first in that it merely explicates what is found in the stipulation. It makes clear who is allowed to find refuge in these cities. However, the first clearly encourages obedience by stating the purpose of the law. The goal is to preserve the community. It asks the individual who is doing well to forego the right to earn a profit by giving a loan at interest so that a fellow Israelite should not become destitute and be forced to move away.

The last categories of motivation clauses are interesting in that they only include those laws which treat the alien and Israelite as equals. The laws requiring charity and the laws of Jubilee do not appeal to principles or penalties as these do. It strengthens the observation that with these laws we are at a new stage in the development of the laws. That many of the laws which claim that the Israelite and alien must be treated as equals are rationalized by appealing to principles indicates part of the process in which the novel status of the alien was achieved. The scribes who were responsible for interpreting and promulgating the law found a new interpretation and application of the law authoritative if it cohered with certain basic pre-established principles.

For example, Exod. 12.48, 49 allows the alien to participate in the Passover if he and all the males in his household are circumcised. This law is followed by two statements of principle. Firstly, it states that no uncircumcised male may eat the Passover meal. This, then, is the reason for requiring the alien and all males in his household to be circumcised. The second principle states that the same law applies to the native-born and the alien. This statement is perhaps unnecessary since the first principle required that the law be applied to all males. However, it may well be that the author(s) are applying the first principle in a new way. Perhaps that first principle was formulated in order to require that all Israelite males be circumcised. Now, however, it is being used to allow the alien to participate in the

Passover if he is circumcised. Hence, to make it clear, the additional principle must be added.

The fifth category of motivation clauses attached to laws pertaining to aliens in the Priestly legislation encourages obedience by stating the result of disobedience.[1] Some of the results of disobedience are punishments meted out to the offender. For example, the Israelite or alien who gives any of his children to Molech will be put to death by stoning (Lev. 20.2). In others, a description of the natural consequences of disobedience is given. The laws concerning capital offenses in Leviticus 18 are backed by a description of what will happen if the land is defiled by these crimes. The land, it states, will vomit them out. This has been categorized as a natural consequence of sin in that the picture of the vomiting up inhabitants is a personification of the people being forced to leave because of war or natural disasters.

The final mode of argumentation is the cosmological. We encounter it in the laws dealing with correct slaughtering technique in Leviticus 17. These laws are backed by explaining what the nature of blood is. Blood carries the life force of the animal and it has been given by God as a means of atonement (Lev. 17.11). This law is based on the nature of created reality. Because blood is this sort of stuff, it has to be handled in a particular way. It may not be eaten (Lev. 17.10), and any animal which is to be eaten must have the blood drained and be covered (Lev. 17.13). The Israelite is asked to submit to the nature and order of the cosmos. The laws also make clear that this order is backed by God. It is God who gives blood as a means of atonement (Lev. 17.11), hence to obey the law is to submit to the God who fashioned the world in a particular way.

In summary, we have seen in the Priestly laws the tendency in the latter stage to back the laws by appealing to undergirding principles, to the results of disobedience, or to the nature of creation. This suggests that at that time the law was being handled by a class of lawyers who were becoming more sophisticated in legal parlance and practice and who understood the law to be an articulation of the norms of the created order. Arguments from principle especially seem to reflect a situation in which the law has become the property of professionals who are adept at interpreting and applying a written legal tradition.

1. These include Exod. 12.19; Lev. 17.8, 10, 12, 13, 15; 18.24-28; 20.2-5; 22.18-20; 24.14-16, 17-22; Num. 15.30.

4. *Characteristics of this Legal Development*

Having briefly traced how the status of the alien, the content of the law, the form of the law and the motivation for obedience have changed through time, I now need to consider whether or not I can characterize the changes that have occurred. I began this study by noting that the dominant way of appraising the development of biblical law in the last century and most of this century has followed Wellhausen's reconstruction. According to his paradigm, the changes that occurred were not progressive but regressive. Law was considered a valid component of the religion of Israel in the pre-exilic period when it was understood as the stipulation of a covenant between God and his people. The covenant context served to ground the law in the history of salvation. At this time in Israel's religious history, it was argued, law was subsumed to gospel. In the post-exilic period, however, when it was claimed that law became divorced from this covenant context, it was described as absolute; an end in itself, petty, meaningless and concerned only with externals.

Levenson has combatted this reconstruction by examining the various understandings of commandment of Israel in the biblical period.[1] Building on the work of Gemser,[2] he demonstrates that we have in the Old Testament a variety of ways in which the laws are understood and validated. Command being a response to the prior act of God, which occurs when laws are presented as the stipulations of a covenant, is one of these ways, but certainly not the only one. He argues that some laws are understood as the particular Israelite articulation of what are universally held norms. The laws that hold for Israel are presented as laws that are good for all. The sermon found in Deut. 4.5-8 is a clear example of this way of thinking. Although the laws are addressed to Israel alone, they are not unintelligible or unattractive to others. They are based on what can be perceived by all to be just and wise. It is precisely because they are based on universal norms that they can function as a means of attracting attention and honor to the people of Israel. Levenson also points out that some commands, such as the Sabbath command in Exodus 20 are grounded in the nature and order of creation—the cosmological argument. He thus expands the number of

1. Levenson, 'The Theologies of Commandment in Biblical Israel', pp. 17-34.

2. Gemser, 'The Importance of the Motive Clause in Old Testament Law', pp. 50-66.

ways in which commands are understood in the Old Testament from one to three.

My study of the laws pertaining to the alien supports his thesis that the Old Testament has a multi-faceted way of understanding laws. We have seen the commands pertaining to the alien understood as a means to an end, as an expression of human kindness, as a response of gratitude to God's kindness, and an articulation of principles.

This variety of ways of understanding law should not be understood as being self-contradictory. Law need not be either a response to prior gracious acts, or grounded in the order of creation or a particular articulation of universal norms. These are not mutually exclusive. The fact that the Sabbath law is grounded in four different ways in the Pentateuch is not a problem of inconsistency, but a testimony to the richness of thinking about law found in the Old Testament.[1]

Often the particular type of motivation employed was determined by the content of the law. Laws requiring charity tended to be backed by clauses encouraging sympathy, and humanitarian concern. These laws could be understood as particular expressions of universal conceptions of justice and goodwill. Dietary laws were backed either by an appeal to creation, in which the law is seen as a means of maintaining the order of the cosmos, or by reminding them of their status as a holy people, in which the law is seen as a response to the prior gracious act of God. The variety of motivating clauses then are not evidence of mutually exclusive understandings of the meaning of law, but testify to the complexity of the theologies of law in the Pentateuch.

Levenson concludes his brief article by pointing to the increase in proportion of motivation clauses through time[2] as evidence of a heightened self-consciousness which has strengthened its legal tradition by grounding it in overlapping theologies of commandment.[3] The increased interest and reflection on law in this later period of Israelite religion is not an indication that it has become lifeless, but is proof of a living tradition becoming more durable. Hence it needs no apologies.

1. Levenson, 'The Theologies of Commandment in Biblical Israel', p. 33.

2. This is documented by Gemser, 'The Importance of the Motive Clause in Old Testament Law', p. 51. He concludes that the Covenant Code has motivation clauses attached to seventeen per cent of its laws, Deuteronomy sixty per cent and the Holiness Code sixty-five per cent.

3. Levenson, 'The Theologies of Commandment in Biblical Israel', p. 33.

My study of the Pentateuchal laws dealing with the alien leads me to concur with Levenson and characterize the development of law as a process of enrichment rather than a process in which law becomes divorced from its moorings. Although the tendency to ground the law in the history of salvation diminishes, law does not become an absolute. It is grounded in the nature of reality, or in universal norms of justice.

The laws dealing with the alien developed and became more inclusive. What began as an appeal for justice for the alien in the Covenant Code (Exod. 23.9), comes to be understood as a legal principle in the Priestly laws: 'There shall be one law for the alien and the native-born'. This then opened the door for the inclusion of the alien into all the rights and privileges of Israelite society. What began as a plea for charity to the alien in the Covenant Code became in Deuteronomy the inclusion of the alien among those Israelites who were socially weak and landless. This tendency went so far as to disallow any double standard between how poor Israelites were to be treated and how poor aliens were to be treated (Deut. 14.21). Again, what began in the Covenant Code as the extension of Sabbath rest to the ox, donkey, slave and alien (Exod. 23.12), led to the complete cultic inclusion of aliens, if they were circumcised, in the Priestly laws. Although this tendency has not been perfectly linear, it is still possible to conclude that the alien who began as an outsider and object of charity has come to be included, if willing, among the people of Israel. This development coheres well with the goal of the chosen people to be a blessing to the nations (Gen. 12.1-3). This was continued in the message of the prophets who looked forward to the day when all would come to the mountain of the Lord (Isa. 2.2-4). The inclusive tendency is the working out, in the legal tradition, of God's purpose to include and save all.

I also noted a shift in how aliens were defined. From being outsiders, ethnically defined, they became outsiders, nationally defined, who were also socially and economically deprived. From there they came to be cultically defined as those who were insiders, having submitted themselves to the rite of circumcision, and who were now considered an equal in all things. As the nature of the alien changed, there was a concomitant change in the concern of the laws. What began in the Book of the Covenant as a body of law concerned mostly with civil and criminal law came in the Priestly legislation to be a body of law concerned mostly with proper ritual.

Hand in hand with this legal development has gone a development in ethics.[1] The transition from a law grounded in their unique history to a law grounded in universal principles or in creation has resulted in a transition in the depiction of the morally responsible agent. When law is based on what God has done for Israel, then the law is applicable only for Israel. It is a particular law for a particular people. However, if the law is based on universally held norms or on the structure of creation, then the law can become pertinent for all people. The moral agent could be the non-Israelite as well as the Israelite. However, it should be noted that alongside the law being grounded in universal norms or in the structure of creation, it is presented as an address by God to Moses, the priests or the people of Israel. Although the laws may be good for all, in the text they are only addressed to the Israelites. In addition, they are placed in the larger context of a covenant made at Mt Sinai after their deliverance out of Egypt. Their authority derives in great measure from their being conceived as the words of God. Hence, even though we can characterize the change in the moral agent as a development from being only pertinent to Israelites, to potentially being pertinent to all; there are also formal characteristics in the text which maintain in all stages that the law is from God and is binding first of all on his chosen people.

Finally, it is necessary to reflect on how this development is to be accounted for. The study of the development of law is a large forbidding area, and I intend to offer only a few limited observations.[2] I have explained the changes that have occurred in the status of the alien by considering social, political, economic and cultural factors. The laws were best understood by considering them in their concrete his-

1. Although not directly feeding into our discussion of the laws, T.W. Ogletree's *Hospitality to the Stranger* (Philadelphia: Fortress Press, 1985), contributes to the discussion on the moral life by using hospitality to the stranger as a metaphor for an ethic which is other-centered rather than self-centered. His prologue contains a rich description of both the risks and rewards awaiting the person who extends hospitality to the stranger.

2. An excellent paper on this topic, 'From Savigny to CLS: Legal Thought and the Biblical Text', was presented by P.J. Haas at the 1988 SBL meeting. He traces the developments in the academic study of the laws in the past two centuries and notes that the changes in the study of biblical law are parallel. His thesis is that developments in the study of the biblical text are part of wider changes that are occurring within academia and the world in general.

torical context. This study, although considering it essential to understand the laws in their historical context, does not support the notion that they are determined by that context. The variety of responses in the legal tradition indicates that, in a given situation, there were several options. The law could treat the alien as a second-class citizen in socioeconomic dealings (Lev. 25.35-38), or could require that the alien be treated as one of their own in socioeconomic dealings (Deut. 14.21). Although the historical context certainly limited the options available, it did not determine which option was chosen.

I have also explained the changes as a result of a culture and legal tradition becoming more mature. This sort of notion is developed, according to Haas, in British scholarship on the Bible which tended to trace the history of legal institutions and legal formulations and see in them a gradual sophistication.[1] This is the sort of development that Levenson's article on the increasing richness in the theologies of commandment would support, and which my study also supports.

Haas ends his survey by describing the now regnant Critical Legal Studies movement which he sees mirrored in the work of Mendenhall and Gottwald in particular. According to this paradigm, there is no overall logic or development to be perceived over time. Rather, law is pictured as the result of competing special interest groups. The changes that occur are not progressive, or even regressive, but *ad hoc*.[2] This paradigm is not helpful, however, in understanding the law pertaining to the alien in the Book of the Covenant and Deuteronomy. The alien is precisely someone who has no power, who could not even compete, and is yet accorded fair, hospitable treatment. The concern to protect the underdog evidenced by these laws cannot be accounted for by this paradigm. Furthermore, the development towards inclusion can be seen as Israel progressively living up to its calling in the legal tradition.

The theologies of commandment which are inherent in the biblical text itself more satisfactorily explain how law develops. In that law is an articulation of universal norms, it cannot be reduced to the result of disputes of competing interest groups. The existence of laws which protect the vulnerable testifies to a universal sense of justice and humanitarian concern. Furthermore, in that the law is a particular articulation of universal norms, or of the order of creation, we need

1. Haas, 'From Savigny to CLS', p. 17.
2. Haas, 'From Savigny to CLS', pp. 20-22.

to take account of the particular situation in which it is articulated if we are to understand it. In addition, we are to presume that as the situation changes, the law will also change. We have seen that the laws do change and develop, and do this as part of an ongoing dynamic tradition which is perpetually grounded in a narrative which recounts Israel's past. The changes that occur in the legal tradition are changes which are limited by the story the community tells to itself about itself. In this way, the laws are the crossroads of the universal and the particular, and both must be kept in mind if the development of law in the Old Testament is to be understood and appreciated.

Appendix

The Translation of גר in the Septuagint

The Septuagint's (LXX) translation of the term גר needs to be taken into account first of all as a witness to the Hebrew text of the Pentateuch. Yet when we study how the LXX did translate the word 'alien' into Greek, we notice that it is more than a witness to the Hebrew text. It is also a witness to the life of the Jewish community in Alexandria in the third century BC. Although this study is not able to enter the discussion on Jewish proselytizing in the Hellenistic world, it also did not seem responsible to ignore the voice of the LXX. The solution has been to include the evidence of the LXX in this appendix.

With the LXX we are at a new stage in the development of the legal tradition in Israel. Changes in the law are no longer being carried out within the confines of what was becoming the canon. Instead, the next stage is discernible by noting how the translation of the Pentateuch into Greek dealt with the laws pertaining to the alien.

The LXX is significant for this study in that it can be characterized as the fundamental document of Hellenistic Judaism.[1] Hellenistic Judaism came into existence in the period following the conquests of Alexander the Great. At that time, not only Jews, but also the adherents of many religions of the Near East learned to speak Greek. The exposure to Greek language and culture resulted in changes at many levels.[2]

Although it is not possible to deal with many of the transformations that occurred as a result of the contact of Judaism with Greek language and culture, this study will focus on the position of the alien. In order to do that I propose first to examine how the term גר was translated into Greek, and attempt to understand the significance of

1. C.H. Dodd, *The Bible and the Greeks* (London: Hodder and Stoughton, 1935), p. xi.

2. Dodd, *The Bible and the Greeks*, p. xi.

that translation. That information will be used to describe the legal and social status of the גר in the Hellenistic Alexandrian Jewish community in the third to second century BC.

Generally, the LXX is thought to have been translated c. 250 BC, to meet the needs of the Egyptian Jewish community.[1] Many of these Jews could no longer understand Hebrew, and the translated Pentateuch was needed for worship and instruction in the Synagogue.[2]

The LXX Pentateuch translates גר either by πάροικος (six times), προσήλυτος (sixty-three times), or γειώρας (once). My study of the meaning and significance of this choice of words is greatly helped by a study of W.C. Allen.[3] In his article he thoroughly examines the meaning of προσήλυτος in the LXX in order to argue against the then prevailing opinion that it was synonymous in meaning with πάροικος. He does this by examining the contexts in which the terms προσήλυτος and πάροικος occur. The resulting evidence is surprisingly clear. It indicates that the translator(s) preferred the word προσήλυτος and only used the word πάροικος when the context indicated that it could not possibly mean proselyte.

For example, πάροικος occurs only twice in Deuteronomy (Deut. 14.21; 23.8). In Deut. 14.21 the law stipulates that if an Israelite finds a dead animal, not properly slaughtered, he may give it to the alien or sell it to the foreigner. Because the law maintains a difference between the Israelite and the alien, the alien cannot be a proselyte. Hence the sense of the law mitigates against translating the word גר with προσήλυτος. Similarly, גר occurs in Deut. 23.8 where it refers to Israel in Egypt. Here also, the rendering of alien with proselyte would not make sense. In the other nineteen instances, גר is translated by προσήλυτος in Deuteronomy.[4] W.C. Allen comments that the translation of גר with προσήλυτος in Deut. 1.16 is strange, since the alien is

1. For the text, with an introduction and notes, see H.T. Andrews's translation in *The Apocrypha and Pseudepigrapha of the Old Testament*, II (ed. R.H. Charles; Oxford: Clarendon Press, 1913), pp. 83-122.

2. S. Jellicoe, *The Septuagint and Modern Study* (Oxford: Clarendon Press, 1968), pp. 55-59.

3. W.C. Allen, 'On the Meaning of προσήλυτος in the Septuagint', pp. 264-75.

4. Deut. 1.16; 5.14; 10.18 (twice in the LXX, once in the MT), 19; 12.18 (MT has no reference to גר in this verse); 14.29; 16.11, 14; 24.14, 17, 19, 20, 21; 26.11, 12, 13; 29.19; 28.43; 29.10; 31.12.

described as 'his' alien.[1] Because the suffix indicates that the גר is in a subordinate position to the Israelite, the translation of it by 'sojourner' (πάροικος) would seem more likely. However, this exception does not threaten his major thesis. A more serious problem is the description of the Israelites in Egypt in Exod. 22.20; 23.9; Lev. 19.34 and Deut. 10.19 as προσήλυτος. These translations are explained by noting that in these instances, the word גר has first occurred in the prohibition, in a context where προσήλυτος was an acceptable translation. Then גר was used again in the motivating clause attached to the prohibition, referring to the Israelites sojourning in Egypt. Because the term in the motivating clause had to be the same as the term in the prohibition in order for the motivating clause to make sense, the Israelites are described as προσήλυτος in Egypt in these four instances.[2] The exceptional case for which neither Allen nor I have an explanation is the single occurrence of γειώρας in Exod. 12.19 (Aquila and Symmachus use προσήλυτος here).[3]

In light of the evidence, the conclusions drawn by Allen seem warranted. The translators of the Pentateuch came to the text with a notion of the proselyte, and took גר to refer to the proselyte except in the cases where the meaning proselyte was impossible.[4]

1. Allen, 'On the Meaning of προσήλυτος in the Septuagint', pp. 268-69.

2. Allen, 'On the Meaning of the προσήλυτος in the Septuagint', p. 271.

3. Allen, 'On the Meaning of the προσήλυτος in the Septuagint', p. 269. The word γειώρας is taken from the Aramaic גיורא, corresponding to the Hebrew גר. J.A.L. Lee, in *A Lexical Study of the Septuagint Version of the Pentateuch* (Chico, CA: Scholars Press, 1983), p. 16, uses it as an example to demonstrate that the everyday language of the Egyptian Jews before they adopted Greek was Aramaic and not Hebrew. γειώρας occurs only twice in the LXX; here and in Isa. 14.1. It is correct, it seems, to conclude that no significance can be attached to these two occurrences of γειώρας. They do not affect the discussion of the meaning of πάροικος and προσήλυτος, and the LXX's tendencies when translating גר.

4. Neither Allen nor K.G. Kuhn, 'προσήλυτος', pp. 727-44, discuss the three places where there is a discrepancy between the MT and the LXX reference to the alien. In Lev. 17.3, Deut. 10.18 and Deut. 12.18, the LXX text has included a phrase referring to the alien (translated as προσήλυτος in all three cases) which is not found in the MT. In his survey, which is otherwise complete, Allen does not include Lev. 17.3 and Deut. 12.18. Kuhn does not discuss them, although when he claims that προσήλυτος is used seventy-seven times for the Hebrew גר, the three discrepancies are included. To be accurate, Kuhn should state that προσήλυτος is used seventy-four times for the Hebrew גר, and three times when there is no corresponding גר in the Hebrew text.

The precise meaning of proselyte at this point is uncertain since the LXX seems to gave coined the term. Allen and Kuhn claim that this word is not found in pre-Jewish or pre-Christian literature.[1] The evidence of the Septuagint for determining the meaning of προσήλυτος is somewhat ambiguous, for as we have seen, the status of the גר has changed from law code to law code, and even within a single law code. Hence, the LXX alone does not tell us what precise meaning the translators had in mind when they translated גר by προσήλυτος.[2] However, the evidence of the LXX does limit the possible range of meaning in that it has consistently distinguished the πάροικος from the προσήλυτος. The meaning of πάροικος as temporary resident or sojourner is made clear by the fact that not only is גר sometimes translated by πάροικος, but that תושב is always translated by πάροικος.[3]

The first definition of προσήλυτος in ancient literature occurs in the writings of Philo. Because he was writing for a Gentile audience, he did not assume knowledge of this unfamiliar word. He described proselytes as people who had left country, friends and relatives, and patriarchal customs, and set themselves under the Jewish constitution. (*Spec. Leg.* 1.51, 52). The term applies to the Gentile who has adopted the Jewish laws and become circumcised.

Is there something to be learned about converts to Judaism in the Hellenistic period in Alexandria by noting that the LXX coined a new word? The phenomenon of conversion at this time was not unique to Judaism, and there were Greek words available which described this phenomenon. Philo himself prefers to use ἔπηλυς, ἐπήλυτος, and ἐπηλύτης to describe converts because these words are familiar to his readers.[4] That προσήλυτος and ἐπήλυτος are synonymous in meaning to him is indicated by his using ἐπήλυτος in one quotation from Deut. 10.17 (*Spec. Leg.* 4.176-77) and προσήλυτος in another (*Spec. Leg.* 1.308). The question concerning the rationale behind the

1. Kuhn, 'προσήλοτος', p. 728; Allen, 'On the Meaning of προσήλυτος in the Septuagint', p. 265.

2. προσήλυτος is a compound of the preposition προ with the stem -ελυ- (with extension -νλυ-), an abstraction from -ηλυσια.

3. K.L. and M.A Schmidt, 'πάροικος', in *Theological Dictionary of the New Testament*, V (trans. G.W. Bromiley; ed. G. Friedrich; Grand Rapids: Eerdmans, 1967), p. 844.

4. Kuhn, 'προσήλυτος', p. 731.

LXX's coinage of a new word has not been explored in any discussion of the meaning of προσήλυτος, nor in any study of the phenomenon of conversion in the Hellenistic world. A.D. Nock's study on conversion at this time does not discuss the various terms used to designate converts to Greek cults or Greek philosophy.[1] He does suggest that conversion to Judaism or Christianity is more analogous to becoming a follower of a certain philosophy than joining one of the cults.[2] However, the word used to describe the effects of listening to a philosopher and changing one's life to live in accord with these teachings is ἐπιστροφή.[3] Hence, although it seems likely that the translators created a new word because they did not want to take over the connotations attached to existing words, we are not in a position to demonstrate that.

Yet we can conclude that the LXX's strong preference for translating גר with προσήλυτος indicates that the phenomenon of conversion did exist, and that there were proselytes in the Alexandrian Jewish community in the Hellenistic era. Without this assumption, we could not explain this tendency, since there were Greek words meaning sojourner, stranger or alien which the translator/s chose not to use. We have to presume that because the translators knew of proselytes, and understood that the laws pertaining to the alien dealt with them, that they translated the word גר by προσήλυτος except when the context made this impossible. This means that what began perhaps as reforming legislation in the restoration period to allow the indigenous population to join the cultic community of the returnees has become a practice in Alexandria which allows converts to join the Jewish community several centuries later.

1. A.D. Nock, *Conversion: The Old and New in Religion from Alexander the Great to Augustine of Hippo* (London: Oxford University Press, 1961).

2. Nock, *Conversion*, p. 62.

3. Nock, *Conversion*, p. 179. This is the word used to describe conversion to Christianity in Acts 15.3.

BIBLIOGRAPHY

Abba, R., 'Priests and Levites in Deuteronomy', *VT* 27 (1977), pp. 257-67.

Ackroyd, P.R., *Exile and Restoration* (Philadelphia: Westminster Press, 1968).

—'The Jewish Community in Palestine in the Persian Period', in *The Cambridge History of Judaism*, I (ed. W.D. Davies and L. Finkelstein; Cambridge: Cambridge University Press, 1984, pp. 130-62.

Allen, W.C., 'On the Meaning of προσήλυτος in the Septuagint', *The Expositor* 4/10 (1894), pp. 264-75.

Alt, A., 'The Origins of Israelite Law', in *Essays on Old Testament History and Religion* (trans. R.A. Wilson; Oxford: Basil Blackwell, 1966), pp. 79-132.

Andreasen, N.-E.A., *The Old Testament Sabbath: A Traditio-Historical Investigation* (SBLDS, 7; Missoula, MT: Scholars Press, 1972).

Astour, M.C., 'Habiru', in *IDBSup* (Nashville: Abingdon Press, 1976), pp. 382-85.

Austin, M.M. and Vidal-Naquet, P., *Economic and Social History of Ancient Greece: An Introduction* (trans. M.M. Austin; Berkeley: University of California Press, 1977).

Bamberger, B.J., *Proselytism in the Talmudic Period* (New York: Ktav, 1939).

Benjamin, D.C., *Deuteronomy and City Life* (New York: University Press of America, 1983).

Bickerman, E.J., 'The Babylonian Captivity', in *The Cambridge History of Judaism* (ed. W.D. Davies and L. Finkelstein; Cambridge: Cambridge University Press, 1984), I, pp. 342-58.

—*From Ezra to the Last of the Maccabees* (New York: Schocken Books, 1962).

Blenkinsopp, J., 'Are There Traces of the Gibeonite Covenant in Deuteronomy?', *CBQ* 28 (1966), pp. 207-19.

—*Ezra–Nehemiah: A Commentary* (OTL; Philadelphia: Westminster Press, 1988).

—*Gibeon and Israel* (SOTSMS, 2; Cambridge: Cambridge University Press, 1972).

—*A History of Prophecy in Israel* (Philadelphia: Westminster Press, 1983).

—'Interpretation and the Tendency to Sectarianism: An Aspect of Second Temple History', in *Jewish and Christian Self-Definition: Two Aspects of Judaism in the Greco-Roman Period*, II (ed. E.P. Sanders *et al.*; Philadelphia: Fortress Press, 1981), pp. 1-26.

—'The Mission of Udjahorresnet and Those of Ezra and Nehemiah', *JBL* 106 (1987), pp. 409-21.

—*Prophecy and Canon* (Notre Dame, IN: University of Notre Dame Press, 1977).

—'The Structure of P', *CBQ* 38 (1976), pp. 275-92.

—'Tanakh and the New Testament: A Christian Perspective', in *Biblical Studies: Meeting Ground of Jews and Christians* (ed. L. Boadt, H. Croner and L. Klenicke; New York: Paulist Press, 1980), pp. 96-120.

—*Wisdom and Law in the Old Testament* (Oxford: Oxford University Press, 1983).

—'Yahweh and Other Deities: Conflict and Accommodation in the Religion of Israel', *Int* 40 (1986), pp. 354-66.

Boecker, H.J., *Law and the Administration of Justice in the Old Testament and the Ancient East* (trans. J. Moiser; Minneapolis: Augsburg, 1980).

Braude, W.G., *Jewish Proselytising in the First Five Centuries of the Common Era* (Providence: Brown University Press, 1940).

Brown, F., Driver, S.R. and Briggs, C.A., *A Hebrew and English Lexicon of the Old Testament* (Oxford: Clarendon Press, 1975).

Carmichael, Calum M., *The Laws of Deuteronomy* (Ithaca: Cornell University Press, 1974).

Cassuto, U., *A Commentary on the Book of Exodus* (trans. I. Abrahams; Jerusalem: Magnes Press, 1967).

Cazelles, H., 'La mission d'Esdras', *VT* 4 (1954), pp. 113-40.

Charles, R.H. (ed.), *The Apocrypha and Pseudepigrapha of the Old Testament.*, II (Oxford: Clarendon Press, 1913).

Childs, B.S., *The Book of Exodus: A Critical, Theological Commentary* (OTL; Philadelphia: Westminster Press, 1962).

Clark, W.M., 'Law', in *Old Testament Form Criticism* (ed. J.H. Hayes; San Antonio: Trinity University Press, 1974).

Clements, R.E., 'Deuteronomy and the Jerusalem Cult Tradition', *VT* 15 (1965), pp. 300-12.

—*God and Temple* (Oxford: Basil Blackwell, 1965).

Coats, G.W., 'The Yahwist as Theologian? A Critical Reflection', *JSOT* 3 (1977), pp. 28-32.

Cody, A., *A History of Old Testament Priesthood* (Rome: Pontifical Biblical Institute, 1969).

Cowley, A.E., *Aramaic Papyri of the Fifth Century BC* (Osnabruck: Otto Zeller, 1967 [repr. 1923 edn]).

Cross, F.M., 'The Priestly Work', in *Canaanite Myth and Hebrew Epic* (Cambridge, MA: Harvard University Press, 1973), pp. 293-326.

Daube, D., *Studies in Biblical Law* (New York: Ktav, 1969).

Davies, D.J., 'An Interpretation of Sacrifice in Leviticus', *ZAW* 89 (1977), pp. 387-99.

Davies, G.H., *Exodus* (London: SCM Press, 1967).

Dodd, C.H., *The Bible and the Greeks* (London: Hodder and Stoughton, 1935).

Douglas, M., *Purity and Danger* (London: Penguin, 1970).

Driver, G.R. and Miles, J.C., *The Babylonian Laws* (Oxford: Clarendon Press, 1952).

Driver, S.R., *Deuteronomy* (ICC; Edinburgh: T. & T. Clark, 1902).

Eichrodt, W., *Ezekiel: A Commentary* (trans. C. Quin; Philadelphia: Westminster Press, 1970).

—*Theology of the Old Testament*, I (OTL; London: SCM Press, 1961).

Eissfeldt, O., *The Old Testament: An Introduction* (trans. P.R. Ackroyd; New York: Harper & Row, 1965).

Emerton, J.A., 'Priests and Levites in Deuteronomy', *VT* 12 (1962), pp. 129-38.

Feldman, E., *Biblical and Post-Biblical Defilement and Mourning: Law as Theology* (New York: Ktav, 1977).

Fensham, F.C., 'Malediction and Benediction in Ancient Near Eastern Treaties and the Old Testament', *ZAW* 74 (1962), pp. 1-9.

—'Widow, Orphan and the Poor in Ancient Near Eastern Legal and Wisdom Literature', *JNES* 21 (1962), pp. 129-39.

Fishbane, M., *Biblical Interpretation in Ancient Israel* (Oxford: Clarendon Press, 1985).
Fohrer, G., *Introduction to the Old Testament* (trans. D.E. Green; Nashville: Abingdon Press, 1968).
Frankena, R., 'The Vassal Treaties of Esarhaddon and the Dating of Deuteronomy', *OTS* 14 (1965), pp. 122-54.
Frick, F.S., *The City in Ancient Israel* (SBLDS, 36; Missoula, MT: Scholars Press, 1977).
Friedman, R.E., *The Exile and Biblical Narrative: The Formation of the Deuteronomic and Priestly Works* (HSM, 22; Missoula MT: Scholars Press, 1981).
Frymer-Kensky, T., 'Patriarchal Family Relationships and Near Eastern Law', *BA* 44 (1981), pp. 209-15.
—'Tit for Tat: The Principle of Equal Retribution in Near Eastern and Biblical Law', *BA* 43 (1980), pp. 230-34.
Gager, J.G., 'Proselytism and Exclusivity in Early Christianity', in *Pushing the Faith* (ed. M.E. Marty and F.E. Greenspahn; New York: Crossroad, 1988), pp. 67-78.
Gammie, J.G., *Holiness in Israel* (Overtures to Biblical Theology; Minneapolis: Fortress Press, 1989).
Gemser, B., 'The Importance of the Motive Clause in Old Testament Law', *VTSup* 1 (1953), pp. 50-66.
Gerstenberger, E., 'Covenant and Commandment', *JBL* 84 (1965), pp. 38-51.
Gilmer, H.W., *The If-You Form in Israelite Law* (Dissertation Series, 15; Missoula, MT: Scholars Press, 1975).
Gottwald, N.K., *The Hebrew Bible: A Socio-Literary Introduction* (Philadelphia: Fortress Press, 1985).
—*The Tribes of Yahweh. The Sociology of the Religion of Liberated Israel 1250–1050 BCE* (Maryknoll, NY: Orbis Books, 1979).
Greenberg, M., 'Some Postulates of Biblical Criminal Law', in *Yehezkel Kaufmann Jubilee Volume* (Jerusalem: Detus Goldberg, 1960), pp. 5-28.
Grelot, P., 'La dernière étape de la rédaction sacerdotale', *VT* 6 (1956), pp. 174-89.
—'Etudes sur le "papyrus pascal" d'Eléfantiné', *VT* 4 (1954), pp. 349-85.
Guterbock, H.G. 'Authority and Law in the Hittite Kingdom', *JAOSSup* 17 (1954), pp. 16-24.
Haas, P.J., 'From Savigny to CLS: Legal Thought and the Biblical Text' (presented at the 1988 SBL Meeting).
Hanson, P.D., 'The Theological Significance of Contradiction within the Book of the Covenant', in *Canon and Authority: Essays on Old Testament Religion and Theology* (ed. G.W. Coats and B.O. Long; Philadelphia: Fortress Press, 1977).
Haran, M., 'Behind the Scenes of History: Determining the Date of the Priestly Source', *JBL* 100 (1981), pp. 321-33.
Harrelson, W., *The Ten Commandments and Human Rights* (Overtures of Biblical Theology, 8; Philadelphia: Fortress Press, 1980).
Hatch, E. and Redpath, H.A., *A Concordance to the Septuagint*, I, II (Oxford: Clarendon Press, 1897).
Hauerwas, S., 'The Moral Authority of Scripture: The Politics and Ethics of Remembering', in *A Community of Character* (Notre Dame, IN: University of Notre Dame Press, 1981), pp. 53-72.
Heider, G.C., *The Cult of Molek* (JSOTSup, 43; Sheffield: JSOT Press, 1985).
Horner, T.M., 'Changing Concepts of the "Stranger" in the Old Testament', *ATR* 42 (1960), pp. 49-53.

Hurvitz, A., 'The Evidence of Language in Dating the Priestly Code', *RB* 81 (1974), pp. 24-57.

Hyatt, J. P., *Commentary on Exodus* (NCB; London: Oliphants, 1971).

Jackson, B.S., *Essays in Jewish and Comparative Legal History* (Leiden: Brill, 1975).

Jellicoe, S., *The Septuagint and Modern Study* (Oxford: Clarendon Press, 1968).

—*Studies in the Septuagint: Origins, Recensions and Interpretations* (New York: Ktav, 1974).

Kaufmann, Y. *The Religion of Israel* (London: Allen and Unwin, 1961).

Kellerman, D., 'גור', in *Theological Dictionary of the Old Testament* (trans. J.T. Willis; ed. G.J. Botterweck and H. Ringgren; Grand Rapids: Eerdmans, 1975), II, pp. 439-50.

Knight, D.A. 'The Pentateuch', in *The Hebrew Bible and its Modern Interpreters*, (ed. A.D. Knight and G.M. Tucker; Philadelphia: Fortress Press, 1985), pp. 263-96.

Koch, K., *The Growth of the Biblical Tradition: The Form Critical Method* (trans. from the second German edition by S.M. Cupitt; New York: Charles Scribner's Sons, 1969).

Köhler, L., 'Justice in the Gate', in *Hebrew Man* (London: SCM Press, 1956), pp. 149-75.

Kooy, V.H., 'Hospitality', in *IDB*, V (Nashville: Abingdon Press, 1976), p. 654.

Kuhn, K.G., 'προσήλυτος, in *Theological Dictionary of the New Testament*, VI (trans. G.W. Bromiley; ed. G. Friedrich; Grand Rapids: Eerdmans, 1968), pp. 727-44.

Lee, J.A.L., *A Lexical Study of the Septuagint Version of the Pentateuch* (Chico, CA: Scholars Press, 1983).

Leggett, D.A., *The Levirate and Goel Institutions in the Old Testament* (PhD Dissertation; Cherry Hill, NJ: Mack, 1974).

Lemche, N.P., *Early Israel: Anthropological and Historical Studies on the Israelite Society before the Monarchy* (VTSup, 37; Leiden: Brill, 1985).

Levenson, J.D., 'The Theologies of Commandment in Biblical Israel', *HTR* 73 (1980), pp. 17-34.

—*Theology of the Program of Restoration of Ezekiel 40–48* (Missoula, MT: Scholars Press, 1976).

—'Who Inserted the Book of the Torah?', *HTR* 68 (1975), pp. 203-33.

Levine, B.A., *Leviticus* (JPS Torah Commentary; Philadelphia: Jewish Publication Society, 1989).

Levison, N.L., 'The Proselyte in Biblical and Early Post-Biblical Times', *SJT* 10 (1957), pp. 45-56.

Lewy, I., 'Dating of Covenant Code Sections on Humaneness and Righteousness', *VT* 7 (1957), pp. 322-26.

Lindars, B., 'Torah in Deuteronomy', in *Words and Meaning* (ed. P.R. Ackroyd and B. Lindars; Cambridge: Cambridge University Press, 1968), pp. 117-37.

Lohfink, N., 'The Option for the Poor: Views of an Old Testament Scholar', Paper presented at the Annual Meeting of the Catholic Biblical Association, 1990.

McCarthy, D.J., *Treaty and Covenant* (AnBib, 21; Rome: Pontifical Biblical Institute, 1963).

McConville, J.G., *Law and Theology in Deuteronomy* (JSOTSup, 33; Sheffield: JSOT Press, 1984).

MacDowell, D.M., *The Law in Classical Athens* (Ithaca: Cornell University Press, 1978).

McEvenue, S.E., *The Narrative Style of the Priestly Writer* (Rome: Biblical Institute Press, 1971).

McKenzie, D.A., 'Judicial Procedure at the Town Gate', *VT* 14 (1964), pp. 100-104.

MacKenzie, R.A.F., 'The Formal Aspect of Ancient Near Eastern Law', in *The Seed of Wisdom* (ed. W.S. McCullough; Toronto: University of Toronto Press, 1964), pp. 31-44.

Maloney, R.P., 'Usury and Restrictions on Interest-taking in the Ancient Near East', *CBQ* 36 (1974), pp. 1-20.

Mauch, T.M., 'Sojourner', in *IDB*, IV (Nashville: Abingdon Press, 1962), pp. 397-99.

Mayes, A.D.H., *Deuteronomy* (The New Century Bible Commentary; Grand Rapids: Eerdmans, 1979).

—'Deuteronomy 4 and the Literary Criticism of Deuteronomy', *JBL* 100 (1981), pp. 23-51.

—'Deuteronomy 29, Joshua 9, and the Place of the Gibeonites in Israel', in *Das Deuteronomium* (ed. N. Lohfink; Leuven: Leuven University Press, 1985), pp. 321-25.

—*Israel in the Period of the Judges* (SBT 2/29; Naperville, IL: SCM Press, 1974).

—*Judges* (Old Testament Guides; Sheffield: JSOT Press, 1985).

—*The Story of Israel between Settlement and Exile* (London: SCM Press, 1983).

Meek, T.J., 'The Origin of Hebrew Law', in *Hebrew Origins* (New York: Harper & Row, 1936), pp. 49-81.

—'The Translation of *Ger* in the Hexateuch and its Bearing on the Documentary Hypothesis', *JBL* 49 (1930), pp. 172-80.

Mendelsohn, I., 'Authority and Law in Canaan-Israel', *JAOSSup* 17 (1954), pp. 25-33.

Mendenhall, G.E., 'Ancient Oriental and Biblical Law', *BA* 17 (1954), pp. 26-46.

Milgrom, J. 'Leviticus', in *IDBSup* (Nashville: Abingdon Press, 1976), pp. 541-45.

—'Religious Conversion: the Revolt Model for the Formation of Israel', *JBL* 101 (1982), pp. 169-76.

Miller, P.D., 'The Gift of God: The Deuteronomic Theology of the Land', *Int* 23 (1969), pp. 14-31.

Moore, G.F., *Judaism in the First Centuries of the Christian Era*, I (Cambridge, MA: Harvard University Press, 1966).

Moran, W.L., 'The Ancient Near Eastern Background of the Love of God in Deuteronomy', *CBQ* 25 (1963), pp. 77-87.

—'The Literary Connection between Lev. 11:13-19 and Dt. 14:12-18', *CBQ* 28 (1966), pp. 271-77.

Morgenstern, J., 'Sabbath', in *IDB*, IV (Nashville: Abingdon Press, 1963), pp. 135-41.

Muntingh, L.M., 'Die Begrip "Ger" in die Ou Testament', *Nederduits Gereformeerde Teologiese Tydskrif* 3 (1962), pp. 534-58.

Nelson, R.D., *The Double Redaction of the Deuteronomistic History* (JSOTSup, 18; Sheffield: JSOT Press, 1981).

Neufeld, E., *The Hittite Laws* (London: Luzac and Co., 1951).

Nicholson, E.W., *Exodus and Sinai in History and Tradition* (Atlanta: John Knox, 1973).

—'The Centralization of the Cult in Deuteronomy', *VT* 13 (1963), pp. 380-89.

—'The Decalogue as the Direct Address of God', *VT* 27 (1977), pp. 422-33.

—*Deuteronomy and Tradition* (Philadelphia: Fortress Press, 1967).

Nielsen, E., *The Ten Commandments in New Perspective: A Traditio-Historical Approach* (SBT, 2/7; Naperville: Alec R. Allenson, 1968).

Nock, A.D., *Conversion: The Old and New in Religion from Alexander the Great to Augustine of Hippo* (London: Oxford University Press, 1961).

North, R., *Sociology of the Biblical Jubilee* (Rome: Pontifical Biblical Institute, 1954).

Noth, M., *Exodus: A Commentary* (trans. J.S. Bowden; OTL; Philadelphia: Westminster Press, 1962).
—*The Laws in the Pentateuch and Other Studies* (trans. D.R. Ap-Thomas; Philadelphia: Fortress Press, 1967).
—*Leviticus* (OTL; Philadelphia: Westminster Press, 1965).
Ogletree, T.W., *Hospitality to the Stranger* (Philadelphia: Fortress Press, 1985).
Patrick, D., 'Casuistic Law Governing Primary Rights and Duties', *JBL* 92 (1973), pp. 180-84.
—'Collective Address in Deuteronomic Law', in *American Academy of Religion Biblical Literature: 1974* (compiled by F.O. Francis; Missoula, MT: American Academy of Religion), pp. 1-13.
—' The Covenant Code Source', *VT* 27 (1977), pp. 145-57.
—'I and Thou in the Covenant Code', in *Society of Biblical Literature Seminar Papers 1978* (Missoula, MT: Scholars Press, 1978), pp. 71-86.
—*Old Testament Law* (Atlanta: John Knox Press, 1985).
Paul, S.M., *Studies in the Book of the Covenant in the Light of Cuneiform and Biblical Law* (Leiden: Brill, 1970).
Pedersen, J., *Israel: Its Life and Culture*, I (London: Oxford University Press, 1973 [1927]), pp. 39-46.
Petersen, David L., 'Max Weber and the Sociological Study of Ancient Israel', in *Religious Change and Continuity* (ed. H.M. Johnson; San Francisco: Jossey–Bass, 1979), pp. 117-50.
Phillips, A.C.J., *Ancient Israel's Criminal Law* (Oxford: Basil Blackwell, 1970).
Polzin, R., *Moses and the Deuteronomist* (New York: Seabury Press, 1980).
Porten, B., *Archives from Elephantine* (Berkeley: University of California Press, 1968).
—'The Jews in Egypt', in *The Cambridge History of Judaism*, I (ed. W.D. Davies and L. Finkelstein; Cambridge: Cambridge University Press, 1984), pp. 372-400.
Pritchard, J.B. (ed.), *Ancient Near Eastern Texts Relating to the Old Testament* (Princeton: Princeton University Press, 1950).
Rad, G. von, *Deuteronomy: A Commentary* (trans. D .Barton; OTL; Philadelphia: Westminster Press, 1966).
—'The Promised Land and Yahweh's Land in the Hexateuch', in *The Problem of the Hexateuch and Other Essays* (Edinburgh: Oliver and Boyd, 1966), pp. 79-94.
Rendtorff, R., *Die Gesetze in der Priesterschrift* (Göttingen: Vandenhoeck and Ruprecht, 1954).
—'Pentateuchal Studies on the Move', *JSOT* 3 (1977), pp. 43-45.
—*The Old Testament: An Introduction* (trans. J. Bowden; Philadelphia: Fortress Press, 1986).
—'The "Yahwist" as Theologian? The Dilemma of Pentateuchal Criticism', *JSOT* 3 (1977), pp. 2-9.
Rogerson, J.W., *Anthropology and the Old Testament* (Oxford: Basil Blackwell, 1978).
Rothschild, M.M., 'Aliens and Israelites–Pt. 1', *Dor le Dor* 9 (1981), pp. 196-202.
—'Aliens and Israelites–Pt. 2', *Dor le Dor* 10 (198–82), pp. 118-21.
—'Aliens and Israelites–Pt. 3', *Dor le Dor* 11 (1982), pp. 35-39.
Schmid, H.H., 'In Search of New Approaches in Pentateuch Research', *JSOT* 3 (1977), pp. 33-42.
Schmidt, K.L. and M.A., 'πάροικος', in *Theological Dictionary of the New Testament*, V (trans. G.W. Bromiley; ed. G. Friedrich; Grand Rapids: Eerdmans, 1967), pp. 841-53.

Schultz, C., 'The Political Tensions Reflected in Ezra-Nehemiah', in *Scripture in Context: Essays on the Comparative Method* (ed. C.D. Evans; Pittsburgh: The Pickwick Press, 1980), pp. 221-44.
Schwarz, W., 'Discussions on the Origin of the Septuagint', in *Studies in the Septuagint* (ed. S. Jellicoe; New York: Ktav, 1974), pp. 110-37.
Shaver, J.R., *Torah and the Chronicler's History Work* (Unpublished PhD dissertation; Theology Department; University of Notre Dame, 1983).
Smith, D.L., *The Religion of the Landless* (Bloomington: Meyer Stone Books, 1989).
Smith, M., 'Jewish Life in the Persian Period', in *The Cambridge History of Judaism* (ed. W.D. Davies and L. Finkelstein; Cambridge: Cambridge University Press, 1984), I, pp. 219-79.
—*Palestinian Parties and Politics That Shaped the Old Testament* (New York: Columbia University Press, 1971).
Soggin, J.A., *A History of Ancient Israel* (trans. J. Bowden; London: SCM Press, 1984).
—*Introduction to the Old Testament* (trans. J. Bowden; Philadelphia: Westminster Press, rev. edn, 1980).
—*Joshua* (trans. R.A. Wilson; Philadelphia: Westminster Press, 1972).
Sonsino, R., *Motive Clauses in Hebrew Law: Biblical Forms and Near Eastern Parallels* (Dissertation Series, 45; Chico, CA: Scholars Press, 1980).
Speiser, E.A., 'Authority and Law in Mesopotamia', *JAOSSup* 17 (1954), pp. 8-15.
—'Cuneiform Law and the History of Civilization', *Proceedings of the American Philosophical Society* 107 (1963), pp. 536-41.
Spina, F.A., 'Israelites as *gerim*: Sojourners in Social and Historical Context', in *The Word of the Lord Shall Go Forth: Essays in Honor of David Noel Freedman in Celebration of his Sixtieth Birthday* (ed. C.L. Meyers and M. O'Connor; Winona Lake, IN: Eisenbrauns, 1983), pp. 321-35.
Stamm, J.J. and M.E. Andrew, *The Ten Commandments in Recent Research* (SBT, 2/2; Naperville: Alec R. Allenson, 1967).
Sulzberger, M. *The Status of Labor in Ancient Israel* (Philadelphia: Dropsie College, 1923).
Sun, H.T.C., 'The Structure, Composition and Date of Lev 25:1-55' (paper presented at the Annual Meeting of the Society for Biblical Literature, 1990).
Talmon, S., 'The Emergence of Jewish Sectarianism in the Early Second Temple Period', in *King, Cult and Calendar in Ancient Israel* (Jerusalem: Magnes Press, 1986), pp. 165-201.
Thompson, R.J., *Moses and the Law in a Century of Criticism since Graf* (VTSup, 19; Leiden: Brill, 1970).
Tov, E., 'Jewish Greek Scriptures', in *Early Judaism and its Modern Interpreters* (ed. R.A. Kraft and G.W.E. Nickelsburg; Philadelphia: Fortress Press, 1986), pp. 223-37.
Van Seters, J., 'The Yahwist as Theologian? A Response', *JSOT* 3 (1977), pp. 15-20.
Vaux, R. de, *Ancient Israel: Its Life and Institutions* (trans. J. McHugh; London: Darton, Longman and Todd, 1961).
Vink, J.G., 'The Date and Origin of the Priestly Code in the Old Testament', *OTS* 15 (1969), pp. 1-44.
—'The Form-Critical Problem of the Hexateuch', in *The Problem of the Hexateuch and Other Essays* (trans. E.W. Trueman Dicken; Edinburgh: Oliver and Boyd, 1966), pp. 26-33.
—*Studies in Deuteronomy* (trans. D. Stalker; SBT, 9; London: SCM Press, 1953).

—*Old Testament Theology*, I (trans. D.M.G. Stalker; Edinburgh: Oliver and Boyd, 1962–65), pp. 187-219.

Wagner, N.E., 'A Response to Prof. R. Rendtorff', *JSOT* 3 (1977), pp. 20-27.

Weber, M., *Ancient Judaism* (trans. and ed. H.H. Gerth and D. Martindale; Glencoe: Free Press, 1952).

Weinfeld, M., *Deuteronomy and the Deuteronomic School* (Oxford: Oxford University Press, 1972).

Wellhausen, J., *Prolegomena to the History of Israel* (trans. J.S. Black and A. Menzies; Gloucester: Peter Smith, 1983 [repr. Meridian Edition, 1957]).

Wenham, G.J., *The Book of Leviticus* (NICOT; Grand Rapids: Eerdmans, 1979).

—'Deuteronomy and the Central Sanctuary', *TynBul* 22 (1971), pp. 103-18.

—*Numbers* (Downer's Grove, IL: Inter-Varsity Press, 1981).

Westbrook, R., 'Biblical and Cuneiform Law Codes', *RB* 92 (1985), pp. 247-85.

—*Studies in Biblical and Cuneiform Law* (Cahiers de la Revue Biblique, 26; Paris: Gabalda, 1988).

Wevers, J.W., 'Septuagint', in *IDB*, IV (Nashville: Abingdon Press, 1962), pp. 273-78.

Whitelam, K.W., *The Just King: Monarchical Judicial Authority in Ancient Israel* (JSOTSup, 12; Sheffield: JSOT Press, 1979).

Whybray, R.N., *The Making of the Pentateuch* (JSOTSup, 53; Sheffield: JSOT Press, 1987).

—'Response to Professor Rendtorff', *JSOT* 3 (1977), pp. 11-14.

Williamson, H.G.M., *Ezra, Nehemiah* (Word Biblical Commentary; Waco: Word Books, 1985).

Wilson, J.A., 'Authority and Law in Ancient Egypt', *JAOSSup* 17 (1954), pp. 1-7.

Wilson, R.R., 'Enforcing the Covenant: The Mechanisms of Judicial Authority in Early Israel', in *The Quest for the Kingdom of God: Essays in Honor of George E. Mendenhall* (ed. H.B. Huffmon; Winona Lake, IN: Eisenbrauns, 1983).

—*Sociological Approaches to the Old Testament* (Philadelphia: Fortress Press, 1984).

Wiseman, D.J., 'The Laws of Hammurabi Again', *JSS* 7 (1962), pp. 161-68.

Wold, D.J., 'The *Kareth* Penalty in P: Rationale and Cases', in *SBL 1979 Seminar Papers*, I (ed. P.J. Achtemeier; Missoula, MT: Scholars Press, 1979), pp. 1-47.

Wright, G.E., 'The Levites in Deuteronomy', *VT* 4 (1954), pp. 325-30.

Zimmerli, W., *Ezekiel I* (trans. R.E. Clements; Hermeneia; Philadelphia: Fortress Press, 1979).

—*Ezekiel II* (trans. J.D. Martin; Hermeneia; Philadelphia: Fortress Press, 1983).

INDEXES

INDEX OF REFERENCES

OLD TESTAMENT

Index of Authors

www.ingramcontent.com/pod-product-compliance
Ingram Content Group UK Ltd.
Pitfield, Milton Keynes, MK11 3LW, UK
UKHW020143290926
15471UKWH00004B/671

9 780567 111401